MW01275273

Henry Addington, Prime Minister
1801–1804

To the British Columbia Archives

from Your Friend

Charles John Fedorak

Series on International, Political, and Economic History

Jack Gieck,
Lichfield: The U.S. Army on Trial

John M. Knapp,
Behind the Diplomatic Curtain:
Adolphe de Bourqueney and French Foreign Policy,
1816–1869

Martha McLaren,
British India and British Scotland, 1780–1830:
Career Building, Empire Building, and a Scottish
School of Thought on Indian Governance

Charles John Fedorak,
Henry Addington, Prime Minister, 1801–1804:
Peace, War, and Parliamentary Politics

Henry Addington, Prime Minister, 1801–1804

Peace, War, and Parliamentary Politics

Charles John Fedorak

The University of Akron Press
Akron, Ohio

02   03   04   05   06   5   4   3   2   1

All inquiries and permissions requests should be addressed to the publisher,
The University of Akron Press, Akron, OH 44325-1703

LIBRARY OF CONGRESS CATALOGING-IN-PUBLICATION DATA
Fedorak, Charles John, 1963–
    Henry Addington, prime minister, 1801–1804 : peace, war, and
parliamentary politics / Charles John Fedorak.— 1st ed.
        p.   cm — (Series on international, political, and economic
history)
    Includes bibliographical references (p.) and index.
    ISBN 1-884836-83-6 (hardcover)
    1. Sidmouth, Henry Addington, Viscount, 1757–1844.   2. Great
Britain—Politics and government—1800–1837.   3. Prime ministers—
Great Britain—Biography.   I. Title.   II. Series.
DA522.S5 F43 2002
941.07'3'092—dc21
                                      2001006778

Manufactured in the United States of America.
The paper used in this publication meets the minimum requirements of
American National Standard for Information Sciences—Permanence of
Paper for Printed Library Materials, ANSI Z39.48-1984.   ∞

For Jacquie

Contents

Illustrations

Be not afraid of greatness. Some are born great, some achieve greatness, and some have greatness thrust upon 'em.

Shakespeare, *Twelfth Night*

Preface

I have incurred many debts of gratitude in the writing of this book. The greatest I owe to two mentors, who provided guidance and encouragement at different stages of my academic life. The first is the late Kenneth Bourne of the Department of International History at the London School of Economics and Political Science, who supervised the doctoral dissertation that evolved into this work. Professor Bourne was an ideal supervisor. He granted me considerable independence in the conduct of my research and writing, but was available whenever I needed his advice or assistance. Sharing with me his unparalleled expertise in the field of nineteenth-century British foreign policy, he also inspired in me a reverence for historical sources and a deep affection for the people we write about. His research explored the personal lives as well as the public lives of leading politicians. He could recite an abundance of entertaining anecdotes about the romantic lives of members of aristocratic society. The historian's task was described by one of my undergraduate instructors as communing with the dead and bringing them to life. Professor Bourne exemplified this approach to history and helped me understand the value of exploring the personal side of the politicians and officials we study.

I also owe a great debt to Edward Ingram of the Department of History at Simon Fraser University. Professor Ingram was the honors supervisor of my undergraduate studies. He first suggested Addington as worthy of study and has continued to provide me with encouragement and support ever since. He possesses the remarkable talent of being able to instill in me a sense of self-confidence tempered by humility. I have always found invaluable his advice and criticism, and the success that I have enjoyed as a historian would not have been possible without his assistance.

I wish to acknowledge the helpful advice provided by the examiners of my doctoral dissertation, Ian Christie and Michael Duffy. Dr. Duffy has also continued to provide me with valuable feedback and advice. I am grateful to Michael Carley, Amy Petersen, and the staff at the University of Akron Press for their support and assistance. I also wish to thank the anonymous reviewers for the University of Akron Press for providing me with suggestions to strengthen my manuscript. I wish to thank John Ehrman for drawing my attention to useful references on Addington contained in the papers of Pitt the Younger and for showing an interest in reading my dissertation. In addition, I am indebted to Anthony Howe, Janet Hartley, David Stevenson, Piers Mackesy, John Breihan, Karl Roider, and Gordon Martel for advice on sources and other aspects of the historian's craft. The Earl of Elgin, Lord Vernon, Francis Sitwell, Giles Adams, and Lieutenant-Colonel Henry Scott were kind enough to allow me into their homes and offices to consult archives in their personal possession. I also wish to thank Christiana Thomas, F. Pacquin, Mary McCormick, Pat Christopher, Celine Silve, Terence Ollerhead, Viscount Sidmouth, Sir Richard Carew Pole, the Earl of Harewood, the anonymous owner of the Liverpool Manuscripts loaned to the British Library, the trustees of the Chatsworth Estate, Service International de Microfilms, Dr. Ing. Schmidl, and the staff at all of the archives and record offices that I have mentioned in the bibliography. I would also like to thank the National Portrait Gallery, London, for permission to include prints of portraits of Henry Addington, George III, William Pitt, and Lord Hawkesbury.

None of my research would have been possible, however, without the generous financial assistance of the Imperial Order Daughters of the Empire, National Chapter of Canada, the Social Sciences and Humanities Research Council of Canada, the Trustees of the Overseas Research Scholarship, and the Central Research Fund, University of London. I wish to thank the former London House for Overseas Graduates (now Goodenough College) for providing me with a place to stay while in London. I am particularly grateful to Barbara and Norman Collier for providing me with a Cornish refuge on several occasions when the noise, soot, and overcrowding of London impinged on my physical and mental well-being. I wish to thank the Royal Ballet School Junior Section for permitting me to write this preface at White Lodge, and especially Robert Dickson-Fuller for taking me on a tour of the building and providing me with a desk at which to write.

I am indebted to my parents, Sandra Cusack and John Fedorak, for providing me with moral and financial support during my undergraduate and graduate school years. Marc Fedorak and Frank Fedorak assisted me greatly by retrieving books that I needed from the University of British Columbia Library. Manuela Myers helped me read German monographs and French documents and acted as an interpreter on my research trip to the foreign office archives in Vienna and Paris. Nadine McGraw assisted me in translating the French quotations that I had transcribed from the French, Austrian, and Russian diplomatic correspondence. Finally, I wish to thank my partner and soul-mate Jacquie Edwards for her love, support, and assistance, which helped me to complete the revision of my manuscript after a hiatus of several years. I dedicate this book to her.

Charles John Fedorak
White Lodge, Richmond Park, Surrey
December 2000

Politicians and Diplomats
Positions Held January 1801 to May 1804

Addington, Henry. M.P. for Devizes 1784–1805; Speaker of
  the House of Commons 1789–1801; First Lord of the
  Treasury (prime minister) and chancellor of the Exchequer 1801–4.

Addington, John Hiley. M.P. for Wendover, Bossiney 1802;
  Harwich 1802. Lord of the Treasury 1800–1801, 1802–3;
  joint secretary to the Treasury 1801–2; joint paymaster-
  general 1803–4.

Bonaparte, Joseph. French plenipotentiary at the Congress
  of Amiens 1801–2.

Bonaparte, General Napoleon. First Consul of France
  1799–1804.

Bragge, Charles. M.P. for Bristol. Chairman of the Ways
  and Means Committee 1799–1801; treasurer of the navy
  1801–3; secretary at War 1803–4.

Canning, George. M.P. for Wendover, Tralee 1802. Joint
  paymaster of the forces 1800–1801.

Cavendish-Bentinck, William Henry, third duke of Portland 1762. Secretary of state for home affairs 1794–1801;
  Lord President of the Council 1801–5.

Cornwallis, General Charles, first Marquess Cornwallis
  1792. British plenipotentiary to the Congress of Amiens
  1801–2.

Czartoryski, Prince Adam. Russian foreign minister
  1803–4; chancellor of Russia 1804–6.

Douglas, Sylvester, first Baron Glenbervie 1800. M.P. for
  Plympton Erle 1801–2, Hastings 1802. Paymaster general

1801–3; vice president of the Board of Trade 1801–4; surveyor general of the woods and forests 1803–6.

Dundas, Henry, first Viscount Melville 1802. M.P. for Edinburgh. Secretary of state for War 1794–1801; president of the Board of Control 1793–1801.

Fitzherbert, Alleyne, first Baron St. Helens 1791. Ambassador to Russia 1801–2.

Fox, Charles James. M.P. for Westminster. Leader of the Whig party in opposition 1783–1806.

Frederick, duke of York and Albany. Commander in chief of the army 1795–1809.

Grenville, William Wyndham, first Baron Grenville 1790. Secretary of state for foreign affairs 1791–1801.

Hobart, Robert, styled Lord Hobart 1793–1804. Secretary of state for War and the colonies 1801–4.

Jenkinson, Charles, first earl of Liverpool 1796. Chancellor of the duchy of Lancaster 1786–1803; president of the Board of Trade 1786–1804.

Jenkinson, Robert Banks, styled Lord Hawkesbury 1796–1808. M.P. for Rye. Master of the Mint 1799–1801; secretary of state for foreign affairs 1801–4.

Jervis, Admiral John, first earl of St. Vincent 1797. First Lord of the Admiralty 1801–4.

Otto, Louis Guillaume. French agent in London for the exchange of prisoners of war 1799–1801; French negotiator for the Preliminary Treaty of Peace 1801.

Pelham, Thomas, styled Lord Pelham 1801–1805. M.P. for Sussex. Secretary of state for home affairs 1801–3; chancellor of the duchy of Lancaster 1803–4.

Perceval, Spencer. M.P. for Northampton. Solicitor general 1801–2; attorney general 1802–6.

Pitt, John, second earl of Chatham 1778. Lord President of the Council 1796–1801; master-general of the ordnance 1801–6.

Pitt, William. M.P. for Cambridge University. First Lord of the Treasury (prime minister) and chancellor of the Exchequer 1783–1801.

Rawdon-Hastings, General Francis, second earl of Moira 1793. Leading member of the Whig party in opposition.

Scott, Sir John, first Baron Eldon. Chief justice of the Common Pleas 1799–1801; Lord Chancellor 1801–6.

Sheridan, Richard Brinsley. M.P. for Stafford. Leading member of the Whig party in opposition 1783–1806.

Starhemberg, Count Ludwig von. Austrian minister in London 1792–1810.

Stewart, Robert, Viscount Castlereagh. M.P. for County Down. Chief secretary for Ireland 1798–1801; president of the Board of Control 1802–4.

Talleyrand-Périgord, Charles Maurice de. French foreign minister 1797–1807.

Tierney, George. M.P. for Southwark. Leading member of the Whig party in opposition; treasurer of the navy 1803–4.

Vansittart, Nicholas. M.P. for Hastings, Old Sarum 1802; special envoy to Denmark 1801; joint secretary to the Treasury 1801–4.

Vorontsov, Count Alexander. Chancellor of Russia 1802–4.

Vorontsov, Count Simon. Russian minister in London 1784–1800; 1801–6.

Wellesley, Richard Colley, first Marquess Wellesley 1799. Governor-general of India 1797–1805.

Whitworth, Charles, first Baron Whitworth 1800. Ambassador to France 1802–3.

Windham, William. M.P. for Norwich, St. Mawes 1802. Secretary at War 1794–1801.

Yorke, Charles Philip. M.P. for Cambridgeshire. Secretary at War 1801–3; secretary of state for home affairs 1803–4.

Yorke, Philip, third earl of Hardwicke 1790. Lord Lieutenant of Ireland 1801–6.

Henry Addington, Prime Minister
1801–1804

Introduction

Henry Addington, first Viscount Sidmouth[1], was one of the most influential men in British politics during the first quarter of the nineteenth century. After serving as Speaker of the House of Commons between 1789 and 1801, he was prime minister for the next three years and held a series of other cabinet offices for fourteen of the following twenty years under four prime ministers. During his term as prime minister he built a following of loyal M.P.s that was larger and more cohesive than that of any other politician between 1806 and 1824. Addington's rise to power was remarkable: when the king appointed him prime minister, he had few personal supporters and no experience in cabinet office. Nevertheless, Addington emerged as the best candidate to lead the government because of a complex series of political, diplomatic, military, economic, and social crises. His performance as prime minister—and the activities of some of his opponents—earned him the political following that was to be the source of his influence for the rest of his career.

Addington has wrongly been depicted as a weak and ineffectual leader, first by his political rivals and subsequently by some historians who have examined his experience as prime minister in the context of a broader theme or in relation to the career of another politician.[2] This book tells Addington's story for the first time from his point of view, in an approach similar to recent biographies of Charles James Fox by Leslie Mitchell and of Georgiana, duchess of Devonshire, by Amanda Foreman.[3] Addington was actually an effective prime minister who dealt with enormous challenges in waging war against France, negotiating peace, restoring government finances, and managing Parliament. This is the story of how he fared. It is an examination of the actions he took, his reasons for taking them, and the domestic and international implications of those actions. While the story touches on the interests and actions of other politicians and other states, its focus is Addington.

When Addington accepted the seals of office in 1801, political power in Great Britain was vested in Parliament, which comprised the king, the House of Lords, and the House of Commons. The relative power of these three components lacked clear definition because there were no constitutional documents delineating a division of power. The British Constitution was essentially unwritten, leaving it open to different interpretations based on tradition and precedent. Everyone concurred that legislation required the approval of the king and both houses of Parliament and that the House of Commons must approve taxation and all other measures of financial appropriation. The most contentious issue was the nomination of ministers. It was customary for the king to appoint the prime minister and other great officers of state. There were occasions, however, when the ministers he had chosen became so unpopular with M.P.s that the government was unable to sustain the majorities in the two houses of Parliament necessary to requisition taxes or pass legislation. If enough M.P.s opposed the king's choice of ministers, they could, in effect, force the king to change them. By the end of the eighteenth century it was clear that, in order to govern effectively, ministers required both the confidence of the king and the support of the houses of Parliament, particularly the House of Commons.

The House of Lords was led by the great landowners but also included members of the royal family, senior officials of the Anglican

Church, and politicians who had obtained peerages for political reasons. The great landowners exercised considerable power because of their wealth, their social connections, and the number of tenants and other individuals who were dependent on them. Some commanded large loyal followings in the House of Lords and controlled the election of many M.P.s in the House of Commons. Many were related through marriage. Although there were no formal political parties in the modern sense, a series of political groups coalesced around particular leaders. None of them were strong enough on their own to control a majority in the House, but if enough of them formed an alliance, they could exert considerable control over the business of the House.

The House of Commons comprised those elected to represent county or borough constituencies. Most members were related to the landed aristocracy. Many were the sons of members of the House of Lords. The right to vote in parliamentary elections was restricted to a fraction of the adult male population, based on wealth or other privilege. Some large constituencies had a few thousand voters; members from these consistencies could exercise political independence when Parliament was in session. Other constituencies had fewer than fifty electors and were effectively under the control of a peer or another M.P. As electors had to declare their votes publicly, the great landowners could control the votes of their tenants and others to ensure that the candidates of their choice were elected. Some members of the Commons were, in effect, leaders of their own parties, which included allies in the Lords. The government also exercised control over some constituencies which elected members loyal to the king or his ministers. Nevertheless, there were too many diverse groups and genuinely independent members in the Commons for any one group to sustain a secure majority.

The extent of the king's power depended on the relative power of the leading parties in Parliament. Whenever the parties remained divided, the king was able to exercise greater latitude in his choice of ministers, but when the king's ministers provoked united opposition among the parties, a majority in either the Lords or Commons could force a change in government. Sometimes the union of the leading parties was strong enough to compel the king to appoint their leaders as ministers. Ministers who forced the king to appoint them against his will, however, did not usually last long in power, as they proved unable to sustain their parliamentary majorities without the king's support.

Securing the necessary majority in both houses of Parliament was not an easy task for any prime minister. As there was no formal party system during the late eighteenth century, the making of a parliamentary majority required a combination of diverse parliamentary elements. If it was clear that the king had confidence in the prime minister, the latter could count on the support of a certain group known as "the king's friends" who would back any government that the king approved. The next ingredient was a group known as placemen, who held offices, pensions, and other financial grants at the discretion of the prime minister. Cabinet ministers, too, brought the votes of their loyal supporters. Thus it was important that the cabinet include some of the great landowners who controlled or influenced the elections of M.P.s. Upon this foundation, the prime minister would add the support gained through electoral patronage: the Treasury controlled a small number of seats and could ensure the election of members who would support the government.

All these votes, however, were still insufficient to guarantee a working majority. There remained a large number of members who were independent of party and liable to change their votes depending on circumstance. The support of these independent members could be volatile and, on any particular issue, liable to be swayed by the quality of the debate. The prime minister and the senior members of the cabinet had to be able, during the course of debate, to persuade independent members to support government policy. Therefore, it was particularly important that the cabinet include effective parliamentary speakers. Finally, the ministers had to ensure that their supporters attended debates and voted with them. Each of these components was necessary to sustain a parliamentary majority. The prime minister could never take for granted the confidence of the king or the support of Parliament, because he could lose either of them suddenly over a clash of personality or a change in government policy. This meant that a change of government could occur almost at any time.

The most influential politician between 1760 and 1801 was King George III. He had studied the role of the monarch in British politics as a boy and committed himself to certain political principles before he became king. He felt that the king should retain the right to choose his ministers and veto legislation. Devoted to the Church of England, he had a strong sense of Christian morality. He disliked corruption, both in politics and in private life. It was his view that, during the course of the eighteenth century, a small group of corrupt politicians had attained a level of political power that enabled them to infringe on the right of the king to appoint his choice of ministers. George III was determined to reassert what he considered to be his constitutional rights and to withstand those politicians who had tried to usurp the powers of the Crown. A frugal man, he tried to set an example with his own personal behavior, and he disapproved of the dissolute lifestyle of many members of the aristocracy and the licentious activities of his two eldest sons.[4]

When George III ascended the throne in 1760, he almost immediately came into conflict with a group of politicians, known informally as the Whigs, who had, over the course of the previous fifty years, become accustomed to holding office. Representing the wealthiest and most powerful landowners, they came to regard themselves as the natural governors of the kingdom. As a result, there was considerable turnover in political office during the early years of the king's reign, while he and the Whigs struggled for ascendancy. During the course of this struggle, there developed a particularly acute antipathy between the king and a young man named Charles James Fox, who was to become the leader of the Whig party in the House of Commons. The clash between the king and Fox was as much a result of personalities as of politics. Fox was the son of Henry Fox, an M.P. who had amassed a fortune and considerable political power through corruption in political office during the reign of George II. He married into the aristocracy and was granted the title Baron Holland for his political services. Charles Fox, both charming and a brilliant orator, was extremely popular and inspired a fierce loyalty among his personal friends and political allies. Nevertheless, he followed a libertine lifestyle of excessive eating, drinking, and gambling, which the king abhorred. Fox became a close friend of the Prince of Wales, and the king blamed him for corrupting his son. Fox, in return, resented the king and openly criticized what he perceived to be the growing influence of the Crown in British politics.

In 1783, Fox and the Whigs built a parliamentary alliance that enabled them to force the resignation of the king's ministers and establish themselves as the only candidates for office who could command a majority in both houses of Parliament. The king was unable to find any alternative candidates who were willing to take office, and had no choice but to appoint Fox and his allies. They took office with William Cavendish-Bentinck, the third duke of Portland, who was one of the most powerful landowners and whose family had been leading members of the Whig party for most of the eighteenth century, as prime minister and Fox secretary of state for foreign affairs. Fox's triumph was, however, only temporary. The king became increasingly resentful of Fox and determined to dismiss him, Portland, and the rest of the government at the earliest opportunity. Although Fox and his allies had sufficient parliamentary support to govern, many independent M.P.s felt that Fox had crossed the bounds of acceptable parliamentary conduct in forcing the king to appoint him. Governing was a partnership between the king and the houses of Parliament. While it was unacceptable for the king to appoint ministers Parliament opposed, it was equally inappropriate for Parliament to compel the king to appoint ministers whom he detested. The king could not dismiss Fox and Portland, however, until he found replacements for them.

This conflict between the king and Fox launched the remarkable career of William Pitt, the Younger, who was to dominate British politics from his appointment as prime minister in 1783 until long after his death in 1806. Pitt was the second son of William Pitt, the first earl of Chatham, who had been a popular politician and a successful war leader during the Seven Years War against France (1756–63). Chatham was a political outsider whose political power derived from his skill at parliamentary debate rather than from his social connections. He educated and trained his son at an early age to become a great public speaker, so that William would also be a successful politician. The younger Pitt exceeded his father's high expectations. He became the most effective speaker ever to debate in the House of Commons, at a time when speaking ability was the most important quality a politician could possess. Pitt often spoke for hours, late into the night, impromptu without notes, and yet every word seemed meticulously selected. His timing was remarkable. He placed precise emphasis on every word to give it maximum effect, as if the whole production had been extensively rehearsed.

Although he was only twenty-four years old and had only a few month's previous experience in cabinet office as chancellor of the Exchequer, he appeared to have the skills and abilities necessary to form a government strong enough to survive the opposition of Fox and Portland. After the king dismissed Fox and Portland and appointed Pitt in December 1783, the new prime minister faced a daunting task. Fox and his allies retained a majority in both houses of Parliament. Pitt persevered in the face of this parliamentary opposition and over the course of a few months won the support of enough members of Parliament to establish a majority. The M.P.s who supported Pitt were not all politically attached to him, but as long as Fox was the only alternative, they preferred Pitt. Pitt called an election in the spring of 1784 in which many new government supporters were elected and a number of Whigs were defeated. This victory was as much a triumph for the king as it was for Pitt, because the electorate identified Pitt as the king's choice, reinforcing the king's position that he had the authority to appoint his own ministers. This triumph for the government also spawned a great personal rivalry between Fox and Pitt. From that moment forward, Fox proclaimed himself "the champion of the people" because he opposed what he considered to be the increasing power that the king was exerting over the people's representatives in Parliament. Fox accused Pitt of being merely an agent of the king. Fox's loyal following in Parliament was strong enough to ensure that Pitt had to manage Parliament carefully to retain his majority and that the king remained dependent on Pitt to keep Fox out of office. This polarized both houses of Parliament, because a solid minority in each house felt that the king had acted contrary to the Constitution when he dismissed the Whigs and appointed Pitt. Pitt and Fox were the only possible candidates for office, and the antipathy that existed between them and between their supporters made remote any possibility of their serving together in office.

Pitt remained in office until 1801. During the 1780s, he was able to sustain a majority on votes of confidence, but he was not able to pass all legislation he introduced. The French Revolution of 1789 and the war that followed in 1793 made managing Parliament even more challenging. The French Revolution acted as a catalyst to a popular movement for parliamentary reform in Great Britain: the French attempts to construct a new system of government upon principles of reason provided a contrast to the British electoral system, in which only a small, privileged portion of the male population could vote and the franchise qualifications varied greatly between constituencies. Some regions of the country were over-represented and others under-represented. Many radical political observers believed that more men should have the right to vote and that a reform of Parliament would lead to better government. The French Revolution and the radical movement in Great Britain also precipitated a conservative reaction. Conservatives believed that any measures of parliamentary reform in Great Britain ran the risk of devolving into the violence and anarchy that occurred in France as a result of the Revolution. The issues that the French Revolution sparked ultimately split the Whig opposition. Fox and a small group of radical Whigs continued to support the parliamentary reform movement in Great Britain even though most of the great landowners in the party led by Portland came to oppose it. Pitt was able to reinforce his parliamentary majority by forming a coalition with Portland and the conservative Whigs in 1794, leaving Fox alone in opposition with a smaller but staunchly loyal band of supporters. The coalition gave the government so much strength that, in 1797, Fox despaired of his situation and ceased to attend Parliament. This left Pitt's parliamentary position virtually unassailable at the time, but that did not mean he was invulnerable over the long term. The challenges of fighting the war with France and the domestic crises that it provoked eventually created the circumstances that compelled him to resign in 1801.

The most important issue in British politics during the final decade of the eighteenth and into the nineteenth century was the war with France. The war lasted from 1793 until 1815 with two brief interludes in 1802–3 and 1814–15. Great Britain and France had fought a series of wars throughout the eighteenth century over conflicting strategic interests. Both were commercial maritime states competing for markets in Europe and control of trade overseas. They developed colonial empires in close proximity in North America, the Caribbean, and India. They competed for maritime trade in the North Sea and the Mediterranean and built large navies for commercial and military purposes. Spain and Holland also had commercial empires, but by the end of the eighteenth century Great Britain and France possessed the two strongest.

The most important region of strategic interest for Great Britain was the Low Countries, comprising modern Belgium and the Netherlands, which contained the best harbors on the Channel coast for both commercial and military purposes. The ports were key trade links between Europe and the outside world. Antwerp had the potential to rival London as the main commercial center in Western Europe. For this reason, Great Britain had arranged through international treaty with the Great Powers of Europe for the closure to all naval traffic of the Scheldt River, which linked Antwerp with Central Europe. It was vital to Great Britain's interests that France not control this region. As France did not have good harbors on the Channel coast, the harbors of the Low Countries would improve the ability of the French navy to attack Great Britain. Control of the commercial centers in the region also would have enabled France to sever important British trade links with Europe. France was interested in obtaining this territory not only for its commercial and strategic value, but also because the southern portion of this region was inhabited by French-speaking people. During the eighteenth century, an important principle of French foreign policy was to expand the territory of France until it encompassed its "natural boundaries."

When the French Revolution began in 1789, Great Britain was satisfied with the international status quo. The territorial settlements that had resulted from the previous wars with France had conformed with British strategic interests. French politics during the early years of the Revolution concentrated on internal affairs to the extent that France became largely inactive in international politics. The Revolution itself was not originally a significant concern for other states. Some observers in Great Britain believed that the French were attempting to establish a constitutional monarchy in imitation of the British model. It was in these circumstances that Pitt told the House of Commons in 1792 that Europe had never had a better prospect of fifteen years of peace.

Anglo-French relations changed almost immediately after Pitt uttered those words. The French were soon at war with Austria and Prussia. Although the eastern monarchies had initial success in battle, the French drove their invading armies out of France, across Belgium, and over the Rhine. France then annexed the territories that the Austrian and Prussian troops had evacuated. Shortly thereafter the French opened the Scheldt River to navigation. The opening of the Scheldt and French annexation of parts of Belgium made war with Great Britain almost inevitable. The French then made an appeal of fraternity to the oppressed people of Europe, calling on them to throw off their oppressors. As this was also directed at Great Britain, it made the resolution of differences between the two states even more improbable. In the end, the French government declared war on Great Britain shortly after beheading Louis XVI in early 1793.

Pitt attempted to fight France the way his father had during the Seven Years War, by paying allies to divert French forces on the Continent and deploying the Royal Navy to attack French trade and colonies overseas. Pitt's strategy was successful in the maritime and colonial sphere. The British captured French colonies in India and the Caribbean, and the British navy won a series of naval battles in the Channel and the Mediterranean which greatly decreased the strength of the French navy. Pitt's European strategy, however, failed miserably. French forces drove out the small army he sent to Belgium. He made loans to the Austrians and granted subsidies to the Prussians to fight the French, but these allies eventually withdrew from the war without driving the French from the Low Countries. The French army, swelled by the ranks of conscripted soldiers, fought with a revolutionary zeal against European armies, comprised largely of mercenaries, who did not have the same vested interest in the outcome of the war. By 1797, France had annexed parts of Belgium, Germany, and northern Italy. Austria and Prussia made peace with France. Spain and Holland, which had begun the war allied to the British, changed sides and joined the French.

Great Britain's other main strategic interest was the Mediterranean Sea. The British had valuable trading interests in the region, but its overriding strategic importance was illustrated by Napoleon Bonaparte's expedition to Egypt in 1798. The French occupation of Egypt, if it were followed by an invasion of Syria, threatened to give France control of the overland routes to India. A permanent French base could also threaten British trade in the Eastern seas. If the French opened a new trade route between Europe and the East through the Red Sea-Suez region (with a projected travel time between France and India of eleven weeks, half the time required for British trade around the Cape of Good Hope), such competition would undermine Great Britain's commercial monopoly in the region.[5] It was for this reason that, in the autumn of 1800, Pitt's administration sent a costly expedition to Egypt to dislodge or neutralize the French presence, so that the French army would be removed as part of a comprehensive peace settlement.[6]

Bonaparte's expedition to Egypt also highlighted the significance of Malta, which was the most important strategic post in the Mediterranean. Bonaparte had captured Malta as a base for his invasion of

Egypt. In so doing, he demonstrated that the Knights of St. John, an international Catholic military order that for centuries had been responsible for protecting the neutrality of the island, could no longer defend Malta. In 1799, the British invaded Malta, defeated the French, and retained a British garrison on the island. The security of British naval interests in the Mediterranean and imperial interests in India required that Malta be secure from French control. British possession of Malta, however, threatened French interests in the Mediterranean. There was also a Russian angle to this issue, as Tsar Paul I, the honorary grand master of the Knights of St. John, wanted the island to be restored to them, free of either French or British control. Therefore, British policy on Malta had an important impact on both Anglo-French and Anglo-Russian relations.

Bonaparte's invasions of Malta and Egypt helped Pitt forge a Second Coalition with Russia and Austria, who also opposed French interference in the Ottoman Empire, to which Egypt belonged. The new coalition experienced initial success during the campaign season of 1799, when Russian and Austrian forces drove the French back through Switzerland and Italy and an Anglo-Russian expedition invaded Holland. The failure of the allies to coordinate strategy or devise compatible war aims, however, weakened the alliance and allowed the French to regain the initiative. The Anglo-Russian forces withdrew from Holland and the French army drove the Russians and Austrians back across Switzerland and northern Italy. By the end of 1800, the Russians had withdrawn from the war and the French had defeated the Austrians decisively in Italy and Austria.

Some British historians of the period have argued that this represented a stalemate between the predominant sea and land powers with neither being able seriously to threaten the other. These assessments fail to appreciate the desperate nature of Great Britain's strategic position.[7] French control of Western and Southern Europe posed a considerably greater threat to British interests than British command of the sea did to French. The British economy was more dependent on international trade than was the French, and Great Britain's most important markets were in Europe. French control of the Mediterranean and Channel ports almost completely severed important British trade links with Europe. Closer to home, the French were in better position to invade Great Britain than the British were to invade France. Far from having fought France to a stalemate, Great Britain was at a considerable disadvantage.

Great Britain's naval policies had also provoked the enmity of other states. The Royal Navy frequently boarded neutral ships in international waters to seize contraband of war destined for France. Denmark and Sweden tried to take over French trade that had been disrupted by the British blockade of French ports, and the Danes and Swedes became extremely annoyed with British interference. They turned to the tsar for protection.[8] The result was that Russia, Denmark, Sweden, and Prussia signed the convention of the League of Armed Neutrality in 1800–1801. The convention had two important results. First, the League denied the British access to Baltic trade in grain and naval stores—masts, tar, pitch, and hemp—which were vital to the Royal Navy. This caused the price of grain in Great Britain to rise and led to severe shortages in some areas. Second, Great Britain was virtually in a state of war against all of Europe, and the Royal Navy had to face the combined naval strength of France and the northern powers.[9]

The Anglo-French War between 1793 and 1801 illustrated several important points about the capacity of Great Britain to wage a Continental war. The British had not won a European war without the assistance of Great Power allies since the triumph of Henry V over the French at Agincourt in 1415. Geography and manpower worked against them. Great Britain was primarily a naval and commercial power on the periphery of Europe and lacked a permanent base on the Continent. Its population was considerably smaller than that of France, Austria, or Russia. This, combined with a political culture characterized by a strong aversion to standing armies, rendered the British unable to compete with the larger armies of the other Great Powers. The result was that the British alone could not defeat the French in battle. The North Sea and the English Channel acted as a defensive barrier for the British, but hampered their ability to put troops into the Continental battlefields. Even the largest British fleet was not capable of delivering a sufficient number of troops into a decisive battle. The Royal Navy could gain command of the seas, but this was insufficient to force the French to retreat from regions of vital British interest. The best the British could achieve on their own was to capture overseas colonies, win celebrated naval battles, and establish naval blockades.

Assertions that Great Britain was the strongest power in the world and recent historical analyses of the foundations of British power obscure an essential point about the nature of that power.[10] Power is relative: relative to other states, relative to particular fields of interest or geographic locations. State power is significant only to the extent that it can preserve the fundamental interests of that state. Despite having the strongest navy, the most extensive colonial empire, and the greatest commercial and financial wealth in the world, Great Britain's most essential economic and strategic interests lay in Western Europe, where on its own it could not defend those interests against Revolutionary and Napoleonic France. Great Britain may have been the most powerful state in the world, but it could not exercise that power effectively where it mattered most. The other Great Powers knew that Europe was the only theater of war that really mattered. That is why they considered the British contribution to the allied war effort to be of secondary importance.

In order to defeat the French, the British required the assistance of allies with larger military resources and the ability to put them into the field effectively. The Russians, Austrians, and Prussians were not, however, always prepared to fight at the prompting of the British or for British strategic interests. Pitt used British gold to entice Continental allies to fight for British interests, but did not succeed. The Russians, Austrians, and Prussians would fight the French only when it was in their interests and they were militarily and financially prepared. The British were at the mercy of developments on the Continent, over which they had little control. By early 1801, Continental politics had left the British in a dangerous situation indeed.[11]

The French Revolutionary Wars of 1792–1801 were complicated by factors of ideology and nationalism. The wars were fought primarily for strategic interests, but the ideological differences between the French Republic and the monarchies of Europe intensified the existing antagonism. The French feared that defeat in war would lead to a restoration of the monarchy, while European monarchies feared that defeat would lead to their overthrow and replacement by republics. From the British point of view, Pitt never claimed that the restoration of the French monarchy was one of Great Britain's war aims, and he did not stipulate that he would not negotiate with the Republic, but he doubted whether any peace settlement could remain secure until there was political stability in France. He also adopted a policy of assisting French counter-revolutionary forces against the Republic, which made the French government distrustful of him, rendering a peace settlement even more difficult. The king and some members of the British cabinet did believe, however, that the restoration of the French monarchy should be one of Great Britain's war aims, and they opposed negotiating with French republicans.

There was also a national animosity between the British and the French. The sense of British national identity that emerged during the eighteenth century was centered largely on antipathy to France.[12] As Great Britain was a culturally and ethnically diverse island, the people derived a sense of unity not from characteristics common to its inhabitants but from their distinctiveness from the rest of the world.[13] In this way, the British distinguished themselves from France, their greatest commercial, military, and cultural rival.[14] Popular patriotic societies, such as the Anti-Gallican Association formed in 1745, were established to combat French cultural influence in Great Britain by promoting British commerce, manufacturing, and indigenous artistic achievement, while denigrating French fashions, food, and literature.[15]

This general antipathy toward France carried over into politics. The British identity defined itself in terms of Protestantism and parliamentary government, in contrast to the Catholicism and arbitrary monarchy of eighteenth-century France and to the atheism and republicanism of Revolutionary France. It was common for both radicals and conservatives to tar their political enemies as dupes of the

French. The series of wars fought between Great Britain and France over the course of the eighteenth century also created the impression that the two states were natural enemies, reminiscent of rivals Rome and Carthage. These nationalist ideas and emotions supported proponents of an anti-French foreign policy, and often fettered the government when British diplomatic interests required an accommodation with France. Foreign policy initiatives that appeared to be pro-French were considered unpatriotic. These feelings ran so strong during times of war that some Englishmen supported fighting France to the end and opposed peace terms that were in any way favorable to France.[16] This made Anglo-French treaties of peace even more difficult to negotiate.

Pitt's inability to win the war or negotiate peace created military and diplomatic crises, and precipitated a serious social crisis that further hampered the government's ability to fight the war. Great Britain experienced a general war weariness that verged on violent dissatisfaction, as the rich were pinched by high levels of taxation and the poor by the high price of grain.[17] The crops of 1799 and 1800 were deficient owing to poor weather. Between January 1800 and March 1801 the price of wheat tripled. As bread was the staple diet of many people, hunger became widespread and resulted in an unprecedented series of massive food riots across Great Britain.[18] Demanding a fair price for bread, large groups of the poor intimidated bakers, corn factors, and farmers. Workers and the unemployed attacked rural farmers who inflated their prices.[19] Protest against high prices often merged with protest against the war, as many blamed the war for price inflation.[20] There was truth in this assumption, as the war prevented the importing of adequate food supplies from the Continent.[21] The British could obtain no grain from France, and Great Britain's dispute with the League of Armed Neutrality cut Baltic supplies of grain, which had provided more than 75 percent of British imports.[22]

The poor and the lower classes were not the only ones affected: the grain crisis also precipitated a drastic and widespread economic recession that caused the domestic market for British commodities to collapse, coinciding with the loss of major European markets for

British goods.[23] While the war provided certain economic benefits (such as stimulating demand for shipbuilding, armaments, and clothing for the armed forces), and new colonial conquests provided sources of raw materials, the war also created large numbers of unemployed who were displaced from traditional industries. At the local level, this caused industrial and commercial decline. The middle and upper classes, already losing revenue because their tenants defaulted on their rents, at the same time had to pay higher prices for goods and higher taxes to finance the war, while making larger contributions to poor relief in order to prevent a severe famine.[24]

The government was in serious financial difficulty. By 1800, Great Britain was importing more than it was exporting and the value of the pound had dropped against European currencies.[25] Government borrowing to finance the war also restricted short-term credit available to commerce and industry and drove up long-term interest rates.[26] Many industrialists and financiers believed that Great Britain required peace, and the stock market noticeably fluctuated in relation to the prospects for peace.[27]

These dire social and economic conditions gave members of the British establishment grounds to fear social revolution. While high grain prices and food riots had occurred often in the past without causing serious alarm, the revolutionary context of the 1790s provided an added dimension to the danger posed by the social unrest. The example of the French Revolution and the publication of radical pamphlets gave an ideological impetus to protest against the existing system of government. A working-class political movement arose in support of parliamentary reform. When this political protest began to use language that verged on sedition, Pitt responded by curbing the activities of radicals through legislation, and in 1794 their leaders were arrested for treason. In 1797, sailors in the Thames and Channel fleets mutinied over poor pay and living conditions. The greatest threat to British security, however, was the Irish Rebellion of 1798. Ireland, with its predominantly Catholic population, posed a strategic liability to Great Britain whenever it was at war with Catholic states in Europe, because the island was an excellent base for an invasion of Great

Britain. British legislation that denied Catholics basic political rights and the brutal manner in which English absentee landlords treated their Irish tenants eventually provoked a rebellion by both Catholics and Protestants. Although British forces quelled the rebellion, British strategic interests remained insecure. As Irish rebels continued to correspond with the French government, British officials expected that another rebellion would coincide with a French invasion.

By 1801, ministers and local officials believed that there was an important connection between food riots and revolutionary insurrection in England. They feared that although most of the rioters were only responding to the distress of the moment, a small group of revolutionaries was trying to use scarcity as an excuse to incite general discontent.[28] The regions where the most serious unrest occurred, such as Nottingham, Yorkshire, Lancashire, and Norwich, were also the centers of skilled artisan labor and the focus of the most extensive activity of the English and Irish revolutionary underground.[29] This mixture of radical ideology, underground organization, unstable industrial relations, and widespread famine was a recipe for insurrection.

The British government felt that it had to take serious measures in the defense of order, but suppressing unrest required armed force. With crises erupting in every region of the kingdom, there were insufficient resources to meet the challenge. Ireland had been relatively quiet since the rebellion of 1798, but lingering uncertainty required a commitment of 16,000 regular infantry and 10,000 cavalry to maintain order.[30] Diverting troops to quell unrest also tied up a large number of British troops needed to fight the French. In order to release more regular troops from the task of suppressing unrest, local authorities often employed regiments of volunteer soldiers as police forces. The experience of the food riots of 1800 brought this policy into question, as volunteers sometimes disobeyed their officers and joined the rioters. This underlined a frightening and real prospect. In the event that rioting became widespread, Great Britain's military resources might not be able to cope if some of the security forces refused to fight or joined the insurrection. The governing classes were an active minority surrounded by an indifferent multitude, and, during a crisis, the government justifiably feared that it might be deserted by high and low alike.[31] This risk increased as the social, commercial, and military crises persisted. An organized revolutionary movement did exist, and although social factors mitigated against a social revolution along French lines, these factors worked largely below the surface of events and were not obvious to contemporaries.[32] The culmination of these military, economic, and social crises led to a change in government in 1801 by which Henry Addington became prime minister of Great Britain.

Addington was the first prime minister who was not related either by blood or by marriage to the formal aristocracy. The Addingtons were gentry who had owned land in Oxfordshire since the fourteenth century. By the time Henry Addington took office in 1801, he owned land in Berkshire, Wiltshire, and Devon. Addington's father, Anthony, came to be renowned as a physician. While Addington's political antagonists exploited his father's profession in order to label him as "middle class" and thus unsuited to the office of prime minister, it should be noted that Dr. Addington was not an ordinary physician. He had been educated at Winchester and Trinity College, Oxford. He had money from land and the opportunity to pursue the more orthodox career paths for members of his social background, but the experience of a near fatal illness while at Oxford sparked a keen interest in medicine. Dr. Addington specialized in mental illness, a field in which little work had been done, and one that had become particularly fashionable and revered. Consequently, it granted him entry to the aristocracy. In 1752, he moved to London and eventually became an important member of the Royal College of Physicians. Dr. Addington became celebrated among the great houses of London as an expert on mental illness, having successfully treated William Pitt, the Elder. He was also one of the physicians consulted about the king's illness during the Regency Crisis of 1788–89. Among the most illustrious members of his profession, he made enough of a fortune from his work to purchase the valuable estate of Upottery in Devon. Nevertheless, members of the aristocracy and their allies would later tar Henry

Addington with the pejorative nickname "the Doctor," on account of his father's profession.

Henry Addington was born in a house on Bedford Row near Gray's Inn and Lincoln's Inn in London on 30 May 1757. From a young age, Addington was social by nature and had a strong desire to be liked, which he retained throughout his life. Unable to develop close relationships with his parents (who sent him to boarding school at Cheam in Surrey when he was only five years old), he built strong relationships with his brother and sisters and acquired a large circle of close friends, many of whom would eventually become his political supporters. He made new friends when he went to Winchester School in 1768 and later at Oxford after 1774. He was a successful student but he did not allow his studies to prevent him from enjoying a social life. He played sports during his early years and spent evenings drinking with friends when he was at Oxford.

Addington demonstrated intelligence in school, attaining high marks in classes with boys several years his senior. One of his teachers at Cheam referred to him as a "genius." At Winchester, he became the favorite student of a junior assistant, who inspired in Addington a lifelong devotion to the Protestant religion, characterized by regular church attendance and a strict sense of personal ethics that he would retain for the rest of his life. A fellow at Brasenose College, which had a reputation for serious study, Addington so loved his academic and social life at Oxford that he stayed on for an extra year after he finished his degree. He demonstrated his intellectual abilities in 1779, when he won the chancellor's prize for the best English essay for a work entitled "The Affinity between Painting and Poetry in Point of Composition."[33] The essay attested to his scholarship and his interest in art and poetry. He loved English and French literature, and would later become a great admirer of the poetry of Robert Burns. He also wrote poetry himself. The best example of his skill in this sphere is a clever metaphorical verse that he wrote one evening at Pitt's home during the Regency Crisis. Addington took a line from the famous eighteenth-century poet Alexander Pope's translation of *The Iliad* "So Shines the Moon pale regent of the Night" as the theme for a verse in heroic couplets (in imitation of Pope's style) about how supporters of the king viewed the prospect of a regency under the Prince of Wales.[34]

After Addington left Oxford he trained as a barrister at Lincoln's Inn in 1780, but his personal life interfered with his training. He fell deeply in love with Ursula Mary Hammond, and married her in 1781 despite the objections of his father. This was significant in that Addington had little money of his own, and Ursula did not have a large dowry. Addington remained devoted and faithful to Ursula for thirty years, and she was a strong support to both his personal and political life. They had seven children upon whom they doted. Addington became so attached to his children that he would interrupt public business to be with them whenever they were seriously ill. Addington demonstrated early on that his family and friends were more important than to him than politics, and in this he never changed.

The most significant friendship that he developed as a boy was with Pitt. Addington met him when Dr. Addington began to treat Pitt the Elder in 1766. Addington was two years older than the shy and reserved young Pitt. Despite the social distinction between their fathers, Addington felt no sense of inferiority toward him. Addington and Pitt met again in 1780 at Lincoln's Inn, where Addington became one of Pitt's closest friends. Their friendship grew steadily during the early 1780s, even after Addington had settled with his wife in Southampton Street and Pitt had entered the House of Commons. Although Addington did not have a seat in Parliament, his friends assumed that his connection to Pitt would lead eventually to his involvement in politics. In early 1783, when Pitt was briefly chancellor of the Exchequer, Addington's friend and future brother-in-law Charles Bragge wrote, "When I left town, I thought the first post would bring me an account of your being called to the service of your country in some honourable station, under the auspices of your illustrious friend."[35] This proved premature, as Pitt was soon out of office. Addington met with Pitt after he became prime minister in December 1783, but Bragge was again disappointed when Addington did not receive a government office.

Addington was one of the many supporters of Pitt elected to the

House of Commons in 1784. His entry into Parliament was facilitated by James Manner Sutton, who had married Addington's sister Eleanor in 1771. Sutton had been M.P. for the borough of Devizes in Wiltshire, which had less than forty voters, and he exercised some influence with them. When Pitt called the election in March 1784, Sutton chose to withdraw from the contest and recommend Addington in his place. Although a number of other candidates took an interest in contesting the seat, all but one withdrew by the time of the vote, and Addington and the other were elected by acclamation. Addington was returned unanimously in 1790, 1796, and 1802, serving as the member for Devizes until his elevation to the House of Lords in 1805.

In his first few years at Westminster, Addington suffered from a lack of ambition and lack of confidence in his speaking ability, characteristics that would continue to hamper his political career. They kept him from taking a visible role in Parliament, even though Pitt persistently encouraged him to speak in the Commons. This did not mean that Addington was idle. He spent time learning about the history and traditions of Parliament. Although he made no speeches, he studied thoroughly the important political issues of the day. Addington was keenly interested in naval affairs and read extensively on the history and theories of taxation. He also took part in some administrative work. Eventually, Pitt decided to force Addington to overcome his reluctance to speak, and selected him to second the address in the House of Commons upon the opening of Parliament in 1786. Pitt wrote, "I will not disguise that in asking this favour of you, I look beyond the immediate object of the first day's debate from a persuasion that whatever induces you to take a part in public, will equally contribute to your personal credit and that of the system to which I have the pleasure of thinking you are so warmly attached."[36] Pitt believed that his friend had the potential to be an effective M.P. and an able administrator, if he could only overcome his personal insecurities and develop a greater sense of ambition.[37]

The House received Addington's maiden speech favorably, but it was not enough to encourage him to overcome his reluctance to speak again for the remainder of the session. He did not make his second speech until May 1787, when he spoke on an issue of taxation. Although it was on a subject in which he was particularly interested, he remained typically self-effacing as to his performance. His sister Charlotte, in describing the speech to their father, stated that Addington "acquitted himself so entirely to the expectation of his most sanguine friends, that they now are convinced he can never again feel more than a becoming embarrassment on a similar occasion."[38]

Pitt's faith in Addington's abilities did not waver and he remained determined that his friend should take a more active role in Parliament. In 1789, the right opportunity presented itself. The office of Speaker of the House of Commons became vacant when Pitt appointed the incumbent, his cousin, William Wyndham Grenville (later Lord Grenville), to the cabinet post of home secretary. Grenville's brief five-month tenure as Speaker had not been popular and Pitt saw the advantages of appointing someone he thought could restore the respect of the House.[39] Addington's knowledge, skills, and personality made him uniquely suited to this role. He had read extensively on the history and traditions of Parliament, and knew and understood the rules and practices of parliamentary procedure as well as anyone. From a technical perspective, his grasp of duties and responsibilities of the Speaker were unparalleled. Addington also possessed a remarkable breadth of mind. He had a rare ability to understand and sympathize with both sides of every issue. This did not mean that he was indecisive, for he made many difficult decisions throughout his career. He understood and respected differing points of view, and could see shades of gray where others saw only black and white.

Addington was also a natural diplomat. He was conciliatory and had the ability to put people at ease when speaking with them about political issues. Sylvester Douglas, Lord Glenbervie, a politician and diarist who often dined with Addington, described his manner of handling people:

> He is a man of considerable address as well natural as acquired, much frankness of manner, but tempered with a sufficiency of reserve; willing enough to speak freely of men, as well as of political transactions and political questions, but that only when he has ascertained what

your opinion is. Not that he is insincere or weak enough to square his own to yours, but if he can he will colour and shade it in to yours if you seem to him to differ from him only in some reconcileable [sic] degree.[40]

The desire to be liked that he exhibited in his childhood was also apparent in his political career. He knew how to get on the right side of people. In contrast to Pitt, whose cold and austere personality annoyed many backbenchers, Addington treated them with courtesy and respect. In fact, Pitt often needed to employ Addington to smooth personal relations between him and other M.P.s.[41]

Addington was also congenial enough to win the friendship and goodwill of many of those who might be thought his political opponents. Treating everyone with cordiality and respect made him universally liked, even among people who disagreed with his policies, beliefs, or actions. He was the only politician to have been, at different times, the favorite of both George III and George IV. The latter came to like and trust Addington more than the rest of the cabinet, including the prime minister, and insisted that he remain in the cabinet after his resignation of the Home Office in 1822. Although one of the closest friends of Pitt, Addington was also seen walking arm in arm with Fox. He was friends with two other leaders of the Whig party, the great conservative orator and philosopher Edmund Burke (for whom he served as pallbearer) and the playwright Richard Sheridan. Both Burke and Sheridan had been bitter enemies of Pitt. The most powerful woman within the Whig party—who was also a devoted follower of Fox—Georgiana, duchess of Devonshire, admitted that, despite her political differences with Addington, she liked him personally.[42] Those who opposed him politically acknowledged that no one could question his honesty.[43]

Although Addington was a close friend of Pitt, opposition members sensed an air of independence about him that set him apart from Pitt's young disciples, whom they held in contempt. Upon Addington's election as Speaker, Sheridan apologized for voting against him for reasons of party, though Addington was about as popular with all parties in the House of Commons as it was possible to be.[44] Addington rewarded their confidence by managing the business of the House with impartiality and a strong sense of fairness. Throughout his career as Speaker, he never lost the confidence of the House, and members of both the government and the opposition praised his conduct.

Addington developed a particularly close rapport with the ordinary, backbench county members. Many of the squires felt a social affinity with him that they did not feel with the leading members of the government and the opposition. They admired his attachment to principle, his even temper, and the respectful manner with which he treated people.[45] While they acknowledged the speaking abilities of Pitt and Fox, some M.P.s found Addington's simple and direct manner more reassuring.[46] Addington also developed a reputation for integrity, through his refusal to accept the types of honors and financial perks that many other politicians grasped at. He turned down the sinecures that were traditionally offered to the Speaker, even though the office did not provide remuneration sufficient for him to meet ceremonial and social duties expected of the office. He also demonstrated his impartiality by entertaining both the government and opposition. He invited government members of the House to dine on the first Saturday of every session, and opposition members the first Sunday, with similar functions throughout the year.

By 1801, Addington had served successfully as Speaker for twelve years and was not interested in higher office. He would have been satisfied to continue as Speaker indefinitely. Members on both sides of the House liked and respected him to an extent that would have been impossible had he been in a cabinet office. He had achieved all that he had desired from a political career. Political power held no attraction for him. It would take compelling circumstances to convince him to trade the comforts of the Speakership for the onerous duties of government.

CHAPTER 1

Exchanging the Mace and Wig for the Seals of the Treasury

While the appointment in early 1801 of Henry Addington, Speaker of the House of Commons, as First Lord of the Treasury (the official title of the prime minister) and chancellor of the Exchequer was surprising and astonishing to many political observers, he was in fact the most suitable candidate, given the extraordinary circumstances. That William Pitt, prime minister for seventeen years, decided to resign was the real surprise. On the eve of Pitt's resignation, no one, except for possibly a few especially perceptive observers, had any reason to expect that he would not remain in office indefinitely. A fixture on the political landscape, Pitt had been prime minister for a longer period than most M.P.s had sat in the House of Commons.

On the evening of 29 January 1801, Addington was celebrating his re-election as Speaker for the new session of Parliament with Prince William of Gloucester and a few of his friends, when he received an urgent letter from the king. The subject was the king's fear that Pitt was about to propose that government remove the existing legal restrictions that prevented Catholics from voting, entering Parliament, or serving in the higher offices

Henry Addington by Sir William Beechey
(By courtesy of the National Portrait Gallery, London)

of the armed forces. Some officials in the Irish and British governments believed that such a policy, which was known by the term "Catholic Emancipation," was necessary to secure order in Ireland. In response to the Irish rebellion in 1798, Pitt proposed that Ireland terminate its status as a colony of Great Britain with its own Parliament and join a formal union with England, Scotland, and Wales. This entailed the abolition of the Irish Parliament and the election of Irish members to both houses of Parliament in Westminster. The issues of Union and Catholic Emancipation were controversial in both Ireland and Great Britain, and it was difficult to secure the majorities in both Parliaments that were necessary to facilitate the Union. Some British officials in Ireland held out the prospect of Catholic Emancipation in order to obtain support for the Union. When Union was achieved in 1800, certain British officials in Ireland pressed Pitt to deliver Emancipation. It was well known, however, that the king adamantly opposed Catholic Emancipation, because he believed it would undermine the Protestant Establishment that he had sworn to uphold in his coronation oath. The cabinet was equally divided on the issue and British political opinion largely opposed it. The Lord Chancellor was one of the members of the cabinet who was opposed, and he had gone behind Pitt's back to warn the king that cabinet was considering introducing the measure.

The king appealed to Addington to persuade Pitt to abandon the issue. Addington went to Pitt immediately. There is no record of the substance of their discussions, but Addington indicated to the king that there was some hope of an arrangement that would be satisfactory to both Pitt and the king. Addington's optimism proved to be unfounded. Two days later, Pitt wrote to the king that he fully supported Catholic Emancipation and, if the king was determined to oppose it, he must resign. The king immediately summoned Addington to discuss the crisis further. He insisted that Addington replace Pitt. Addington respectfully refused and returned to Pitt to persuade him to facilitate a reconciliation, but was unsuccessful. Not only did Pitt refuse to reconsider his resignation, he pressed Addington to accept the king's request to take office. After Addington told the king the results of his conversation with Pitt, the king wrote to Pitt that, although he could not change his mind in regard to Catholic Emancipation, he entreated Pitt to remain in office. Pitt responded on 3 February that, if the king's position remained firm, he wished to resign as soon as possible. When the king received this reply, he insisted that Addington succeed Pitt. On 4 February, Addington agreed to become prime minister.

It appeared to many observers at the time, and to historians since, that Pitt resigned over the issue of Catholic Emancipation and that the king appointed Addington because the Speaker was an opponent of Emancipation. This is an oversimplification and an exaggeration. There was much more to Pitt's resignation than a constitutional impasse with the king.[1] There is strong evidence that Pitt, rather than wholeheartedly supporting Catholic Emancipation, was actually of two minds on the issue. His assertion that the government believed the measure necessary for the king's service was misleading, because the cabinet was almost evenly divided over it. The cabinet also could not agree over war aims and strategy. Members differed over how to resolve the grain crisis and how to respond to social unrest. Addington did not come to power as the result of a momentary disagreement between Pitt and the king that could easily have been patched over. The change of ministries was the culmination of long-term forces that were bound to have serious consequences for British parliamentary politics, even if the issue of Catholic Emancipation had never arisen. Members of the cabinet recognized that the government could not continue much longer without some change in personnel.[2] Pitt's strong parliamentary position obscured the fact that the cabinet had ceased to function effectively. Seventeen years in power and eight years of war had also taken a toll on Pitt's health. During the previous six months, Pitt had been on the verge of mental and physical collapse, and his health remained poor for the next five years until his death.

It is also misleading to conclude that Addington was a firm opponent of Catholic Emancipation. Addington had stated in the House of Commons in 1799 that, while he opposed Catholic Emancipation unless Ireland first joined in Union with Great Britain, he might support it subsequent to a Union. It is likely, however, that in any discussions with the king on the issue, Addington would have given him the impression of agreeing with his position, because Addington typically discussed political issues in a way that found common ground with the position of the person to whom he was speaking. In addition, it is unlikely that he would have disagreed openly with the king on any issue. Once the king had declared his inalterable intention to oppose Catholic Emancipation, Addington understood that it would be pointless to promote the issue.

Addington became prime minister because both the king and Pitt concluded that he was the best candidate. The king was a man of principle and integrity, and he believed that Addington possessed similar values.[3] During his term as Speaker, Addington had developed a close relationship with the king. Their friendship was extraordinary in that the king, who maintained a strictly formal court in which considerations of rank were paramount, did not normally associate with anyone who was not of the formal aristocracy.

Addington met the king for the first time in 1788, and thereafter the king gradually grew attached to him. The king's regard for Addington was such that in 1800, when Pitt informed him that Addington had proposed new financial arrangements for the officers of the House of Commons, the king responded, "I fully authorize Mr. Pitt to give my consent to the Bill proposed, as it has the approbation of the worthy and excellent Speaker of the House, who would not countenance the measure if not advantageous to the public."[4] He always felt that he could trust and rely on Addington. Although Pitt had served the king as prime minister for many years, the king did not warm to him personally as he did to Addington. This was partially because Pitt was formal and austere with all but his closest friends. It was also because between 1795 and 1801, Pitt had increasingly neglected to consult the king on issues of policy and even failed to inform him of decisions of government, as was customary. In 1800, he had gone six weeks without even seeing the king.[5] Pitt remained in power during this period because there appeared to be no one who could replace him other than Fox. The king welcomed the prospect of Addington replacing Pitt.

Pitt agreed that Addington was the candidate best suited to succeed him because he had long believed that Addington possessed the skills, knowledge, and abilities required for cabinet office. He so valued Addington's opinions that, whenever the House was in session, he dined frequently at the Speaker's residence for the purpose of discussing government business. In 1793, he offered Addington the Home Office when the incumbent, Henry Dundas, expressed a wish to retire.[6] Addington refused because he preferred to retain the office of Speaker. Nevertheless, Addington's preference for the Speaker's chair did not alter Pitt's opinion that he was well suited for government office. Pitt also continued to involve him in decision making. Throughout the war, he briefed Addington on major foreign and domestic developments. Addington functioned in effect as an informal member of the cabinet, and Pitt often confided in him about policy more than he did with some of his cabinet colleagues.[7] Addington also conversed regularly with other members of the cabinet and corresponded with naval officers and imperial administrators. No one outside the cabinet knew more about developments in the war or the formulation of policy. Pitt and other members of the government often asked for his advice. By 1800, Pitt relied on Addington as his sounding board on the issues of war, peace, and the grain scarcity. When Pitt became seriously ill in October 1800, he went to recuperate at Woodley, Addington's home near Reading. Addington consequently knew as much about the state of foreign and domestic affairs as any of Pitt's cabinet colleagues. It was not surprising therefore that Pitt, when informing his brother, the earl of Chatham, of his decision to resign, declared that he had long expected that Addington would succeed him.[8]

The choice of Addington as prime minister was easier because there were no viable alternatives. There was no one in Pitt's cabinet, or the lesser offices of state, who would have made a more effective candidate. As Glenbervie noted at the time, Pitt had never given any of his younger colleagues sufficient opportunity to let their talents shine or to establish any degree of independence based on their own character and abilities.[9] The most skilful administrators and debaters within the cabinet also happened to be the ones who supported Catholic Emancipation and therefore resigned along with Pitt. Of those who remained, there was no one of the caliber to run the government. The only possible successor to Pitt was Portland, who had filled the office in 1782–83 (and would fill it again 1807–9) but had functioned largely as a figurehead supported by strong ministers in the key portfolios.[10] The situation in 1801 was quite different. As there were no strong candidates available to support the prime minister, the cabinet required a strong leader. Portland, who had once been talented and industrious, had become physically and mentally exhausted by 1801. He was not the man to be prime minister. Outside of the cabinet, only Fox and his allies possessed the talents and abilities required to run the government. The king would have vetoed their appointments, because of his strong personal differences with Fox. In 1797, the king had said of Fox that "from personal pique at me and my administration he is become an open enemy of his country."[11] Pitt also certainly did not wish to see his rival in office.

Addington was the only alternative. Twelve years in the role of Speaker had given him the stature and degree of independence that was required of Pitt's successor in the circumstances. It was clear that the new prime minister ought to be neither a devoted follower of Pitt—for then he would have felt obliged to resign—nor a member of the opposition. As there was no one else who had a solid party behind him, the successful candidate required the respect of both sides of the House of Commons to sustain a parliamentary majority. Although Addington owed his position as Speaker to Pitt, he had never been considered an ardent Pittite, but was one of the few M.P.s who were on good personal terms with all leading politicians.[12]

In spite of support from the king and Pitt, Addington was reluctant to become prime minister. He was comfortable with his position as Speaker, which suited his mild temperament, and the salary and the Speaker's residence provided a good living. Taking the premiership meant sacrificing this comfort and security for onerous responsibilities and a precarious future.[13] As someone who wanted to be liked, he dreaded the prospect of making personal and political enemies. Beyond these considerations, the diplomatic and political problems of the day were so intractable that their resolution appeared remote. The men who accepted office at this time risked their careers and faced seemingly certain failure.

Addington agreed to take office only under heavy pressure from the king and after Pitt agreed to advise the new ministry. In his own words, "I have done no more than my duty; and being actuated by that alone, and having no object but the good of my country, I have sought no political connections; but shall steadily pursue those measures which my own mind approves, and which I therefore venture to hope will be approved of and supported by parliament and the public." The atmosphere surrounding Addington, his family, and friends was surprisingly somber considering that he had just acceded to the highest office in government. "You may guess," one sister observed, "how he feels both the arduousness of the undertaking and the sacrifice of private comfort: but what *is for the best* in the present crisis can be the only consideration, *and of that* all seem perfectly agreed. His own struggle is over, and he seems calm and collected, and to look forward with confidence, though not without anxiety. The great thing is to keep up his spirits, to carry him through what he feels it his duty to undertake." One politician told Addington, "Sir, I cannot do as others are doing, give you joy; for I pity you sincerely." Another told him he was sorry that he had taken the government. Within a few days of agreeing to take office, Addington appeared pale and agitated. This is not surprising as he had agreed to assume the burden of serious problems that Pitt with all of his talent and experience had been unable to resolve.[14]

Although Addington was uneasy about accepting office, the king was delighted that he was to have a friend as his chief minister. He demonstrated his gratitude in strong terms. He realized that Addington in resigning the Speakership lost his only house in London. The king then offered him the White Lodge in Richmond Park. Shortly after Addington moved in, the king arrived unannounced with a present, a copy of Sir William Beechey's recent portrait of him in military uniform. The king found no one at home, but he waited there until Addington returned. This was remarkable, as it was not customary for kings to wait for anyone. The king had not made such personal gestures to any of Addington's predecessors, but they were typical of the generosity that he would display toward Addington. Although Pitt had once been the champion of the king's prerogative, Addington was the king's minister in a more personal sense.

Selecting Addington to replace Pitt was easy compared to finding replacements for the members of the cabinet who had also resigned with Pitt. In order to ensure a majority in both houses of Parliament, it was necessary to include men with different qualities, including landed magnates who controlled the election of M.P.s and able speakers who could swing the votes of independent members to support the government. Selecting the best ministerial team could be difficult enough during peacetime; it was all the more complicated under the extraordinary and serious pressures of war. The unique consequences of Pitt's resignation after seventeen years in office limited options even further. Nevertheless, Addington's new cabinet contained a nucleus of capable and promising young politicians. Although in normal circumstances they may not have attained such high office at this early stage in their careers, they were subsequently to enjoy long and successful careers.

Addington, having no parliamentary following of his own, did not have any lieutenants to bring into office with him, as new prime ministers usually did. Lacking any significant formal support among M.P.s made it all the more important for Addington to find men of weight and influence in Parliament to join him. The departure of the most able members of Pitt's cabinet and many capable diplomats and administrators from non-cabinet offices meant that there were fewer qualified men from whom Addington could choose and many vacancies to fill. To make matters worse, the ministers who would have liked to remain in office were indolent and ineffective.

Addington's inexperience and lack of connections made his task difficult, but he was fortunate that Pitt was willing to assist him in recruiting candidates for office. While Pitt had placed Addington in a very difficult position as the new prime minister, he worked hard to support him and set him on his feet. Pitt was not obliged to help Addington form a new ministry. In fact, it was virtually unprecedented for a departing prime minister to offer such assistance to his successor. From the time he tendered his resignation in February until the end of the year, Pitt acted out of a spirit of friendship, devotion to the king, and a commitment to what he believed to be the best interests of the country. He suggested several of the candidates who finally accepted office, persuading some against their own inclination to join Addington.[15] They were reluctant to take office after Pitt resigned because they considered him to be their political leader.[16]

Given Great Britain's desperate diplomatic position, the most important post that Addington had to fill was that of foreign secretary. He selected Lord Hawkesbury, formerly Robert Banks Jenkinson, whom Pitt recommended highly. Addington had lately taken him into his confidence and considered him one of the few good candidates for cabinet office. Hawkesbury was the son of Charles Jenkinson, the first earl of Liverpool, who at the time was the president of the Board of Trade. Hawkesbury attended Christ Church College at Oxford and got off to a quick start in politics. His father arranged for him to be returned for two boroughs in the 1790 election, a few months before he had reached the age of majority and could take his seat in the House. He had traveled in Europe the previous year, and had witnessed the storming of the Bastille in Paris on 14 July 1789. When he took his seat in the Commons, he made a good beginning. Although not particularly witty or eloquent, Hawkesbury demonstrated in debate a sound understanding of complex subjects and a mastery of detail.

Hawkesbury held a variety of minor offices, including posts at the Board of Control of the East India Company and the Board of Trade. An efficient administrator, he appeared destined for higher office. He was close to Pitt, who recognized him as second only to Fox as a man of business. The king also looked favorably on Hawkesbury on account of his father. On giving the seals of the Foreign Office to Hawkesbury, the king said that he had never given them away with such pleasure. Hawkesbury quickly became Addington's lieutenant and closest confidant in the cabinet.[17]

On the choice of First Lord of the Admiralty, Addington consulted Pitt, who recommended John Jervis, the first earl of St. Vincent. The retiring First Lord seconded the recommendation, and the king concurred. St. Vincent was a career seaman and one of Great Britain's most respected admirals, renowned particularly for an important victory at the battle of Cape St. Vincent in 1797. He was a popular choice with the public, and enjoyed the support of most naval officials. Given the challenges posed by recent developments in the war, the Admiralty required an administrator of vigor and ability. St. Vincent understood the workings of the Admiralty. He also expressed a fervent desire to reform abuses in the system and to improve the supplying and maintenance of the fleets. Addington possessed a thorough knowledge of naval affairs and understood the need for naval reform. Having supported reform in other branches of the government, he was keen to appoint reformers.[18] Neither St. Vincent's political connections to M.P.s who often voted with the opposition nor his vote for a motion for parliamentary reform in 1793 deterred Addington from appointing him. Addington's goal was to develop the strongest cabinet possible, by appointing the most qualified candidates, regardless of their political alliances or how they had voted on political issues in the past.

The other office crucial to the prosecution of the war was the secretary for War. Addington selected Robert, Lord Hobart, eldest son of the third earl of Buckinghamshire. Although his father associated with the opposition, Hobart was a career army officer who had allied with Pitt during the 1780s. Hobart had five years' experience as chief secretary for Ireland and governor of Madras. Addington believed that Hobart would work well with St. Vincent, and it was vital to the war effort that the War Office and Admiralty collaborate. Hobart, like Addington, was initially reluctant to take office but agreed after discussing the issue with Pitt.[19]

Addington had a few political connections and he appointed them to some of the non-cabinet offices in government. Charles Yorke, a schoolmate from Cheam, Addington appointed secretary at War. Yorke was a hard-working administrator, well-suited to the role of implementing the policies of the secretary for War and coordinating the supply of men, equipment, and food between the different military departments. He was the younger brother of Philip Yorke, the third earl of Hardwicke, whom Addington appointed Lord Lieutenant of Ireland. Yorke, like Addington and Hobart, was reluctant to take office. He spoke for many, including Addington, when he told his mother:

> the consenting to fill the Breaches . . . is considered by us all as a matter of *necessity* & *Duty,* not of *Choice,* as a means of preventing the country from falling into the very worst hands & the K[ing] from being delivered up to some of his worst enemies. For my own part, I reflect upon it as a most arduous, responsible & difficult task which I have undertaken. . . . But I think as a great and terrible conflict may be expected that it is more glorious to combat in the *front Ranks* than in the *Rear.*[20]

For the two secretaries to the Treasury, Addington appointed his brother Hiley and another school friend from Cheam, Nicholas Vansittart. Pitt had appointed Hiley a Lord of the Treasury in 1800, but it was clear that he did not have the skills and abilities for more senior office. Hiley was ambitious and aspired to cabinet office, but Addington knew his limitations and refused to appoint him, which remained a sore point with Hiley. Vansittart had not held office before, but he had a good grasp of financial issues and provided valuable assistance with the financial reforms that Addington introduced. Addington appointed as treasurer of the navy Charles Bragge, a school friend from Winchester who had become his brother-in-law. Pitt considered Bragge to be a procedural specialist and arranged for him to be balloted for the Select Committee on the Bank of England in 1797 and appointed chairman of the Commons' Committee of Ways and Means in 1799.[21] Bragge was a shrewd debater, but unfortunately had bad enunciation and a dreary voice which detracted from the quality of his argument. As a testimony to the substance of his speeches, some of his opponents admitted that "he took better than any other the point of a case, and it was a common thing for those who followed him on his own side later at night, when the House was fuller, to use the materials of his speech over again."[22] Of these three men, Vansittart and Bragge proved successful administrators and served many years in cabinet office.

Addington enjoyed the benefits of his close relationship with the king, but also suffered from its drawbacks. The king insisted that he appoint two members of the cabinet who proved problematic. The king had decided in 1799 that John Scott, first Baron Eldon, should become the next Lord Chancellor. Eldon had considerable experience in legal offices, having been solicitor general 1788–93, attorney general 1793–99, and chief justice of the Common Pleas since 1799. A devoted follower of Pitt and concerned about his own livelihood, Eldon preferred the Common Pleas to a post in the cabinet under Addington, fearing that he would lose his job if Addington fell. The king pressed him to become Lord Chancellor, and he complied after Pitt promised him a pension of £4,000 in the event that Pitt returned to office and dismissed him. These circumstances undermined Eldon's relationship with Addington, because he considered himself appointed by the king and "indebted to the King himself, and not as some supposed, to Mr. Addington." As the king's chancellor, he assumed a degree of independence, which in the end was one of the major factors that undermined Addington's leadership.[23]

The king also forced Addington to appoint Thomas Pelham, who proved to be a difficult cabinet colleague. Pelham, the eldest son of

the first earl of Chichester, had administrative experience as chief secretary for Ireland in 1783–84 and 1795–98. As a nephew of the duke of
Newcastle, whose ancestors traditionally had been powerful landed
magnates, he brought a number of loyal votes in the Commons. Politically, he had been allied to the conservative Whigs who had followed
Portland into office with Pitt, but was also a good friend of the
duchess of Devonshire, who remained an intimate ally of Fox. In that
sense, Pelham had more in common with St. Vincent than he did
with the rest of the cabinet.

Addington did not want to include Pelham in the cabinet, and he
found satisfying Pelham to be almost impossible. Pelham was vain
and did not get along well with his colleagues. He was jealous regarding what he considered to be the jurisdiction and responsibilities of
his office. These were not the qualities that Addington was seeking in
a cabinet colleague, but both the king and his second son, Frederick,
the duke of York, who was commander in chief of the army, insisted
that Pelham be included in the cabinet. They suggested that Addington offer Pelham the War Office, which suited York, who had to work
closely with the secretary for War. Pelham refused the post once, but
the king insisted that Addington try again. He refused a second time.
Again at the insistence of the king, Addington offered Pelham the
presidency of the Board of Control, but he insisted on a cabinet
office. Addington eventually became exasperated by all the royal pressure to conciliate Pelham, who seemed adamantly opposed to joining
the ministry. He once threw up his arms and demanded of one of the
king's friends, "Would you have me go on my knees to him?" York and
the king continued to insist that Addington include Pelham in the
cabinet, however, and the new prime minister wanted to avoid making political enemies at such an early stage. In the end, Addington
found a solution. Pelham took the leadership in the House of Lords,
and the position as home secretary, which Portland agreed to vacate.
In the end, the arrangement for Pelham pleased the king, but it did
not bode well for cabinet solidarity.[24]

Another drawback of Addington's favored relationship with

George III was that the king's mental health was fragile. If he became incapacitated, there would need to be a regency under the Prince of Wales, who, as he was on bad terms with his father, was likely to dismiss his ministers and appoint Fox. The king's health became an issue for Addington almost immediately after he agreed to take office, as the king suffered another attack of porphyria in mid-February and became incapacitated for about four weeks beginning on 20 February. This created a great political uncertainty, as Pitt and most of his colleagues who intended to resign had to remain in office until the king became well enough to accept their resignations. Addington and Pitt agreed that both the new and the old ministers should attend cabinet meetings together until after the king recovered. During the king's illness, the Prince of Wales and his Whig associates exacerbated the political crisis by reacting as though the king would not recover. Addington also experienced personal uncertainty. He had resigned the Speakership and his parliamentary seat, as it was required of M.P.s taking government office to resign their seats and face a by-election. Pitt did not have the opportunity, however, to return his seals of office to the king before he became ill. Addington's by-election could not be held until he took office, which could not happen until the king recovered.

The king recovered in March to a sufficient extent to rule out a regency, but immediately afterwards a development occurred that was to have enormous consequences. Upon hearing on 6 March that Pitt had enquired after his health, the king replied, "Tell him I am now quite well—quite recovered from my illness; but what has he not to answer for who is the cause of my having been ill at all?"[25] Pitt understood this to mean that the king believed that the reason that he became ill was because Pitt had raised the issue of Catholic Emancipation. This distressed Pitt, and he immediately promised never to raise the Catholic issue again during the king's reign. When the news of this got out, a group of Pitt's supporters led by George Canning considered that the Catholic question was no longer an obstacle to Pitt's returning to office. Canning was a young and talented politician who held minor office under Pitt. He was quick-witted and an elo-

King George III by Sir William Beechey

(*By courtesy of the National Portrait Gallery, London*)

quent speaker, but he was excessively vain and jealous. He was also fanatically devoted to Pitt and resigned his own post of Treasurer of the Navy because he would not serve under anyone but his mentor. His strong emotional attachment to Pitt clouded his judgment and led him to conclude that Addington was responsible for Pitt's fall. For this reason he despised Addington, and became determined to do all that he could to force Addington's resignation.

Canning and his associates pressed Pitt to reconcile himself with the king for the purpose of facilitating his immediate return to office. This put Pitt in a difficult situation. He had pressed Addington to succeed him on the basis that remaining in office himself was impossible. He could hardly go back to Addington, as Canning suggested, and tell him that he had changed his mind and wanted his old office back. Pitt's reluctance did not deter Canning, who proposed to send a message to Addington requesting his resignation on the grounds that there were no other obstacles to Pitt's returning to office. When Pitt heard about this plot, he ordered Canning to desist. Pitt knew it would be unfair and unreasonable to expect Addington to resign after all that had happened. Nevertheless, Pitt's having forsaken Catholic Emancipation removed the only intractable obstacle to his return to office, and Canning and a small group of Pitt's youngest supporters were determined to resort to any means necessary to secure that end.

The roles that Pitt and the king played in facilitating Addington's appointments to cabinet led a few observers to speculate incorrectly that Addington was not really in charge. Fox, for one, supposed that the whole arrangement was a juggle or a "*dessous des cartes.*" In Addington's own mind, however, he was not merely a caretaker. He had agreed to take office only when Pitt had demonstrated that his differences with the king were irreconcilable. From the start, he was determined to be the effective head of the government with complete control over policy. He was prepared to take any course of action that he believed right, regardless of whether Pitt agreed.[26] At the end of February, prior to discussing with his cabinet colleagues the major questions facing the government, Addington warned them that they must be ready for tough debates and could not count on the support of the previous ministers.[27] He told the French envoy in London, Louis Otto, that he trusted his own judgment and made all of the most difficult decisions himself.[28] During the first few months in office, he often consulted Pitt, but this does not mean that Pitt was directing the government from behind the curtain. Addington relied less on Pitt as time passed and he became more comfortable in office. That most of Addington's cabinet had served under Pitt did not mean that he was still in control. It was common for there to be continuity of personnel in cabinet after a change in prime minister. Moreover, most of Addington's ministers were not loyal Pittites. Portland, Pelham, and St. Vincent had once opposed Pitt. Addington's ministry, like its predecessor, was a coalition of members of different political factions.

The reaction to the news of the impending appointment of Addington and the rest of his cabinet was mixed. Some of Pitt's supporters were angry. Other observers compared Addington's inexperience and speaking ability unfavorably with Pitt's longevity and reputation as a great parliamentary speaker. Some members of the Foxite opposition laughed when they heard that Addington had been appointed, but then they had also laughed when Pitt had been appointed in 1783. They discriminated against Addington because he was the first prime minister who was not related by either blood or marriage to the formal aristocracy. They believed that it was not appropriate for a man of his class to lead the government. Moreover, they were disappointed because, for seventeen years, they had assumed that Pitt was the only obstacle that stood between them and returning to office. Now, their hated enemy had finally fallen, but Addington had stepped into the breach, denying them their chance at office.

Other observers reacted to the news of Addington's accession more positively. Eldon rejoiced at Addington's elevation as a man of strong Protestant principles.[29] Chatham felt that "the king could not have acted more wisely, than in having recourse to the Speaker, on every account, and on none more than that, I am sure, no one man, will feel a more sincere concern than himself, for the occasion which has called him forth."[30] The governor-general of India, Richard, the first Marquess Wellesley, had known Addington at Oxford and expressed great respect for him: "I never can conceive any system to be tainted with the least touch (of public or private dishonor or incorrectness) which is conducted by Addington, in whose virtues & talents I place the most cordial reliance; I therefore wish him to succeed in his Enterprise, if success be attainable with such instruments, & under such strange circumstances."[31] Some backbench M.P.s actually preferred Addington's talents, personality, and manner to Pitt's. One observer had said of Pitt prior to Addington's appointment, "At the close of every brilliant display an expedition failed or a kingdom fell. God send us a stammerer!"[32] After Addington took office, another thanked God for a ministry "Without one of those confounded men of genius in it."[33]

This is not to say that Pitt had become unpopular, but that there was a consensus that Addington was the only suitable candidate to fill Pitt's place. He was "not only the best but the only man that could be found."[34] There was "no alternative but Mr Addington or Mr Fox."[35] Yorke accurately summed up the attitude within ministry: "That some parts of the new Administration are greatly inferior in Talents & Abilities to those of the former no man living can doubt; that it is to be deplored & regretted but it *must* be formed as it is, or Messers. Sheridan, Grey, & Tierney sent for."[36]

Addington's cabinet, like all others, had weaknesses and strengths. The two important weaknesses were speaking ability and a lack of landed magnates. Although they all spoke well on occasion, no one on the front bench was consistently eloquent and convincing. During Addington's first few months in office, Pitt provided valuable assistance, but Addington could not rely on him indefinitely. The problem was not that Addington had appointed poor speakers instead of good ones, but that great debaters were not available. The ministry was also short on landed magnates who controlled parliamentary seats. While

Portland had a considerable pedigree and several M.P.s under his control, he and John Fane, the tenth earl of Westmorland, who held the position of Lord Privy Seal, were the only two members of the landed aristocracy in the cabinet. This was important because issues of class influenced whether some members of the landed aristocracy would support the government.

The lack of nobility in the cabinet underscored its deficiency in the skill of parliamentary debate. Liverpool explained this connection: "nobility joined to Talents, produces a wonderful Effect upon the Minds of men; and Talents, where there is no Nobility, must be very conspicuous, to compensate for the Want of it;—This is exactly the State of Mr Addington: a worthy and good man, and with a certain Degree of Talents, but not sufficient to hold him up, against the Aristocratic Feelings of Mankind."[37] Addington would have required extraordinary talents to compensate for his lack of pedigree in the eyes of many in the aristocracy.[38] Pitt's ministry had also been short on magnates, but his eloquence on the floor of the Commons often made up for that. In the short term, Addington's lack of command of the Commons was offset by Pitt's support and the fractionalized opposition. In the long term, however, his failure to manage Parliament adequately ultimately caused the fall of his ministry three years later.

These deficiencies should not overshadow the ministry's several important attributes. Addington, Hawkesbury, Hobart, St. Vincent, and Pelham were as competent and businesslike as many who had preceded them.[39] They proved effective in formulating sound policies in extremely difficult circumstances, when more eloquent members of the opposition were advocating unrealistic alternatives. Their strengths were their sound common sense and willingness to make tough decisions.

On balance, the prospects for the long-term survival of Addington's government were good. After it survived the series of initial crises, more people began to think that it would continue. The wife of Fox's nephew observed, "The first laugh over people begin to think this Administration may last, and if they commence a negotiation [for peace with France] they will even become popular."[40] Pitt believed that even though Addington was not a great orator, he could survive, if he were well supported.[41] Glenbervie even prophesied that if he could "stand up firm for a few weeks while attacked by all the invective, vehemence, sarcasm, virulence, menaces, affected contempt and ridicule which will be used in order to bully or laugh him out of his place, the Opposition or the House will get tired of that sort of warfare, and men of property, rank, and talents will then cling to him."[42] The greatest challenges for Addington were the military, diplomatic, and political crises left by Pitt, and his political survival depended on the effectiveness of his policies in resolving them.

CHAPTER 2

Peacemaking

*T*he most pressing issue facing Addington when he took office was the threat to British security posed by the military, economic, and social consequences of the war with France and by the naval dispute with the League of Armed Neutrality. Great Britain had been at war with France for eight years. From a military perspective, the British were losing. The French armies had destroyed two Grand Coalitions, and all of Great Britain's Great Power allies had withdrawn from the war. France had driven the allied armies from the Low Countries and across Central Europe and had incorporated a large portion of this territory under French rule. The states that bordered France from the Mediterranean to the North Sea had also become allies of France. French troops remained in Egypt, threatening the security of British India. Not only had Great Britain lost its most important allies, the practices of the Royal Navy in dealing with neutral powers on the open seas had provoked the hostility of Denmark, Sweden, Prussia, and Russia, who formed a naval alliance to resist the Royal Navy by force. Great Britain was virtually in a state of war against all of Europe with the exception of Austria.

British conquest of the colonies of the French and their allies in the East and West Indies could not compensate the British economy for the harm caused by the war. The most important British trading interests were with Western and Northern Europe, and by 1801 British commercial ties in these regions were severed almost entirely. A French embargo imposed on British trade had a devastating effect on British commercial interests, which depended on European import and export markets. Business and personal bankruptcies were increasing, as were the ranks of the unemployed. The British economy required a respite from the conditions of war and a restoration of traditional markets. The British Treasury, the Bank of England, and other financial institutions needed a relaxation of the wartime restrictions on the money supply. The British pound was declining in value on the international currency markets, hurting commerce further. Supplying the armed forces required increasing levels of taxation and relying on large government loans, which exacerbated the strain on the economy. Government finances had been stretched so far that it was doubtful whether the British could continue to fight for an extended period. The Royal Navy was in poor repair, lacking naval stores that the Baltic states refused to sell, while the army was short of artillery, weapons, and ammunition. The armed forces needed a period of restoration. Short-term prospects for the British war effort were poor. On another level, the effects of the war had drained the British emotionally and psychologically. The British public was tired of the war and of the hardships it imposed.

Most important of all, however, was the starvation caused by the failure of the recent harvests and loss of access to European food supplies. Lord Grenville, Pitt's foreign secretary, heard from his brother that "the scarcity of bread and the consequent distress of the poor, if it continues, will, I believe, force you whether you will or no to make your peace with France."[1] As the social strains increased and the prospects of winning the war diminished, the war became increasingly unpopular.[2] The *Annual Register* of 1801 claimed, "Though the difficulties and dangers, that encompassed Great Britain, from the commencement of the war, had been very great, the situation of this country in the three first months of 1801, had become critical and alarming almost beyond any former example. . . . It was now quite apparent, that the country was plunged into a situation of difficulty and distress, from which nothing but a speedy peace could relieve it."[3]

Addington appreciated the gravity of the military, economic, and social crises and their interrelationship long before he became prime minister. He was a proponent of peace as early as October 1797, considering "the state of the country as to its interior to be so bad that we cannot, in strict duty venture to reject . . . [a French] offer, which may at least give us some interval of rest for doing what we have to do at home."[4] Bonaparte proposed peace in December 1799, but Pitt and Grenville refused, and Addington criticized them for doing so.[5] In September 1800, he expressed despair about the course of the war and the state of internal affairs.[6] At that time, Pitt was convalescing for several weeks at Woodley. This gave Addington the opportunity to discuss the grain crisis, and he pressed Pitt to intervene in the market to increase the supply of grain.[7] Addington had reached this conclusion after analyzing the causes of the crisis and studying the fluctuations in the price of grain.[8] Above and beyond his concerns about national security, Addington was also personally concerned about the plight of the poor. He was a member of "the Society for Bettering the Condition and Increasing the Comforts of the Poor" and expended some of his own limited resources financing and administering soup kitchens in the neighborhood surrounding his estate in Devon.[9]

Addington supported ending the war because of the desperate political and economic situation. Upon taking office, he faced a dangerous diplomatic tangle and increasing difficulties in financing the war. Confronting popular dissatisfaction and the internal threat posed by social unrest, Addington recognized that Great Britain required an interval of peace, however short. Pitt too had been just as eager to end the war, but had encountered two major obstacles. First, his cabinet had become so divided that it could not agree on terms. Second, the French did not believe peace could be negotiated with Pitt. This was a view also held by many British observers.[10] Hence, in seeking to end the war, Addington was following a policy Pitt endorsed but could not implement.[11]

Bringing the war with France and the dispute with the League of Armed Neutrality to an end was, however, more difficult than it appeared. British public and parliamentary opinion demanded peace, but on terms favorable to Great Britain. Addington felt that, at a minimum, the French must evacuate Egypt and the British must retain some colonial conquests to compensate for the growing power of France in Europe. The British had to resolve the naval dispute with the League of Armed Neutrality on terms that would allow the Royal Navy to retain its supremacy. Great Britain also had to improve relations with Russia, after France the most powerful state in Europe. Russia had the power to harm British interests, but also to provide effective assistance in the struggle with France. Therefore, before the British could achieve the breathing space they required, they had to dissolve the League of Armed Neutrality, restore a favorable relationship with the Russians, and negotiate a treaty of peace with the French that would address Great Britain's essential security interests.

THE LEAGUE OF ARMED NEUTRALITY AND RUSSIA

Addington took a more direct role in the formulation and conduct of British foreign policy than was customary for the prime minister. He and Hawkesbury worked closely together on all major decisions. They gave priority to addressing the conflict with the League of Armed Neutrality, which, combined with the embargo on British trade in the Baltic, posed a more urgent threat to British wealth and naval power than did the war with France. The League united the strongest navies of Europe in an alliance formed to enforce the rights of neutral shipping. Great Britain's dispute with Denmark and Sweden concerned the rights of belligerent and neutral powers on the seas. The League supported the position in maritime law that belligerent powers could not board, search, or seize merchant ships that were flying neutral flags or being escorted by warships. As British power was based on maritime and commercial dominance, Great Britain could not accept these principles of maritime law. On the other side, the neutrals objected to the high-handed manner in which

British authorities searched their ships and the obvious pro-British bias of the British Admiralty Courts, particularly those in the Caribbean.

The British approach to the League of Armed Neutrality was to deal with one member at a time. Denmark was first in line. Pitt and Grenville decided to be firm with Denmark, and Addington and Hawkesbury agreed to continue this approach. In response to the declaration of the League of Armed Neutrality to resist searches, Pitt had sent a fleet to Copenhagen to secure passage of the Sound between Denmark and Sweden and to coerce the Danes into renouncing the treaty. A large force under Admiral Sir Hyde Parker, with Horatio, Viscount Nelson, as second in command, assembled at Yarmouth in February 1801. Their instructions were to proceed to the Baltic as soon as it was free of ice, in order to arrive before the Swedes and Russians could send their navies to support the Danes. Once the Danes had surrendered, the fleet was to sail to Revel and Kronstadt to attack the Russians.

There were advantages to attempting to resolve the dispute through negotiation, however, provided that it could achieve the same goals of preserving Great Britain's naval and commercial security. In early February, the Foreign Office received an anonymous letter, believed to have been sent by Prince Charles of Hesse, father-in-law to the Prince Royal of Denmark, indicating that the Danes wished to negotiate. Dispatches from William Drummond, the British minister in Copenhagen, corroborated this information, and Addington and Hawkesbury sought to resolve the crisis diplomatically. They had three options. The first was to proceed with the naval attack in the Baltic, as planned by the previous administration. The drawback to this approach was that provoking a naval war would exacerbate the impression—prevalent at the time both at home and abroad—that the British government was not interested in peace. The second option was to suspend naval operations and resolve the crisis through negotiation. A diplomatic strategy unbacked by the threat of war, however, was not likely to succeed in forcing the Baltic powers to abandon the principles of the League of Armed Neutrality. Grenville, who continued to advise the new government on diplomatic issues, counseled against accepting the Danish offer to resolve the dispute through negotiation. The third option was to proceed with the naval operation but also negotiate with the Danes until the fleet arrived in the Baltic. Addington and Hawkesbury chose this option. If negotiations were successful, war would be averted. If negotiations failed, Great Britain at least would have demonstrated the inclination to resolve the dispute peacefully. As the fleet could not reach Copenhagen before the end of March, no time would be lost in the attempt.[12]

A diplomatic solution was preferable because it might repair the damage that the previous government had caused to British relations with the other European powers. Most of the courts of Europe found Grenville's diplomacy to be haughty and high-handed.[13] British war policies during the First Coalition with Austria and Prussia, 1793–97, and the Second Coalition with Austria and Russia, 1798–1800, had also caused resentment. The British focused their attention on conquering enemy colonies, while expecting the Austrians, Prussians, and Russians to face the brunt of the French army in Europe. As a result, Great Britain gained the reputation as an ineffective and unreliable ally.[14] By persevering in the war after all their allies had made peace with France, the British appeared to be warmongers, the only obstacle to a European peace that everyone expected would provide commercial benefits to all of Europe. It was important for the new British government to demonstrate to the rest of Europe that British diplomacy was changing. Accepting Prince Charles's offer to negotiate was the first step.

Addington sent Vansittart as special envoy to meet Prince Charles in Schleswig. Vansittart's orders were that, if the Danes appeared willing to abandon the League of Armed Neutrality and to regulate permanently the question of neutral law, he was to join Drummond to assist with the negotiations.[15] Despite wishing to appear conciliatory, the British were determined to convince the Danes that they would remain firm: they could accept nothing less than the termination of

the League of Armed Neutrality. To drive home this point, Hawkesbury sent a stern note on 25 February to the Danish ministers warn-
ing that, if they did not accommodate, the British would resort to
force. That same day he sent an order to the Admiralty "to capture or
destroy the Navy & weaken as much as possible the Maritime
Resources of Denmark in the Port of Copenhagen, or wherever they
may be found and can be attacked."[16]

Vansittart's mission proved unsuccessful, however, because the
Danes felt that they were not in a position to agree to Great Britain's
terms of surrender. As one of the lesser powers of Europe, Denmark
was subject to the influence of the Great Powers, particularly Russia,
the predominant power on the Baltic Sea because it also exercised
influence over Sweden and Prussia. The Danes knew that they could
not afford to alienate the Russians on the issue of the League of
Armed Neutrality. Furthermore, as a signatory of the convention with
Sweden and Prussia, Denmark feared that it would lose face by abandoning the League, and might provoke considerable animosity from
two of its closest neighbors. The Danes particularly wished to avoid
giving the Swedes an excuse to invade the Danish province of Nor-
way. The Danes believed that the consequences of abandoning their
allies would be greater than the price to be paid by a naval war.[17]

Hawkesbury sent Drummond an ultimatum with his note of 25
February stating that, if the Danes did not come to terms within
forty-eight hours of receipt of the dispatch, the issue would be turned
over to the Royal Navy.[18] The fleet that left Yarmouth on 12 March
arrived off Copenhagen eight days later and attacked Danish shipping
and artillery in Copenhagen harbor on 2 April, commencing the first
Battle of Copenhagen.[19] After defeating the Danish fleet, Parker and
Nelson signed an agreement with the Danes on 9 April. The terms of
the accord included an armistice of fourteen weeks to provide for
direct negotiations between Copenhagen and London, on the conditions that the Treaty of Armed Neutrality be suspended during the
negotiations and that the British fleet be allowed to obtain provisions
in Copenhagen and free passage of the Sound. This agreement pre-

served British interests in the Baltic for an interval that permitted the British to turn their attention to improving relations with Russia, the real threat behind the Armed Neutrality.

The principal focus of foreign policy of the new British government was Russia. Rapprochement with Russia was necessary to the British, not only as a means to strengthen their political and military position prior to negotiating peace with France, but also as an end in itself.[20] The primary British objective, which became obvious to the Austrian ambassador in London, Count Starhemberg, was "to do everything to separate Russia from France" and then to secure a diplomatic and military alliance.[21] This policy followed an established trend, for during the eighteenth century British official and popular opinion had considered Russia a natural ally in European affairs. Both states had interests in opposing the dominance of France. As two powers situated at opposite ends of the Continent, they had few conflicting interests. The reason the British had not achieved a strong alliance with the Russians in the past was that they had proved unwilling to make the diplomatic or financial sacrifices the Russians required.[22] The British and the Russians fought as allies against France during 1798–1800, and mutual blame and recrimination over their defeat by the French soured their relations thereafter. The major Anglo-Russian initiative during the war was a joint invasion of North Holland in 1799, which had to be withdrawn after only a few weeks. Each side blamed the other for the failure of the expedition. The British had also decided to retain troops on Malta, which contravened an agreement that they had made with the Russians to return control of the island to the Knights of Malta once the French troops had been expelled. In response, the Russians had joined the League of Armed Neutrality and made a diplomatic overture to France. Addington and Hawkesbury sought to repair Anglo-Russian relations and even held out a faint hope that they might be able to forge an alliance if Franco-Russian relations ever deteriorated again.[23]

While the new cabinet was deliberating over whether to propose peace to the French, it also decided to make a conciliatory overture to the Russians. As the tsar had expelled the British representative in St. Petersburg in June 1800, Hawkesbury sent the offer on 24 March through the British minister in Berlin. He instructed him "to endeavour, in the first instance to negotiate a Treaty on Maritime Law, . . . but if you should find the Russian Government unwilling to enter into Engagements of this nature, His Majesty will be satisfied with a formal Renunciation of the Convention signed at [St.] Petersburgh [*sic*] on the 16th of December, and will, on this Condition, and on that of the Embargo being immediately taken off, consent to the Terms which have been proposed respecting Malta."[24] These instructions signaled an important change of direction in British foreign policy: the new government was prepared to evacuate Malta in order to facilitate an Anglo-Russian reconciliation. This change of policy coincided with an important change in Russia. On the day that Hawkesbury wrote the dispatch, a conspiracy of Russian aristocrats assassinated Paul I in St. Petersburg. His son and successor, Alexander I, was more favorably disposed toward Great Britain, because he wanted peace and did not share his father's concern about Malta or support for the League of Armed Neutrality. He was also generally inclined to turn the attention of the Russian government away from foreign entanglements and toward reform at home.[25] Accordingly, he sent messages through his chancellor, Count P. A. Pahlen, and the former Russian minister in London, Simon Vorontsov, that he wished to reestablish diplomatic relations and resolve outstanding Anglo-Russian disputes.[26]

Addington and Hawkesbury were delighted at the sudden turn of events and determined to take advantage of them. They took pains in selecting a new ambassador to negotiate a settlement over the Armed Neutrality, wanting to appoint someone who would be agreeable to Alexander I. After careful consideration, they chose Alleyne Fitzherbert, Baron St. Helens, who was an experienced diplomat with knowledge of Russia (he had been envoy extraordinary to Russia during the reign of Catherine II) and a personal friend of George III. St. Helens was the ablest and most distinguished of British diplomats. It was hoped that his appointment would flatter the tsar and that the new ambassador would be able to negotiate a treaty favorable to British interests.

Great Britain's diplomatic position had changed with the new developments in international affairs. The recent victory at Copenhagen and the death of Paul I had strengthened the British position. Accordingly, the British did not need to offer as many concessions to the Russians as Hawkesbury had instructed the British minister in Berlin to offer.[27] Nevertheless, Anglo-Russian diplomacy required a conciliatory approach. Alexander I was prepared to fight the British if they demanded unreasonable terms. In order to sustain Russia's prestige with the Baltic states, the tsar required at least some small concessions from the British on behalf of his allies before he would abandon the Armed Neutrality.[28] The new British government would have to be more willing to compromise than its predecessor had been, if it were to succeed in improving Anglo-Russian relations.

Addington and Hawkesbury were ready to compromise, because removing the threat of war and restoring diplomatic relations were their main objectives. They sought more that just peace with Russia. They desired a diplomatic understanding that could be used to contain the power of France. Before they could achieve this goal, they had to remove sources of Anglo-Russian friction, the most serious of which was the dispute over maritime law that had precipitated the formation of the League of Armed Neutrality. The challenge was to persuade the Russians to allow the British navy to continue its practices of blockade and searching neutral ships for the purpose of seizing enemy property.

This first major diplomatic initiative of the new ministry was remarkably successful. St. Helens arrived in St. Petersburg on 18 May, and although Count N. P. Panin, the Russian negotiator, tried to obtain concessions, he did not prove intransigent. After two weeks of bartering, they signed an agreement on 17 June.[29] The treaty achieved all of the major British objectives at relatively little cost. The convention recognized the rights of search and seizure, subject to restrictions the British had been willing to make all along. St. Helens also obtained a relatively loose definition of blockade, while the tsar even consented to overlook the continued British occupation of Malta, so as not to impede the agreement.[30] Alexander I's main concern was to end hostilities with Russia's most important trading partner. He was also pleased that the British had offered him enough concessions in terms of restrictions on the right of search and seizure to allow him to save his face with his Baltic allies, even though the treaty had the effect of sacrificing the rights of neutrals that the Armed Neutrality had been formed to protect.[31]

Once peace with Russia had been achieved and the threat of the League of Armed Neutrality dissolved, Addington and Hawkesbury tried to take the Anglo-Russian reconciliation one step further by proposing an alliance. They sought a close commitment with Russia because it was "the only Power on the Continent capable of balancing the Influence of France."[32] The Austrians had direct strategic interests in Germany and Italy that gave them more of a stake in the war with France than any other power, and they had done most of the fighting on the Continent during the course of the war. Nevertheless, the Austrians were financially and militarily exhausted by 1801. They were also reluctant to commit all of their military resources against France, out of fear that Russia and Prussia would take the opportunity to expand their territory and influence Eastern Europe.[33] Russia was the most powerful state in Europe other than France, exercising considerable influence in Austria, Prussia, Turkey, and the Scandinavian states. Therefore, the British policy of pursuing a grand coalition against France could not succeed without the support of Russia.[34]

Addington and Hawkesbury hoped that once Anglo-Russian relations improved, they could persuade Russia to join the war against France. While St. Helens was negotiating the convention in St. Petersburg in May 1801, Franco-Russian relations broke down, and this rupture presented an opportunity to form an Anglo-Russian alliance. In order to take advantage of that opportunity, it was necessary to find an issue where British and Russian interests coincided. The Russians had joined the war against France in 1798 after Bonaparte had invaded Egypt, and this demonstrated that the security of the Turkish empire was one issue upon which the British and Russians could agree. On 19 May, Hawkesbury instructed St. Helens to discover whether the Russians would agree to a joint Anglo-Russian guarantee of Egypt to Turkey to prevent the French from invading Egypt again. St. Helens must "impress on their minds, that His Majesty is actuated by no views of ambition and aggrandizement, but solely by a desire of restoring Peace to Europe, on Terms which may insure its duration." Addington expressed the same desire for an alliance to Vorontsov, who had resumed his post as Russian minister in London. The British were offering the Russians an equal, if not a predominant, role in any joint military and diplomatic efforts.[35]

The conclusion of the Anglo-Russian convention gave the British an important edge. Starhemberg speculated, "The plan is certainly to coordinate with Russia, for the purpose of forcing the other powers of Europe, under the pretext of a concert adopted in common, to propose to France, at gunpoint, the conditions of the peace of which the British cabinet would be the principal arbitrator."[36] This, of course, was something the Austrians dreaded. A peace settlement dictated by the British alone, or by the British and the Russians together, was unlikely to meet the needs of Austria. Throughout the war, the British had expected the Austrians to become the third partner in a Continental alliance and could not understand the Austrians' reluctance. While the Austrians wished to contain the territorial expansion of France, they did not wish to weaken it entirely, because a strong France was necessary to counterbalance the power of Russia in Eastern Europe. Therefore, a new territorial settlement dominated by Russia was not in Austria's interest, because if the Russians became too powerful and expanded their territory in Eastern Europe, they could threaten Austria's existence as a Great Power.[37] This would also threaten British interests in the Near East. The failure to recognize that a collapse of French power would pose a serious risk to the balance of power in Eastern Europe and the Near East was a critical flaw in British foreign policy during the French Revolutionary and Napoleonic Wars.

Unfortunately for the British, but fortunately for the Austrians, the Russians refused in 1801 to join an alliance against France. While recognizing that Great Britain was one of Russia's "natural allies," the tsar wished to avoid commitments likely to offend Bonaparte. He had not made peace with Great Britain for the purpose of fighting France.[38] "I will mostly strive to follow a national system, that is to say a system founded on the advantages of state, and not, as it has often been, on a preference for one or another power. I would be, if I would judge useful for Russia, on as good terms with France for the same reasons that motivate me now to cultivate the friendship of Great Britain."[39] He wished to improve Russian agriculture and industry, and the administrative system, all of which required that the first principle of his policy "must be to maintain peace."[40]

The failure to gain the assistance of Russia in the war against France should not obscure the important diplomatic achievements of the new British government. It took office when Great Britain faced the dangerous prospect of a Franco-Russian alliance. Within three months, careful diplomacy had removed the Russian threat and terminated the League of Armed Neutrality without sacrificing any important British interests on the question of neutral rights. Naval action and firm diplomacy had also removed any threat to British interests posed by Denmark. By the summer of 1801, the diplomatic position of Great Britain had greatly improved from what it had been at the beginning of the year. Moreover, while the British had been negotiating with the Russians, they had also been negotiating with the French, with the same ultimate objective: to secure a peace settlement that would preserve Great Britain's essential security interests.

NEGOTIATING PEACE WITH FRANCE

Addington had been a proponent of peace for several years and, upon taking office as prime minister, decided to attempt to negotiate a treaty with France. At a meeting on 19 March, the new cabinet decided formally to request the permission of the king to commence the negotiations. Addington conveyed this message to the king and received his consent that same day.[41] Hawkesbury invited Otto, the French agent in London for the exchange of prisoners of war, to meet on 21 March at his home in Sackville Street where negotiations began.

He suggested to Otto that they should make written records only by
mutual consent in order to minimize the potential for proposals to be
leaked to the British press, which might cause popular outbursts that
would prejudice his bargaining position. Rumors of progress during
the course of previous negotiations had caused considerable fluctua-
tion in the London financial markets.[42]

Although the French tried to take advantage of Hawkesbury's lack
of diplomatic experience, they had little success. Bonaparte instructed
Otto to suggest a maritime armistice as a preliminary to the peace,
but Hawkesbury refused, for he recognized that it would have allowed
the French to reinforce their army in Egypt and left them unimpeded
on the Continent, while, at the same time, it would have deprived the
British of their strongest weapons.[43] Otto then attempted to pressure
Hawkesbury into accepting one of two alternatives regarding Egypt,
which he regarded as the critical question in the negotiations.[44] He
characterized these alternatives as "whether France should relinquish
Egypt, Great Britain relinquishing the whole, or some part of her
Conquests; or whether France should retain Egypt, Great Britain preserving her Conquests."[45] Hawkesbury refused both of these alternatives. The British could agree neither to surrender all of their conquests nor to allow France to keep Egypt, because it would continue
to threaten British India. The British did not intend to acquire Egypt
for themselves. As Hawkesbury explained to the Russians and the
Turks, the British had always intended to restore Egypt to the Turks
once peace was concluded.[46] Any advantage to be gained by keeping
Egypt would be outweighed by Russian and Turkish animosity.

Addington followed Pitt's policy of seeking to restore Egypt to the
Turks by either military or diplomatic means. In March 1801, an
amphibious force successfully invaded Egypt and defeated the French
forces in several key battles. The British army was unable, however, to
force the French to surrender. Although the British had reason to
expect that they would eventually achieve victory, no one could pre-
dict how long it would take. Moreover, owing to the rudimentary system of communication available at the time, news from Egypt took
almost two months to reach Paris and London. Therefore, until they

heard the results of the fighting in Egypt, the British were prepared to relinquish some of Great Britain's conquests in return for the French evacuating Egypt.[47]

The arrival on 13 April of the Russian chancellor's letter to Hawkesbury announcing the death of Paul I strengthened the British bargaining position with the French by reducing the likelihood of a Franco-Russian alliance, but it did not remove the incentive for the British government to seek peace. Internal pressures for peace were increasing, and, according to Otto, the ministers remained concerned about the consequences of social unrest. This assessment was correct. On 1 April, Addington moved in the Commons for a secret committee to examine evidence of disaffection in Ireland and England. By 13 April, the committee concluded that there was a strong connection between radicalism and distress, and the fear of a French invasion combined with the expiry of Pitt's repressive legislation could facilitate an insurrection. The committee recommended the reintroduction of the expired legislation, and Addington complied.[48]

Hawkesbury continued the negotiations but took a stronger position, making a counteroffer to Otto on the subject of Egypt. On 14 April, Hawkesbury explained that the cabinet had rejected the French offers because, in the event of their evacuating Egypt, the British kept nothing to compensate for France's other acquisitions. He then proposed that, if France restored Egypt to the Turks, Great Britain would return all conquests except Ceylon, Malta, Trinidad, Tobago, Guadeloupe, and Martinique, but stipulated that the British would withdraw this offer if they received news of an evacuation of Egypt by the French forces.[49] The French rejected this proposal, however, and the fundamental difference of opinion over the future of Egypt caused the negotiations eventually to bog down.[50] Otto confirmed that "All eyes are fixed on Egypt," and as long as the fate of Egypt was undecided, it would be impossible to obtain better terms.[51] It would take until 14 May for the British to learn that on 21 March their army had won a major battle but had not forced the French to surrender. The British, though confident of eventual victory, knew it would take a few more months.

Although the British position was improving, continuing the war indefinitely was not a viable option. Hawkesbury explained to the British minister at Vienna that, although prospects were brighter, the government was still determined to seek peace, because the British could not carry on the war alone and there was no prospect of another European power joining in the near future. He added:

> It is impossible not to lament, for the Sake of Europe, that the Two great Confederacies of which this Country made a part, should have unfortunately failed in the attainment of the End which they had in view—but, to whatever cause their Failure may be ascribed, it is by no means probable, that, at this time, a third Confederacy could be formed, which would have the same Chance of success as the Two preceding ones; and, even if it could, the Difficulty of raising the necessary Supplies (notwithstanding the abundant Resources of the Country) is become so great from the long Continuance of the War, that it could not be wise, under existing Circumstances, to run the Risk of a Third Failure, unless we were forced to it by absolute necessity.

Hawkesbury remained determined to cultivate good relations with Russia, Austria, and Prussia, even if they could not be of help in the immediate future, for "whatever their Sentiments may be respecting Peace, We ought never to forget that it is possible we may have no Choice, and that we may be reduced to the necessity of trying again the Chances of War; and, even if Peace should be concluded, the Power of France, on the Continent of Europe is become so formidable, that it is of the utmost Importance that a good understanding should subsist amongst the other Great powers of Europe."[52]

Finding terms that would be acceptable to both the British and the French, however, remained difficult. Bonaparte was not prepared to trade France's territorial acquisitions in Europe for the return of a few colonies.[53] Accepting a settlement on those terms might have provoked serious opposition in France and undermined his position. He was prepared to evacuate French and Spanish troops from the territories of Great Britain's allies—Portugal, Naples, and Turkey—but nothing more. On the other hand, if the British refused to relinquish their colonial conquests, France would continue to occupy Italy and

Portugal, threatening British commercial and strategic interest in the Mediterranean. From the middle of April until the end of May, the negotiations were alternately resumed and suspended as Otto and Hawkesbury had difficulty establishing common ground. Hawkesbury sought a settlement that would give the British security and allow them to keep some of the colonial conquests to compensate for the expense of the war. Bonaparte wanted the settlement to reflect the military reality: a triumph for France. Both sides were reluctant to make major concessions.

As reports of the British success in Egypt reached London, Otto realized that his bargaining position would weaken if news of a final French surrender arrived. On 1 June, he pressed for a resumption of negotiations. Hawkesbury responded by re-offering the British terms of 14 April, arguing that this constituted a concession because Great Britain's diplomatic position had improved.[54] Otto tried to counter the British demands by threatening Portugal: Spain and Portugal had signed a peace treaty, but the First Consul refused to ratify it (leaving Portugal subject to further conquest) unless the British offered more concessions. At this point, the negotiations reached another stalemate when the French insisted that the British return all conquests except Ceylon, a demand the British considered unacceptable.[55]

This was a decisive point in the negotiations for the British. Addington and Hawkesbury wished to avoid making further concessions but dreaded the only alternative, which was to continue the war. Great Britain's strategic position was once again deteriorating: Prussian troops had occupied Hanover, and the French were threatening to overrun Portugal as they had Naples. In Egypt, there was little hope of a final French capitulation in the near future. The new ministers had made a considerable political investment in the negotiations, and they feared losing the faith of British and foreign opinion, which favored peace. Some M.P.s representing commercial and financial interests would support the government only if it demonstrated a disposition toward peace. Nevertheless, the British negotiators could not agree to return all colonial conquests except Ceylon, judging that such terms would neither protect Great Britain's strategic interests nor be acceptable to Parliament, the king, and the public, despite its desire for peace.[56]

After a long meeting on 28 July, the British cabinet decided to attempt once more to get Otto to improve the French offer. This time Hawkesbury presented a new proposal that proved a decisive step toward a final agreement. One of the major stumbling blocks in the negotiation was the British occupation of Malta. The French wanted the British to evacuate, but the British feared that the French would invade again at the next opportunity. Hawkesbury broke the impasse on 5 August by offering to neutralize Malta.[57] This appeared to be a major concession in the negotiations and an important step toward achieving peace, but in fact the British already intended to evacuate Malta in order to placate Russia.[58] As the Knights of St. John were not strong enough to defend the island, Hawkesbury proposed to Otto that it should be garrisoned by a third power, ideally Russia.

In return for this concession, Hawkesbury demanded that the British be permitted to retain a number of colonial conquests in the Caribbean. Bonaparte agreed to Hawkesbury's offer on Malta but claimed that Great Britain did not require more territory in the West Indies. He did not want Great Britain to achieve the same hegemony there as in the East Indies.[59] Otto offered to allow the British to keep Tobago in addition to Ceylon. Hawkesbury, though pleased with the change in the French tone, insisted that to protect Great Britain's interests in the West Indies, the British must retain another colony in addition to Tobago. The British were still eager for peace, but the terms the French were offering remained unacceptable.[60]

At this point, conflicting reports from Egypt sent the negotiations into turmoil. When an unconfirmed report of the fall of Cairo arrived, Otto decided a quick agreement was necessary and requested permission from Charles Maurice de Talleyrand, the French foreign minister, and Bonaparte to accept Hawkesbury's offer of 5 August, with Tobago and St. Lucia remaining in British hands, while Demerara, Essequibo, and Berbice were to become free ports.[61] Bonaparte refused, however, and instructed Otto to dilute as many of the British demands as possible. Otto then made a further proposal. As Talleyrand had previously given him permission to offer Trinidad to the British, Otto proposed to Hawkesbury that the British could keep it if they renounced Tobago, Demerara, Essequibo, and Berbice.[62] The British, however, demanded both Trinidad and Tobago.

As the end of summer neared, the French became resolved that the negotiations must be concluded, whether there was an agreement or not. On 17 September, Bonaparte complained that the suspension of hostilities during the negotiations was stagnating his army. Autumn was approaching and, if there was to be war on the Continent, he must campaign before winter. He also was planning an expedition to recover St. Domingue (Haiti). Peace must be signed before 10 vendémiaire (2 October) or not at all. Nevertheless, he would offer no more concessions to the British. "They risk losing all," he said, "if they seek for more."[63] Otto delivered the ultimatum on 22 September along with a project for a treaty of peace, but Hawkesbury still remained dissatisfied.

During the last week of September Addington and Hawkesbury realized that the negotiations had reached the decisive phase. There had been a number of critical points along the way, but in those cases the question was whether to accept the French terms or continue the negotiations. This time the discussions could no longer be continued indefinitely. Their choice was either to propose terms the French would accept or to continue the war. The critical decisions they made at this point must be the focus of any assessment of their performance.

In order to end the war, the British had to make one more overture to the French, and this time it had to succeed. Great Britain's diplomatic position had undergone some significant changes since the commencement of the negotiations in March, and two new issues had moved to the forefront. The first was the prospect of a French invasion, which the British began to take more seriously by the end of August. During September, Addington had discussed the defense of southern England with Pelham, Pitt, and the Royal Engineers. On 26 September, Glenbervie noted in his diary that "The expectation of an invasion is greater than I ever remember."[64]

The other issue, and Addington's predominant concern, was the future of the country's finances. He doubted whether the economy could stand the strain of further war, and there was some question as to whether the government could secure another loan on reasonable terms. Those who controlled the money markets in the City seemed to desire peace, as it was generally believed that Bonaparte would reopen European markets to British goods. In addition, the income tax was extremely unpopular, and Pitt had borrowed heavily, using the projected yield of the tax as security. Yorke predicted that, if they carried on the war for two more years, the financial position might force the government to make peace on even worse terms.[65]

At this vital juncture, a difference of opinion emerged between Addington and Hawkesbury. The former argued in favor of peace and the latter opposed any further concessions. Addington decided to consult Pitt for help in resolving this impasse. On 26 September, Addington, Hawkesbury, and Pitt stayed up most of the night discussing these issues. In the end, Addington, with Pitt's support, persuaded Hawkesbury that peace was worth the price, on two conditions. The first was to better secure the neutrality of Malta. The second was to get the French to agree to allow Great Britain's allies, Portugal and Naples, to accede to the treaty.[66]

With these goals in mind, on September 28, Addington intervened in Hawkesbury's meeting with Otto and effectively took the reins of negotiations from the foreign secretary. Citing the pretext that the mutual goal of Great Britain and France in negotiating peace was not merely to cease hostilities but to reconcile their two nations, Addington argued that it was necessary to secure the neutrality of Malta, which would otherwise remain a point of contention between them. He also insisted that inviting Great Britain's allies to accede to the treaty was a matter of diplomatic courtesy to which Otto could not object. Whether Addington had deployed his natural charm and diplomatic skills to greater effect, or his position as prime minister gave him greater weight in the negotiations, is not clear. Regardless, Otto stated that Addington was a more effective negotiator than Hawkesbury had been. The next day, Otto delivered another draft treaty, both sides made some minor modifications, and then they shook hands. The deal was done.[67]

Addington earnestly sought the necessary approvals for the treaty. He convened the cabinet to consider the treaty early on 1 October. After a lengthy debate, his cabinet colleagues overcame their doubts and formed a consensus in favor of the treaty. One major hurdle remained though, for the king had been a strong proponent of continuing the war. Immediately after the cabinet meeting concluded that afternoon, Addington went to the king and asserted he would have to resign unless the treaty were approved, because it would not be possible to obtain better terms from the French. The king acquiesced. Hawkesbury then summoned Otto to the Foreign Office and early that same evening they signed the Preliminaries of London.

Starhemberg later stated that it would have been impossible for anyone to have exerted more effort than Hawkesbury had in the negotiations with Otto.[68] His diligence, combined with Addington's intervention at the critical point, had finally achieved their goal. Great Britain and France had signed a Preliminary Treaty of Peace, which settled the major points of contention and provided for a formal peace congress to be conducted in Amiens to finalize the outstanding issues. Under the terms of the treaty, Great Britain returned all French, Spanish, and Dutch conquests except Ceylon and Trinidad, with the Cape opened to all as a free port. Egypt was returned to the Ottoman Empire, whose territorial integrity the treaty guaranteed. The French agreed to evacuate Naples and the Papal States and to restore Portugal's European territory. Great Britain returned Malta to the Knights of St. John under the guarantee of an unnamed third power, with the details to be worked out at Amiens.[69]

From the time they took office until October 1801, the foreign policy of the new British ministers was remarkably successful, despite the way some contemporaries represented it. They had achieved their three goals: dissolving the League of Armed Neutrality; reestablishing cordial relations with Russia; and terminating the war with France. Having come to power at a dark moment in the war, Addington and Hawkesbury had resolved Great Britain's most pressing external and internal threats within eight months. Conscientious and careful diplomacy, combined with some military good fortune, enabled them to succeed where their predecessors had failed. They defeated the Danes and achieved all of Great Britain's essential objectives with regard to the Russians. In return, Great Britain made only a few minor diplomatic concessions.

Negotiating with the French had been difficult because France held the stronger hand. Addington and Hawkesbury hoped to achieve peace while retaining more of Great Britain's colonial conquests, particularly Malta and the Cape. Nevertheless, even if the French had agreed to let the British retain Malta, the Russians would not have. The goodwill of the Russians, which they had worked so hard to achieve, was far more important than retaining Malta, as long as it remained out of French hands. The importance of the Cape was largely as a refueling station on the route to India, and, as a free port, it would still meet this need. Great Britain's real security interests were the Low Countries, the Iberian Peninsula, southern Italy, and Egypt. The treaty addressed these concerns by providing for French withdrawal from Portugal, Naples, and Egypt. Given the military situation in 1801, it is inconceivable that retaining a few more colonial conquests would have significantly improved British security. Placed within the context of the possible social, economic, and political costs of continuing the war, the Preliminary Treaty was a significant achievement.

CHAPTER 3

The Treaty of Amiens and the Deconstruction of Parliamentary Politics

PARLIAMENT AND THE PRELIMINARY TREATY

The Preliminary Treaty had been difficult to negotiate, and Addington expected that there would be some public and parliamentary opposition to the terms, but popular opinion toward the peace proved more supportive than he had anticipated. General rejoicing erupted throughout the country in response to the announcement of the signing of the treaty. A friend of Addington's sister in Bath reported that the people shouted, "Long live the King, Addington for Ever."[1] In London, the populace celebrated in the streets for days. Those taking part in the festivities demanded that all houses be illuminated as a mark of support for the celebration, and threw stones at the windows of those that were not. When the French envoy arrived in London with the French government's ratification of the treaty, the mob disengaged his horses and pulled his carriage through the streets. Otto put a banner in his window that read "concorde," but some of the semi-literate in the street misread it as "conquered" and stoned his house until he took the banner down.

Although these activities on London streets were not necessarily accurate indicators of public opinion, the celebrations and the lack of demonstrations of dissatisfaction appeared to indicate that the country on the whole either supported or at least did not oppose the peace. Foreign diplomats such as Otto and Starhemberg asserted that the peace was extremely popular.[2] The general reaction enabled Lord Chancellor Eldon to overcome his doubts that the cabinet had made the right decision: "I think I have discovered that we ought to be hanged, and that *Parliament* had so *forewarned* us, if we rejected such a Peace, as we have made."[3]

The peace was of crucial significance to party politics, when Parliament reconvened to debate the terms of the treaty. Addington had managed Parliament fairly easily during the spring session. Pitt's friends had continued to support the government, and, after the first few weeks, the opposition had become remarkably quiescent. The reaction in Parliament to the terms of the Anglo-Russian Convention and the Preliminary Treaty, however, upset party alignments, and the results affected the course of British politics for the next twenty years.

Pitt supported the treaty and told Addington that he would have signed on those terms with pleasure.[4] As Pitt explained in Parliament, "It was undoubtedly the duty of every government in negotiating a treaty of peace to obtain the best possible terms; but it was sometimes difficult to know how far particular points might be pressed without running the risk of breaking off the negotiation." As to the colonial possessions that Addington and Hawkesbury had surrendered, "They would only give us a little more wealth; but a little more wealth would be badly purchased by a little more war." He summarized by stating that "the government had undoubtedly endeavoured to obtain the best terms they could for the country; and he was ready to contend, that the difference between the terms we had obtained and those of retaining all which we had given up, would not have justified ministers in protracting the war."[5]

Pitt also solicited the support of his friends for the treaty and many complied.[6] George Rose, Pitt's secretary to the Treasury, was a close friend and resented Addington for displacing Pitt, but this did not prevent him from supporting the treaty. He told Addington:

> I have no Hesitation in expressing the most un-qualified approbation of the Terms of the Peace which you were so good as to communicate to me; they are according to my Judgement most highly creditable to the Country; and on the whole as advantageous as could reasonably be expected; I should have thought so even if the Cape had been un-conditionally restored, and I am confident that no Hope of getting something better terms [*sic*] Twelve Months hence could have justified the incurring another Year's Expense with the Consequences thereof.[7]

Several others including Canning expressed similar sentiments,[8] but not all of Pitt's former colleagues agreed.

Grenville, the former foreign secretary who had rejected Bonaparte's peace overture in 1799, was the first one to break ranks with Addington and Pitt over the treaty in October. Grenville had agreed with Pitt that they ought to support Addington to keep Fox out of office. He also understood the difficulties that the new ministers faced and persuaded his colleagues to assist Addington. Back in February he had told the British minister in Berlin, "I will not conceal from you that I have a personal interest in making these suggestions to you, considering as I do, our own honour as very deeply concerned in the avoiding all (even the slightest) appearances, of giving either by ourselves, or by those intimately connected with us in alliance & friendship, any trouble to those who, at a crisis so very arduous, are to undertake a task from which the strongest nerves might shrink."[9] He continued to support and advise Addington and Hawkesbury until the summer. According to Glenbervie on 24 October, "Lord Grenville six weeks ago said he knew no measure of this Ministry that he did not approve of, and that he could not easily foresee any which he could bring himself to oppose."[10]

Nevertheless, soon after the peace was announced Grenville wrote to Addington, Pitt, and the king to say that he disapproved of the treaty and would oppose it in Parliament. He stated that "nothing but a sense of indispensable duty could have led me to this separation from those for whom I entertain sentiments of friendship and regard, and whose measures I was most sincerely desirous of supporting."[11] Despite Pitt's warnings to the contrary, he believed that he could oppose the treaty without entering into a systematic opposition or endangering the position of the government.[12] Several of Pitt's allies wrote to Grenville trying to convince him to change his mind. One claimed that he thought the "Peace, even as it is, preferable to the continuance of the War, under all the circumstances of it." Another commented on the terms: "But from the anxiety to obtain Peace, (on which subject the Country is as usual after a long war, so madly anxious, that it is hardly possible to fancy terms which would not be acceptable in the first instance) I am not surprised (considering the circumstances) at the Terms agreed upon." A third warned of the consequences of attacking the government, for if it were demolished "I do not fore see that it will open the way to a better."[13] These entreaties did not move Grenville.

In the parliamentary debate in the House of Lords, Grenville criticized Addington and Hawkesbury for failing to use the principles of *status quo ante bellum* or *uti possidetis* as a basis of the negotiations, meaning that the territorial settlement after the war should reflect either the territorial situation as it was prior to the war or at the time the war ended. Why he believed that these were the only acceptable bases for negotiations is unclear, given that neither had been the basis of the previous Anglo-French treaties of 1714 and 1763. He predicted that surrendering the colonies as required by the treaty would cause Great Britain's strategic position to deteriorate. Eldon and Viscount Nelson retorted that, even had the British kept all of their conquests, the dangers that Grenville envisioned would not have been better provided against. Nevertheless, Grenville proceeded to provoke a division in the Lords, which the government won 114 to 10.[14]

In the Commons, William Windham was the major opponent of the peace. Windham was a conservative Whig who had been an ally of Edmund Burke in opposing the principles of the French Revolution. He was one of the Portland Whigs who joined Pitt's cabinet in 1794, taking the position of secretary at War. He believed that the primary aim of the British war effort should be the restoration of the French monarchy. Addington had expected that Windham might dislike the treaty but hoped to persuade him that it was still in the country's best interests. He wrote to Windham immediately after the treaty was signed, "I think when I see you which I hope I shall before you leave London I can satisfy you that it is not clear even upon your own Principles that we are wrong."[15] But Windham condemned the peace without even bothering to find out what the terms were: "the Country has received its death blow."[16] Addington and his colleagues still felt that it would be worthwhile to discuss the issue with him, but Windham was unrelenting. The decision to sign the treaty was not just a mistake, it constituted national suicide. In Windham's words, Addington and Hawkesbury "in a moment of rashness and weakness, have fatally put their hands to this treaty, have signed the death-warrant of their country. They have given it a blow, under which it may languish for a few years, but from which I do not conceive how it is possible for it ever to recover."[17] It is difficult to believe that Windham, a man with considerable intellect, really could have believed what he was saying.

The motivation behind the opposition of Grenville, Windham, and other opponents went deeper than a dispassionate assessment of the terms of the treaty. The language used in commenting on the treaty indicates the extent to which the influence of national pride distorted the reactions of politicians. This is suggested by Sheridan's favorite description of the treaty as "a peace which every man ought to be glad of, but no man can be proud of," and the lament of Grenville's brother Thomas that "To have been victorious, and yet to have treated as a vanquished nation, was a galling reflexion to a British mind."[18] As the idea that the British had won the war was absurd, the real origin of this erroneous remark lay in the highly emotional nature of the Francophobia that pervaded Great Britain during the eighteenth century. There were some Englishmen who, regardless of the actual military situation, supported fighting what they considered to be their natural enemy to the end and were appalled at a peace treaty that they construed as more favorable to

France than to Great Britain. Such sentiments were common among outspoken critics over the course of the eighteenth century whenever the government negotiated an agreement with France.

There were others whose opinions were less favorable than Pitt's, but more favorable than Grenville's. Henry Dundas was Pitt's loyal Scottish lieutenant, who served with him as home secretary 1791–94 and secretary for War 1794–1801, and president of the Board of Control 1793–1801. He supported peace in principle but disliked the terms. Although he cared little about Europe or the French monarchy, he disapproved of returning the colonial conquests, especially the Cape and Malta. Nevertheless, he was too personally devoted to Pitt to differ from him publicly. While expressing his views to colleagues in private, he decided not to attend Parliament, to avoid the dilemma of having to vote against either his conscience or Pitt. The distress that this dilemma caused Dundas made him seriously consider resigning from politics.[19] Canning and his allies felt that loyalty to Pitt was the most important consideration and were concerned about how the issue was dividing his supporters. If the party split, Pitt's parliamentary standing would deteriorate and the chances of his returning to office in the future would diminish. They tried desperately, but in vain, to patch up the differences and keep Pitt's party together. The split that arose between Pitt and Grenville on the issue of the treaty never completely healed.[20]

Ironically, while members of the former ministry were withdrawing support from the new government, members of the former opposition were beginning to back it. Fox had advocated peace from the moment the French declared war in 1793. In the debate in the Commons on the treaty, he stressed the social damage that the war had wrought, referring to the increase in poverty and the failure of charity to deal with it. He argued that the rapid decline in the price of grain when the peace was announced proved that high prices were linked to the war. "Can any man doubt under such circumstances," he added, "whether it be not better for the people to eat, than that we should possess the Cape, or even Malta . . . ?" Noting that the joy expressed at the news of the peace was greatest among the lower classes who evinced no interest in the terms, he concluded "that the people were so goaded by the war, that they preferred peace almost upon any terms." His only regret was that it had not come sooner.[21]

As the opposition to the war had been one important political issue holding the Foxite Whigs together, Addington's peace treaty provoked dissension within their ranks. After a decade of opposing every measure of the government, the Whigs faced an issue that they could only support. Consequently, party unity began to dissolve, as it had among Pitt's supporters.[22] Fox had once been the unifying force behind the party, but his influence had waned since his voluntary secession from Parliament in 1797. Moreover, morale was low. Even though their two greatest aspirations had been achieved—Pitt removed from office and the war ended—they were still as far as ever from obtaining office themselves.

The signing of the Preliminary Treaty and the parliamentary debates that followed completely changed the complexion of Parliament. As Yorke had predicted, new parliamentary groups were aligning.[23] George Tierney, one of the Whigs who tried to fill the leadership void within the opposition, highlighted the significance of these developments: "The fact is that the overthrow of an administration 17 years old, had necessarily loosened an infinite number of political Ties, and it will be some time before such new arrangements can be made as will present the Idea of a firm & settled Government."[24] Grenville and Windham had broken from the government ranks, taking their adherents into opposition. This was counterbalanced by the support of most of the Foxite Whigs. The split in Parliament placed the few Whigs who opposed the peace on the side of Grenville and Windham against Addington, who had the support of the rest of Parliament. As a result, Addington's position was stronger than it had been before the treaty, because the number of Foxite Whigs who supported it was considerably larger than the small band of Grenvillites who defected. Nevertheless, Addington was not comfortable with these developments. He wrote to Windham, "As to the *Measure* [the peace], to which you advert, I should indeed have Cause for Shame if the Principles upon which it is disapproved of by you, were not far more congenial to my own mind, than those upon which some Persons are disposed to support it."[25] He would have preferred that Grenville and Windham continue supporting him and that Fox continue opposing. This was because, while he had lost the votes of Grenville and Windham, he could not be certain of maintaining those of the Foxites. Grenville and Windham did not control many votes, but they were strong debaters and had the potential to win over a following. This highlighted again the need for Addington to obtain the assistance of talented debaters.

Addington was aware of his cabinet's strengths and weakness, and throughout his term in office explored every chance to upgrade its talent. The political realignments that occurred during the debate on the treaty presented one of these opportunities. During November and December 1801, rumors spread that he was negotiating a coalition with the Foxite Whigs. Given Fox's historic antipathy toward Pitt and the king, some observers considered it surprising and unethical for Addington to have contemplated a deal with some of Fox's allies. The idea of a coalition with the Whigs was consistent, however, with British parliamentary practice. Political adversaries had often joined forces to form a government. Differences of policy or principle mattered little in comparison with the government's need to recruit men with administrative ability and to sustain a working majority in Parliament. Addington's government already comprised a coalition of different parties, including Portland, St. Vincent, and Pelham, who were once classed as Whigs. Support for peace provided a basis for a coalition between Addington and the Whigs.

Most of the discussions toward a coalition took place between Addington and Tierney, who among the Whigs was the most supportive of an alliance. It was obvious that there was no question of including Fox in the arrangement, because the king would never allow it, but it was not necessary to include him anyway. His hold on the Whig party had deteriorated over the previous few years as a result of his growing antipathy to politics and his frequent absences from Parliament. Tierney, Sheridan, and Francis Rawdon-Hastings, the second earl of Moira, had grown to be stronger political figures in their own right, and became more closely identified with the Prince of Wales than with Fox. There was also a fundamental point of divergence between Fox and them. His antipathy was directed toward the king, while their antagonism was directed toward Pitt. With Pitt out of office, the major obstacle to their joining the government had disappeared, and the desire to keep Pitt out gave them a strong incentive to support Addington. The most important point was that, while Addington and the Whigs had disagreed on certain issues, they always had respect for one another. Thomas Erskine, a Whig M.P. and lawyer who had become famous for successfully defending the accused in the treason trials of 1794, explained:

> I thought and think still that Mr Addington's temper and character were most happily constituted to produce the best consequences to the country, I thought and think that he had great confidence to expect from the public from the manner in which he had made the peace; and I thought and think that I might safely confide in him as a private man from his personal Honour and character, and from the esteem which he had uniformly professed for me for many years that notwithstanding the differences of opinion which we entertained upon particular subjects and which we still entertain.[26]

Over the years, the war had been the source of the greatest difference of opinion between Addington and the Whigs. Addington's having made peace removed the only major obstacle to most of them working together.

Addington negotiated with Tierney, and Moira arranged for St. Vincent to negotiate with Charles Grey. Grey was an excellent debater but one of the more radical members of the Whigs. The stumbling block in the negotiations with Moira was that he refused to join a cabinet that included Portland, whom he despised for betraying his friends by joining Pitt's government in 1794. Grey also placed conditions upon accepting office. He would join the cabinet only if it became, in essence, a Whig government. He explained to Tierney that he would take office only if preceded by "the adoption of some great & leading measures which would speak for themselves, or by the admission into the administration of such a number & description of

Persons on our side, as combined with the removal of those whose conduct has been the most obnoxious on the other, would give us a sufficient influence over the general measures of Government, & afford an unequivocal proof of a change of system." For Grey, Addington's reluctance to raise the issues of parliamentary reform or Catholic Emancipation was problematic, because he was committed to both causes. As Addington was unable to meet the demands of Moira and Grey, the negotiations terminated by the end of December. A month later, the Prince of Wales pressed Addington to try again. Addington met with Moira in February, but they failed to reach agreement and the negotiations collapsed.[27]

The demands made by the Whigs were too great for Addington to accept, for he would not surrender his control of the government to them. Rather, he hoped to gain further talent and support for the government by offering lesser offices to Tierney, Grey, or Erskine. He desired only partial changes to the administration. As it was already a coalition of men from different parties, he felt that the addition of one or two more Whigs could strengthen the cabinet without undermining his authority. The negotiations failed because Moira and Grey were not willing to enter the cabinet without fundamental changes.

After the failure of the negotiations with the Whigs, Addington could console himself that his parliamentary position remained strong, at least for the short term. Opposition to the treaty in the Commons was so weak that Windham did not bother to move for a division, and the division in the Lords provoked by Grenville resulted in a strong majority for the government. Addington understood, however, that his parliamentary situation was less secure than it appeared. He confided in Hiley that he considered the position of the government to be precarious.[28] He could not count on the support of the Whigs and had strong reason to believe that some of Pitt's friends might drift into outright opposition. This was important for, as the negotiations for the definitive treaty dragged on, he began to doubt whether peace would last.

THE CONGRESS OF AMIENS

Although the signing of the Preliminary Treaty was a considerable achievement, it did not prove a final resolution of Anglo-French diplomatic conflict. During the negotiations of 1801, both Hawkesbury and Otto had wanted to announce an agreement as early as possible. Finding that agreeing in principle was easier than spelling out the details, they signed a Preliminary Treaty that was to serve as a set of guidelines for a final treaty to be settled at a Congress of representatives of France, Great Britain, Spain, Holland, Portugal, and the Ottoman Empire. Hostilities ceased, but the peace would not be firm until the signing of the definitive treaty. In the interim, Great Britain and France were not at war, but neither were they completely at peace. Addington assumed that the signing of the definitive treaty would prove a mere formality, but this proved to be a miscalculation, as the Congress actually dragged on until the end of March. The delay in the negotiations, and the expansion of French influence in Europe during the interim, exacerbated the natural suspicion between the British and French that would poison future relations. It also pushed Addington to the brink of resuming the war.

The British selected George, the first Marquess Cornwallis, as the British negotiator. There were rumors that the British would send another more seasoned diplomat to Amiens, but Addington told Otto that the frank and conciliatory character of Cornwallis was more suitable. Cornwallis liked France and was averse to diplomatic ploys.[29] A career soldier, he had commanded British forces in the American War of Independence and in India. He had also proven a successful administrator as governor-general of India 1786–93 and Lord Lieutenant of Ireland 1798–1801. As the Preliminary Treaty had apparently settled all the essential points at issue between Great Britain and France, it was more important for the British envoy to inspire the respect of Bonaparte than to be an expert diplomat.[30] Hawkesbury wrote to the king that he was "convinced that the military reputation and character of Marquis Cornwallis will give him advantages in treating with the French Government which no other person would possess in an equal degree."[31] A treaty should be ready quickly and no later than the middle of November.[32]

From the moment Cornwallis arrived in France, however, French naval movements began to arouse the suspicions of the British government. On 7 November, Otto informed Hawkesbury that the French were sending a fleet of twenty-three ships of the line, sixteen frigates, and twenty thousand men to St. Domingue to crush a slave rebellion that had occurred on the island. The size of the fleet Bonaparte sent to the Caribbean, a region where the British had important colonial possessions, was alarming, and the British felt obliged to send an equivalent force to shadow the French fleet. Hawkesbury instructed Cornwallis to inform the French that, while the British did not object to the expedition per se, moving a large military force into a region of strategic interest to Great Britain could harm Anglo-French relations.[33]

Upon arrival in Paris, Cornwallis met privately with Talleyrand and Joseph Bonaparte. Although Hawkesbury had told him that he could settle the principal points in Paris before they left for Amiens, Cornwallis told Hawkesbury that he did not wish to stay because "I should have to deal with Talleyrand on the spot, instead of negotiating with him through the medium of Joseph Bonaparte, who had the character of being a well meaning, altho' not a very able Man, and whose near connexion with the first Consul might perhaps be in some degree a check on the spirit of chicanery and intrigue which the Minister of the exterior so eminently possesses."[34] Cornwallis's first impression of Joseph Bonaparte was mistaken, but he was misled by the agreeable manner of their first meeting in Paris, at which they appeared to concur on most of the terms. Cornwallis's sense of optimism dissolved, however, when he met the First Consul four days later. Bonaparte contradicted his brother's position on many of the terms and raised a new issue by suggesting that the fortifications of Malta should be destroyed in order to neutralize the military value of the island.[35]

Realizing that he was making little progress in Paris, Cornwallis insisted on proceeding to Amiens, where he arrived on 1 December. He believed that once he and Joseph Bonaparte sat down together, without the interference of Talleyrand or the First Consul, they would soon conclude the treaty. He told Hawkesbury, "I have little Doubt, as soon as I shall receive it [a proposal for a definitive treaty] from Your Lordship, together with His Majesty's final Commands in regard to Malta, that this Business will be arranged with Expedition."[36] Hawkesbury was pleased with this report and on 16 December sent a treaty proposal.[37] In a private letter accompanying the dispatches, he added,

> I hope we shall be able to form some Judgement in the Course of a week or ten Days of the probable Duration of the Negotiation. I confess I should be very much inclined Personally (but This is not official) if every other point could be satisfactorily settled and a Spanish Minister should not arrive within a certain time to sign the Treaty with the Plenipotentiaries who were at that time at Amiens & to insert an article similar to that respecting the Ottoman Porte inviting the King of Spain to accede to the Treaty.[38]

Cornwallis's assistant at Amiens remarked, "They are in such a Hurry at Home . . . that we are even authorized to conclude and sign before the Arrival of the Spanish P[l]en[ipotentiar]y if there should be a Prospect of any Delay in the Consequence of his non-Presence."[39]

Joseph Bonaparte could sense that Cornwallis was eager to conclude the treaty, and he assumed that the longer the marquess remained at Amiens, the more impatient and ready to concede better terms he would become.[40] When Cornwallis delivered the British project on 21 December, instead of discussing the terms, Joseph presented a counter-project. Cornwallis's assistant described the counter-project as tending "no less than to take away in some instances, to leave in doubt in others, all the Advantages given us by the Preliminaries in return for the Sacrifices we have made."[41] This counter-project threw the negotiations into disarray. When Cornwallis proposed that both sides have their secretaries draw up an official protocol, they could not agree what was to be written down. Cornwallis concluded that Joseph Bonaparte's strategy was to "throw upon me the Odium of the Delay (which now appears to be the aim of the French Government) and, upon the whole, to create a Confusion in our Proceedings."[42] Unfortunately for the British, Cornwallis proved unable to meet the challenges that he faced at Amiens. He became visibly upset at the new demands that the French introduced in the negotiations and did not defend British interests effectively. It turned out that he lacked the diplomatic experience and mental and physical stamina required to deal with Joseph Bonaparte.

The British cabinet, which had expected the business to have been completed during November, became quite anxious when the negotiations dragged into January. Addington's policy was to keep "clear of the extreme of distrust on the one hand and of credulity and weakness on the other," but he was beginning to lose patience with the French. As doubts grew over whether the treaty would be concluded, public confidence in the government began to wane. This uncertainty also impeded the formulation of policy in other important areas. Hawkesbury informed Cornwallis on 10 January that "it is difficult for us to arrange our Finances till the Peace is actually concluded. As Parliament must meet for the Dispatch of Business before the End of this Month it will be impossible for Mr Addington to bring forward the Budget before the Completion of the Definitive Treaty & we may therefore be placed in a very embarrassing Situation and shall certainly be exposed to perpetual Importunities." Addington was anxious to bring in a peacetime budget, as there was more evidence of financial and social pressures on the government. The good harvest and the announcement of peace in October had an initially positive economic and social effect. As the negotiations at Amiens dragged on, however, there was a loss of confidence that peace would last, which undermined the economic and social situation in Great Britain. The price of bread began to rise again despite the good harvest, and according to Starhemberg, "It is impossible for the government to reduce any of the taxes, and consequently the people are still aggrieved, poverty increases, and discontentment has recurred."

There was considerable pressure on the government to sign a treaty as soon as possible.[43]

The delay in the negotiations was beginning to sap any remaining goodwill for the French on the part of the British. Bonaparte had expanded his power by having himself appointed, in a public ceremony at Lyons, the president of the new Cisalpine Republic that he had recently created in northern Italy. Bonaparte also forced the Spanish to cede Louisiana to France. This appeared to indicate that France would continue to make territorial acquisitions in Europe and overseas despite the peace. Hawkesbury instructed Cornwallis that it was even more essential for him not to make further sacrifices: "The Business of Lyons however makes it important for us to be more firm than ever upon our own Rights and more determined than ever to resist all new Pretensions as far as respect British objects on the Part of the French government. If we do not adopt this as our policy We shall be exposed to perpetual insults."[44]

Addington and Hawkesbury realized that they could not allow the negotiations to drag on, and became determined to reach a settlement as soon as possible. At the end of January, they even considered sending the undersecretary in the Foreign Office to Amiens to take over the negotiations.[45] After dismissing that idea, they decided that if the treaty were not concluded soon, they would have to resume the war. On 12 February, the same day that Hawkesbury ordered Cornwallis to be firmer with Joseph Bonaparte, Hobart instructed the Admiralty to prepare for war. Three weeks later he ordered the Admiralty to send six ships of the line to the West Indies to join those already sent to follow the French fleet.[46] The cabinet was unable to make any final decisions at that time, however, because Addington and his daughter were seriously ill. Addington spent most of the month of February at home recuperating and watching over his daughter, who nearly died. By the beginning of March, the cabinet doubted whether, in Yorke's words, the "Infinitive" treaty would ever arrive. Addington and Hobart, among others, began to fear that the negotiations would break off.[47]

Although the uncertainty of the negotiations was impeding the formulation of policy, resuming the war might have outraged parliamentary and popular opinion.[48] The British were prepared to declare war, however, if the final treaty did not reflect the minimum terms of the Preliminary Treaty. Addington and Hawkesbury resolved to take a two-pronged approach. They would try to succeed through negotiation, while at the same time ensuring that Great Britain was ready for war. This approach was to combine the threat of naval mobilization with a softening of terms on minor points in the treaty. It proved successful: Joseph Bonaparte was surprised and alarmed at the prospect of British naval armament and suddenly became amenable to British terms on some of the outstanding articles.[49]

Hawkesbury then directed Cornwallis to present an ultimatum to the French, and sent a copy of a new draft treaty. He added ominously that

> If, however, any new demands should be insisted on, or if the Plenipotentiaries of the other Powers should object to signing the Treaty conformably to the Articles, of the inclosed Draft, it is His Majesty's Pleasure, that you inform the Minister of the Congress, that you have gone to the utmost extent of you instructions, and that in obedience to the orders of your Court, you must leave Amiens in eight days from the period of that Declaration; unless the Treaty is concluded within that time.[50]

The British proposal was similar in many respects to the latest French project, but included amendments to the article concerning Malta. Hawkesbury reiterated, however, that this was a final offer.

Napoleon Bonaparte had not intended to draw out the negotiations this long. On 1 December 1801 he predicted that "the definitive peace will be signed promptly." At the end of December, he told Joseph that he expected to hear soon that the treaty would be signed as "it does not appear to be that there are any remaining serious obstacles." He became displeased when he heard that the British refused to sign unless the Turkish government was invited to accede to the treaty to approve the terms relating to Egypt, as stipulated by the Preliminary Treaty. Bonaparte wanted to sign a separate peace with Turkey to prevent the British from having influence as to the terms. He told Joseph that he did not trust the British cabinet and felt that the delay in signing the treaty was their fault. He opposed making any concessions to the British, who, he felt, would have to sign the treaty because, considering the state of Europe, they could not carry on the war. Otto had warned him, however, that if the treaty were not signed soon, Addington might be forced to resign. This, Otto suggested, "must be regarded by all of Europe as a calamity" as it could lead to the return of Pitt, who would be less conciliatory. Joseph eventually admitted responsibility for the delay in signing the treaty. He deliberately drew out the negotiations to break the patience of the British, in hopes that they would accept terms more favorable to France. Bonaparte eventually tired of the delay. When Joseph indicated that the British would sign immediately, if the French would allow the Turks to sign, Bonaparte "accepted with regret that the Turks be invited to accede to the present treaty," but he insisted that British sign immediately.[51]

Cornwallis presented Hawkesbury's "final" proposal to Joseph Bonaparte on 17 March but, because he found the latter disposed to agreement, withheld the threat of the ultimatum as "it might indicate strongly a Disposition of a contrary Tendency." The French envoy claimed that, although there were still many differences, they were more of wording than substance.[52] As he had during the negotiation of the Preliminary Treaty in September, Addington took a more active role at the climax of the Amiens negotiations. He wrote to assure Cornwallis that the government approved of his discretion in not issuing the ultimatum, and agreed to a few more alterations to the terms of the treaty. As he was under great pressure to settle the finances, he stressed that "Under the present Circumstances, Dispatch is of the utmost Importance on all Accounts, & particularly with a view to the financial Arrangements for the Year."[53]

In order to overcome the remaining difficulties, which Cornwallis thought to be merely semantic, he made some modifications to the language of the proposed treaty. Joseph Bonaparte found them acceptable. On the evening of 24 March, Cornwallis and Joseph hammered out the final details, and 27 March the official treaty was completed. Six months after the signing of the Preliminary Treaty, and one year after commencing the negotiations, Addington finally had achieved a definitive peace. In the end, the Treaty of Amiens very closely resembled the Preliminary Treaty. The most important change was the provision for Malta, which constituted a compromise. Where the Preliminary Treaty stipulated that a third party, understood to be Russia, would occupy and defend Malta, under the terms of the Treaty of Amiens, the garrison was to be Neapolitan, and the British, French, Austrians, Prussians, and Spanish would join the Russians in guaranteeing the neutrality of the island. This change was necessary because the tsar could not afford to garrison the island, owing to the state of the Russian finances.[54] Therefore, although the Treaty of Amiens failed to meet all British expectations, it did adequately settle the issues left outstanding by the Preliminary Treaty.

This did not mean that the situation was as favorable as it had been in October 1801, or that public and Parliament received the terms of the definitive treaty as well as those of the preliminary. For the European scene had indeed changed. France had sent a large fleet to the West Indies, and Bonaparte had increased his power by having himself elected the president of the Cisalpine Republic and acquiring Louisiana. Prior to the signing of the Preliminary Treaty, the British did not anticipate that Bonaparte would expand French territory in Europe or overseas during the peace. The experience of the Amiens negotiations, however, showed that ending the war did not prevent France from making new acquisitions that threatened British strategic interests. It also suggested that peace might be of a shorter duration than the British had originally hoped.

The announcement of the final terms exacerbated the new divisions in Parliament. In the eyes of Grenville and Windham, the previous six months had justified their opposition to the Preliminary Treaty. Pitt continued to support the peace, but conceded that the prospect of an enduring settlement seemed remote. Addington agreed with him. The political climate in Great Britain had certainly deteriorated between the signing of the Preliminary Treaty and the conclusion of the Treaty of Amiens. He and Hawkesbury had expected that the Congress would be short and mostly a formality. Instead it dragged into a complicated negotiation that produced final terms slightly less favorable to the British. In addition, British public and parliamentary opinion on the peace soured with each new French gain.[55] Addington still felt that the benefits of the peace outweighed the costs of renewing the war. He was less inclined, however, to believe that the peace would endure.

CHAPTER 4

The Necessary Breathing Space

The social and economic turmoil of 1801 that precipitated the peace did not disappear entirely once the treaty was signed. Peace was merely a prerequisite to the resolution of these problems: the termination of the war eliminated certain expenditures, injected greater confidence into the stock market, and led to a further decrease in the price of wheat. Nevertheless, the government finances remained in disarray and social tension continued. There was also a need for reform in the civil administration of the navy, which suffered from inefficiency and abuse. The Peace of Amiens gave Addington and the First Lord of the Admiralty, the earl of St. Vincent, the opportunity to address these issues. Addington consequently shifted his attention from foreign policy to domestic issues for the next six months. While the termination of the war relieved the intensity of the pressure on him, there were high expectations of the benefits of the peace. The wealthy demanded a reduction of taxes, including the repeal of the income tax. Commercial interests anticipated a revival in trade with Europe. The poor were counting on an increase in imported food supplies. Radicals and reformers were hoping for the relaxation of government repression. The members of the armed forces looked forward to demobilization.

Naval administrators wished to restore the fleet. Addington thus faced the challenges of financial and economic retrenchment, social pacification, and administrative reform.

FINANCIAL POLICY

Addington's primary concern was the state of the government finances. During the previous summer, he had concluded that the government would soon require drastic and unpopular measures to remain solvent. War expenses increased every year. At the same time government revenue was becoming more difficult to obtain. Wartime taxes were extremely unpopular and insufficient to meet expenditure, forcing the government to resort to large loans. The money markets were increasingly restricted, as the interruption of foreign trade and the collapse of domestic consumption (caused by the high price of wheat) cut profits. As a result, the City had less money to lend, and this led to a steep rise in interest rates.[1] High interest rates and the scarcity of money restricted the capital available to private commerce, which in turn intensified the general economic slump. As long as the war continued, the government and economy were caught in a depressing cycle with no relief in sight.

The signing of the Preliminary Treaty brought initial respite, but the delay in the negotiations at Amiens caused further uncertainty in the money markets. The risk of lending money, even to the government, was great as long as peace remained uncertain. If Addington had tried to negotiate a major loan at that time, he would have had to accept extremely disadvantageous terms. Therefore, he postponed the loan and the budget until after he knew whether the Amiens negotiations would succeed.[2]

When the news of the treaty arrived on 29 March, Addington began immediately preparing Great Britain's first peacetime budget in ten years. His goal was to respond not merely to the financial needs of the government but also to the larger pressures that pervaded all aspects of his policy-making. Addington sought to secure the benefits of peace immediately.[3] The only means of achieving this end was to reduce taxes by cutting expenditure, and the largest item of expenditure—besides interest payments—was the military. The end of the war naturally permitted large cuts in the army and the navy, but he knew that the peace would remain precarious. He suspected that the French might take advantage of British demobilization and disarmament to increase their influence in Europe or even to provoke a renewal of war.[4] Therefore, he decided to maintain British forces on a footing that would facilitate rapid mobilization. Balancing the priorities of reducing expenditure without sacrificing British security was, however, a considerable challenge.

Addington's first budget, which he introduced in the Commons on 5 April 1802, was extraordinary in many respects. The budget addressed several new issues, the most important of which was the repeal of the income tax. The public had tolerated Pitt's new tax, but only grudgingly, because it was necessary to address the financial strains of the war in 1799. Although Parliament and taxpayers recognized the necessity of the new tax, they considered it a distasteful temporary expedient. As the war dragged on, extra-parliamentary opposition to the tax grew, and criticism of it began to carry over into criticism of the war in general. During the interlude between the Preliminary Treaty and signing of the Treaty of Amiens, the City of London had petitioned Parliament for the repeal of the income tax.[5]

Addington had long decided that repeal of the tax was necessary for both political and practical reasons.[6] The tax was unpopular because it hurt the economy. On the practical side, the tax was inefficient to administer. It was an extraordinary measure implemented to meet the extraordinary financial demands of the war. He believed, as he told the Commons, that "this burthen should not be left to rest on the shoulders of the public in time of peace, because it should be reserved for the important occasions which, he trusted, would not soon recur."[7] If continued during peace, the tax would eventually be treated as a routine source of revenue, and the government would have to find another source to meet the increased demands whenever war resumed.

Addington's next major concern was the peacetime military establishment. Army and navy spending could be reduced, but two concerns prevented him from cutting expenditure as drastically as some observers were expecting. First, disbanding regiments and decommissioning ships took time, up to six months or more for those overseas. Second, as he suspected that the peace might not last, he had to be ready to remobilize British forces at short notice. This could only be done if he retained a large peacetime establishment. Addington's challenge was to retain an effective force at the least expense.[8] His response was to provide only for the first five months of the budget year, and defer the request for funds for the following seven months until later in the year, when he would have a better idea of the forces required.[9] He thus budgeted for an initial naval establishment of 130,000 seamen, and he returned in June to ask Parliament provision for 70,000 for the rest of the year. He reduced the regular army to 95,000, but this was still twice the number of the first peacetime establishment following the American War of Independence in 1783. He also provided for a militia of 48,000 with 24,000 in reserve and an Irish militia of 18,000.[10]

Addington implemented a series of financial reforms. One of his budgetary reforms involved the Civil List. At that time, the Civil List provided for the salaries of government officials as well as the expenses of the royal family, according to a rate schedule set in 1786. The result was that, while the king had exercised remarkable economy in managing his household, the Civil List had run into arrears because of the growing expense of government and the diplomatic service during the war. To resolve this problem, Addington asked Parliament to pay the accumulated debt of the Civil List. He then removed the government charges from the Civil List, and arranged for them to be paid directly by Parliament out of the annual budget. Thereafter, Parliament rather than the king was responsible for the expenses of government.[11]

Abolishing the income tax, retaining a large peacetime establishment, and paying off the debt on the Civil List were costly. Addington had to make up for the deficiencies of some of Pitt's financial projections; contribute to the reduction of the national debt; and pay off some exchequer bills and the interest on the rest. He faced a serious dilemma. He had to obtain sufficient revenue to meet these costs, while at the same time relieving the country of the financial burdens that Pitt had imposed during the course of the war. When the income tax failed to produce the revenue projected, Pitt met the shortfall by raising loans on the security of future revenue. This had the effect of mortgaging the tax for another ten years, while the interest on those loans absorbed one-third of the revenue.[12] In all, Addington had to find the means of raising in excess of £100 million.

His solution to the problem of meeting all of the required expenditure, despite the loss of a major source of revenue, was to raise an extraordinarily large loan. This was controversial because, according to Pitt, financial orthodoxy dictated that the government should raise loans only in wartime and rely on taxes in peacetime. In this case, however, it would have been impossible for Addington to have raised the amount he required. His decision to negotiate the loan met little opposition in Parliament; even Pitt recognized that unusual financial and political circumstances demanded extraordinary measures. The major drawback was that the loan increased the national debt during peacetime, but Addington calculated that this would be the least onerous means of meeting all the government's financial needs. As long as there were sufficient funds in the money markets, government loans provided an attractive investment without injuring the economy.

Having repealed the income tax, Addington had to provide for the loans which Pitt had secured upon it, amounting to more than £56 million. To meet this, along with other expenses, he raised a total loan of almost £98 million. His timing proved excellent. Owing to the conclusion of peace, and the expectation of reduced government borrowing in the future, there were seven applications for the loan and the bids were competitive. Addington was thus able to obtain the loan at a lower rate of interest that was a "bargain . . . perfectly satisfactory and auspicious to the greatest degree."[13] Pitt agreed and asserted that, after nine years of war, Addington had obtained a loan "at the very same price of stocks at which, in the first year of the war in 1793, with all the accumulating resources of ten years of peace, we made a loan for only four millions."[14] Addington calculated the annual interest on the loan at just over £3 million but cautiously raised additional taxes to cover £4 million.

Another controversial financial measure was the suspension of cash payments. Until 1797, British banknotes could be exchanged for their equivalent value in gold. The economic and financial strains of the war forced Pitt to suspend cash payments and increase the number of banknotes in circulation. There was a general expectation, however, that peace would lead to a resumption of the gold standard. In theory, once the war ended, the suspension was no longer required. The suspension led to disadvantageous exchange rates between sterling and other currencies, but reestablishing the gold standard would have severely contracted the money supply, thus hurting British trade. British commercial and industrial interests demanded relief from the war, and a further recession would have ruined the recovery that they so desperately required. Another consideration was that the Bank of England requested a recuperation period of at least six months before resuming cash payments. Addington decided that it would be prudent to wait until he could assess the effects of peace on British trade before abolishing the restrictions. His decision met little opposition, even from Whig financial critics.[15]

Despite the enormous challenges Addington faced in formulating his budget, it proved a remarkable political success. Even Canning, who was becoming Addington's most bitter enemy, grudgingly admitted that "Pitt's [being] at the head of the Treasury is no longer essential to the salvation of the Country."[16] The tax hikes, though regrettable, were generally accepted as necessary in order to permit the abolition of the income tax. In the end, the tax increases did not prove onerous, because peace permitted a revival of overseas trade and the fall in the price of wheat aided internal markets. The budget did not, however, satisfy everyone. Fox, in particular, questioned the need to retain larger establishments in the armed forces than was customary during peacetime and the rise in the national debt. Addington demonstrated a better grasp of the larger picture by recognizing that, as Great Britain's diplomatic interests and economic interests pulled in different directions, a compromise was necessary. His policy was to provide a military and naval force sufficient for national security without being too expensive. Fox complained that the force was too large, while war hawks, like Grenville, complained that it was too small. Addington's compromise struck the right balance by providing the country with most of the benefits of peace, while at the same time leaving the military prepared for a sudden renewal of war. Pitt and the king supported Addington firmly, and he was extremely popular during the months immediately following the conclusion of peace and the budget.[17] Otto reported, "Mr. Addington triumphs completely. . . . These circumstances together have given to Mr. Addington unparalleled popularity. Everyone in high society is talking about him, and the people bless him for bringing down the price of food."[18] Fox noted that Addington was the most popular prime minister since the accession of George III.[19]

Addington had faced almost insurmountable odds. A man with no previous experience in office, he reluctantly took over the government when Great Britain was facing a series of crises that experienced and talented ministers were unable to resolve. Improbably, he succeeded where these others had failed. He restored favorable diplomatic relations with the Great Powers of Europe, ended the war with France, and restored the finances of the British government. He accomplished all this and gained the almost universal approbation of the public in the course of just one year.

Addington introduced a second peacetime budget on 10 December 1802 that both represented an important new step in the evolution of modern budget presentation and had an impact on the underlying strength of Addington's parliamentary position. In his budget speech, Addington inaugurated what would become an enduring feature: he provided a general overview of the British economy by describing at length the financial and commercial situation of the country.[20] Former budgets had been merely accounts of projected revenue and expenditure for the following year. Addington offered a more extensive examination of the finances to justify his measures, and so provided Parliament and the public with information that they had not previously received. This facilitated a better understanding of the working of the economy and provided a more complete context in which to evaluate the budget itself. Successive chancellors of the Exchequer adopted this method, and it became traditionally one of the highlights of every session of Parliament.

The parliamentary implications of Addington's second budget were the effects that it had on Addington's relationship with Pitt. From March through November 1801, Pitt had supported Addington, particularly in defending the terms of the Preliminary Treaty. But after that, Pitt stayed away from London, dividing his time between Bath and Walmer Castle, his residence on the coast of Kent. Time and physical distance undermined the connection between him and Addington. The schemes of Canning and his associates exacerbated the deterioration of the friendship. Canning's attempts to turn Pitt against Addington eventually succeeded. While Pitt was away from Westminster all information he received about Addington was distorted through the filter of Canning and Rose, whose persistent personal attacks Addington did not have the opportunity to refute.

Although Pitt supported Addington's first budget, he gradually became more critical of Addington's financial policies. This first became clear in response to Addington's second budget. Pitt objected to Addington's borrowing money to pay for the military establishment proposed for 1803, because Pitt believed that it was bad financial policy to resort to loans in peacetime. He felt that all expenses should be met through taxation.[21] Nevertheless, Addington did not face a normal peacetime situation. French expansion on the Continent continued to threaten British interests and forced Great Britain's military to remain on a war alert.[22] These unusual circumstances demanded a level of expenditure far beyond a typical year of peace. Addington had to increase either taxes or the national debt. A tax increase of £11 million would have provoked serious opposition both in Parliament and in the country, and he calculated that the increase in trade since the beginning of the war would permit the money markets to handle the

loan without harming the economy.[23] He also wished to avoid impos-
ing further burdens on the taxpayer.

The other area of disagreement was over Addington's projections
of government revenue. Addington estimated the surplus for the
entire year would reach £6.5 million, but Pitt and Rose believed that
this was an overestimation of almost £2.8 million.[24] In the end, the
actual surplus was only £5.1 million, but Addington based his budget
calculations on the expectations of raising only £4 million.[25] Addington's projections that the revenue would be higher had no effect on
government finances because he had officially budgeted for a more
conservative amount.[26]

Placing Pitt's criticisms in perspective, it is important to note that
Addington's second budget was even more successful and popular
than his first. Castlereagh, who had just joined the cabinet as president of the Board of Control of the East India Company in October,
asserted that "Mr Addington has opened the most prosperous budget
this country has witnessed, not even excepting 1792. The revenue has
risen above three millions, and the export of British manufactures
has increased to an equal amount upon the rated value, between six
and seven millions. The effect of this statement has been to raise the
funds above four percent."[27] Liverpool observed that the foreign
exchanges had changed in Great Britain's favor and that the merchant
interests supported the government.[28] Yorke, the secretary at War,
believed that the budget speech did much to stabilize support for the
ministry.[29] Pitt's physician, Sir Walter Farquhar, who was also a political observer, praised Addington: "I can not suffer this opportunity to
escape me of congratulating the prime minister upon the impression
which his conduct has made upon the Country in general, & in a
more particular point of view, the Electrical effect upon the Public
mind, by his animating, and impressive Speech of Friday last. It has
warmed every heart, & enlivened every Countenance. It has inspired
Confidence, & met the Feeling of the Country at large."[30] Even some
of Addington's fiercest opponents admitted that the budget was successful and would strengthen his position.[31]

As a financial reformer, Addington compares favorably with Pitt, whose reputation in this field is exaggerated.[32] Pitt's achievements were modest and confined almost exclusively to his first few years in office: he virtually abandoned his program of reform once the war with France commenced in 1793. Addington returned the issue of economic reform to the agenda of government and established a trend that his successors would follow.[33] Addington also introduced a number of important innovations. The renewal of war would deny him the opportunity to pursue his reformist policies with the same vigor as during peacetime. Nevertheless, Addington's two peacetime budgets demonstrated imagination and a willingness to implement reforms. He failed to achieve some of his fiscal goals because he could not isolate his financial policies from the need to retain large peacetime military and naval establishments. Given that he was able to sustain the military and naval establishments at approximately double their prewar size, it was remarkable that, as Pelham reported, by the end of 1802 "the total savings already resulting from the peace amounted to twenty-five millions sterling annually."[34] Addington had thus achieved the general financial aims of his peacetime administration.

SOCIAL UNREST

The three major issues that Addington faced upon taking office were the war, the state of government finances, and alarming levels of social unrest. Having ended the war and set the finances on a firmer foundation, Addington shifted his focus to the issue of social unrest. He understood the role that unemployment, poverty, and famine played in fomenting riot and insurrection, but he felt that this could not detract from his responsibility to provide for the security of the Crown and preserve the interests of the propertied elite as represented in Parliament. Addington developed a reputation as a staunch reactionary, but he was no innovator of repressive measures and he resorted to them less than had some of his predecessors. He demonstrated a greater concern for the plight of the poor and underprivileged than had Pitt or Portland. He was, at heart, a Christian philanthropist, who throughout his life supported charitable causes, such as the establishment of soup kitchens for the poor and the building of hospitals. He sympathized with the unemployed and underpaid, and felt that employers should address some of the grievances of their employees. He supported government measures to increase the supply of food. The conclusion of peace improved food supplies, and thus lower prices undermined radical opposition to the government. And the end of the war removed a major target of radical criticism of the establishment. Home Office reports of riots and other seditious activities declined after the Preliminary Treaty was signed in October 1801. While there is some disagreement as to the length and extent of the resulting lull in radical activity, radicalism and social unrest did subside below the alarming levels of the early months of 1801.[35]

Addington realized that peace and the resumption of trade were not sufficient to redress all of the sources of social unrest. Repressive legislation, most notably the Seditious Meetings Act and the suspension of habeas corpus for treason implemented during the 1790s, was a cause of popular discontent. Addington did not feel that the social and political challenges presented by the French Revolution and the war required excessive security measures. He had supported the resumption of repressive legislation in April 1801, but only after the special committee of Parliament had received persuasive evidence of an insurrectionary movement. He had favored these extraordinary security measures to prevent a potential social revolution. Once the war was over and social unrest had subsided, Addington allowed the repressive acts to lapse and released most of the state prisoners.

Addington and Pelham, the home secretary, employed the traditional machinery of government in dealing with social unrest, but they were less aggressive than their predecessors. When Portland was home secretary under Pitt, he encouraged magistrates to be more vigorous in implementing the laws against riots and seditious activities, even when they were reluctant to do so. Pelham took a less forceful approach, while the war continued, and with the conclusion of peace, Pelham became even more relaxed about pursuing those involved in riots and radical agitation.[36]

Addington and Pelham also faced violence stemming from industrial disputes. Between April and September 1802 there were frequent outbreaks in the clothing districts of Yorkshire and Wiltshire, provoked by unemployment and low wages. The establishment of new mills and factories deprived many traditional artisans of their livelihood, and there was no community or state infrastructure—other than the minimal amount of relief available through the poor laws— to assist them. As many of them began to starve, they became desperate and resorted to breaking machines and setting fire to cloth factories, mills, and ricks of manufacturers. They also fired guns at both workmen and manufacturers. In many ways, this violence foreshadowed the Luddites of the next decade. In Yorkshire, the workers' grievances centered on their declining wages, which resulted from employers replacing workers with machines and adopting employment practices that contravened legislation regarding apprenticeships. In Wiltshire, the problem was a surplus of agricultural labor exacerbated by the return of ex-servicemen, who increased the ranks of the unemployed.[37]

Pelham initially refused to act and left the problem to the local magistrates, but as the violence continued through the summer, they persisted in pressing him for military assistance.[38] In August, he traveled to Salisbury to consult Wiltshire magistrates. As the disturbances continued, he and Addington saw that, rather than being a series of isolated incidents, the violence in Yorkshire and Wiltshire was related. They concluded that the only way to avoid further violence was not only to punish the law breakers, but also to address the grievances of the workers. Pelham explained to a Wiltshire magistrate:

> It appears to me from these accounts that the successful Establishment of the Machinery is a Subject of great National Importance in as much as the Preeminence of our Cloths in great measure depends upon it, at the same time the immediate Interest of the Sheermen & others who may be deprived of their accustomed support & Means of living is not to be disregarded, however irregular & dangerous their mode of Maintaining their Interest may have been; It has occurred to me that a Meeting of some of the principal Clothiers from Yorkshire & Wiltshire might be of use in devising Means for satisfying those People who are likely to be affected by this Machinery, in order that, when Govern-

ment shall have convinced those who have attempted to redress themselves by Acts of Violence, that the Laws cannot be transgressed with Impunity, there is a disposition to attend to their reasonable complaints & to prevent a recurrence of the same outrages.[39]

The nature of Addington and Pelham's approach to social unrest is illustrated by the way they dealt with two attempted revolutionary insurrections. The first was known as the Despard conspiracy. Colonel Edward Marcus Despard was an Irish ex-soldier who felt that he had been treated unfairly by the British government when it dismissed him from his position as king's Superintendent of British Honduras in 1780. Unemployed and bitter, he joined the Irish and English radical associations. He was arrested in 1799 for implication in the Irish Rebellion, but released when the suspension of habeas corpus lapsed in April 1801.[40]

During 1802, Despard came to believe that discontent was widespread and he planned an armed revolt in London intended to precipitate a revolutionary insurrection. He recruited from among disaffected soldiers, whom he assembled regularly at a number of different taverns in working-class areas of London. After several months of planning, they chose to strike on 23 November (the day of the opening of Parliament), as the king rode in from Windsor. The plan was first to attack the Tower to gain munitions, then to capture the Bank, and finally to kill the king. Unfortunately for Despard, the government had become aware of the conspiracy during the summer.[41] On 16 November, London, Surrey, and Kent patrols raided the Oakley Arms tavern in Lambeth and arrested Despard in the company of forty working men and soldiers.

Despite the discovery of a planned insurrection, Addington and Pelham decided not to reimpose the repressive legislation of the 1790s, as they did not believe that the conspiracy posed a serious threat to the security of the Kingdom.[42] The atmosphere surrounding the trial and execution of Despard reinforced this assessment. The new French ambassador in London claimed that the affair made little sensation.[43] Despard did not receive the infamous attention usually granted to state executions. As Fox noted, "Of Despard nothing is said more than of any housebreaker, who may have been hanged the same day."[44] The poet Robert Southey, who followed British politics closely and frequently commented on them, described Addington's dealing with Despard: "With such lenity are things conducted in England. No arrests have followed, no alarm has been excited; the people are perfectly satisfied of his guilt, and only say What a blessing that it did not happen under Pitt—Never had a nation a more perfect confidence in the rectitude of their minister."[45] Despard called Nelson as a character witness at his trial, and just before the execution, he sent Nelson a petition for reprieve. Nelson passed it on to Addington, who sincerely empathized with the tragedy of Despard's circumstances, but could not excuse his crime.

While Addington and Pelham felt that no extraordinary legal measures were required in response to the Despard conspiracy, the circumstances of an abortive insurrection in Dublin in July 1803 were different. United Irishmen, under the direction of Robert Emmet, had stored arms for an insurrection planned to occur simultaneously with a French invasion of Ireland. An accidental explosion at their arms cache in July 1803 alerted British authorities, and Emmet decided to move prematurely. The Lord Lieutenant received news of the plot on the eve of the insurrection, but the Irish commander in chief played down the reports. As a result, British forces arrived on the scene several hours late. Fortunately for them, only a few hundred of the expected several thousand rebels materialized, and the security forces crushed the insurrection easily, but not before the Lord Chief Justice of the King's Bench and several others were murdered.[46] In this case Addington suspended habeas corpus and invoked martial law in Ireland.

Addington and Pelham's approach to social policy was generally consistent with that of their predecessors and successors. The Home Office responded to reports of serious social unrest with instructions to implement existing laws to punish the ringleaders, but deployed troops sparingly. They had some sympathy with the circumstances that drove individuals to violence, but the government upheld the law. When riots occurred, the government believed that law enforcement officials should punish the leaders of riots and insurrection and let their followers go. Nevertheless, Addington and Pelham differed from Pitt and Portland to a small but perceptible degree. Fox's nephew, Henry Fox, the third Baron Holland, was a politician who recognized the difference. He remarked that "Mr. Addington seemed disposed to lower the high and insolent tone which his predecessors had assumed both at home and abroad." This, he said, "had a very beneficial effect on the country, and assuaged, if it did not heal the wounds which the anti-revolutionary and jealous spirit of Mr Pitt's government had inflicted."[47] Southey was another observer who drew an even more stark distinction between the policies of the governments of Addington and Pitt: "The system of terror, of alarm, and of espionage, has been laid aside, the most burthensome of the taxes repealed, and a sincere desire manifested on the part of the new minister to meet the wishes of the nation. . . . They call him the Doctor . . . a minister of healing he has truly been; he has poured balm and oil into the wounds of the country, and the country is blessing him."[48] Addington did not change the direction of government social policy, but he was slightly milder and less reactionary than his predecessors in implementing it.

NAVAL REFORM

The Royal Navy was a pillar of state power and national pride. It was the lifeline for trade and commerce, the linchpin in the British Empire, and the first line of defense against invasion. Over the course of the French Revolutionary War, naval victories were a welcome pretext to light beacons and ring church bells during the long periods when reports of the military situation on the Continent brought nothing but bad news. They boosted public morale and enabled ministers of government to forget, for just a moment, how poorly war on the Continent was going for Great Britain. The Royal Navy was an integral part of the British identity during the late eighteenth and early nineteenth centuries. Consequently, naval policies were often the subject of parliamentary and public scrutiny. St. Vincent's naval reforms proved to be the most controversial of Addington's peacetime initiatives and had the most important long-term consequences for the Royal Navy and parliamentary politics. Their origins lay in the experience of the war. The consequences of St. Vincent's commission of naval inquiry would stretch beyond the fall of Addington and have an important impact on the course of parliamentary politics for the next decade.

The idea of reforming the navy took shape in the 1780s. It had been apparent after the American War of Independence that the dockyards wasted public funds through carelessness and corruption. Although inefficiency was not peculiar to the navy, it was particularly conspicuous there because the navy received a large proportion of both government expenditure and political attention. Despite growing considerably in size and importance, the administration of the dockyards had hardly changed since the seventeenth century. During the 1780s and 1790s, political pressure for efficiency and economy compelled the Admiralty to force the Navy Board to reform dockyard procedure. After the Finance Committee of the House of Commons recommended an inquiry in 1798, Pitt's administration commissioned Brigadier General Samuel Bentham (brother of the famous philosopher Jeremy Bentham) to reform the dockyards. Bentham constructed a comprehensive and worthy plan, but in the midst of war, the Admiralty postponed many of the reforms. The Admiralty made a promise, however, that an inquiry would be made after peace was concluded.[49]

The system of fraud and abuse was pervasive across the administration of the navy. Corruption was apparent at three levels: the dockyard workers, the contractors, and the Navy Board. Workers were guilty of widespread theft and fraud. While custom had legitimized the practice of workers taking unusable wood "chips" home for firewood, it became common practice for workers to cut up good pieces of timber into chips so that they could take them home. The loss of this timber had grave consequences when the circumstances of the war cut off Great Britain's foreign supplies of timber. Even more serious, some workers stole copper bolts required to hold the ships together and disguised the theft by cutting off the ends, replacing the middle section with wood, and putting them into the ships being repaired. At least two ships were lost when such bolts failed to hold together at sea. The dockyards also frequently charged for work they never completed. At Portsmouth, some artificers were paid for working twenty-one hours of overtime in one day. A government survey found that there were 2,361 more men on the payroll than actually worked in the dockyard. The government was also grossly overcharged. Cooperage at Deptford that cost £37 was charged at £1,000. As a result of such fraudulent practices the HMS Dedalus, for example, cost £8,788 to build, but £13,802 to repair. Theft and fraud combined robbed the government of at least £1 million per year.[50]

Contractors made enormous fortunes by defrauding the government further. The worst abuses concerned timber, as contractors often charged top prices for rotten wood. The government also suffered from poor contract management. Many contracts remained in the same families for generations, denying government the benefits in terms of quality and cost savings that would have been offered by a system of competition among suppliers. For example, at Plymouth, the Navy Board gave block contracts to William Taylor of Southampton for periods of seven or more years at a time, without considering bids from any other firms. Taylor then subcontracted out to other firms for a commission of 10 percent. The cooperage contract at Plymouth remained in one family from 1714 to 1782, after which it was given to another. In cases where competitive bids were issued, some firms were able to beat the system by bidding very low and then arranging to increase the price after receiving the contract.[51] This would not have been possible without the compliance of officials of the Navy Board, who, instead of preventing these abuses, often abetted them. Some officials accepted bribes. The board was also afraid of antagonizing the workers or contractors, preferring inefficiency to the disruption that might have resulted if they had tried to correct it.[52]

St. Vincent had been aware of these abuses long before he became First Lord of the Admiralty. During the war, ships under his command often suffered the consequences of faulty workmanship, and he obtained first-hand knowledge of the dockyards when he was in Gibraltar. His experience convinced him that the navy required important reforms. He often said that he would change the system if ever given the power. Upon his appointment as First Lord, he expressed his intention to act: "There is much to do, and a late attempt of my great Predecessor meets with every species of opposition and obloquy. I mean 'a partial reform in our Dock Yards' and comparing small things with great (which must come, or we are ruined) I shall have a very difficult task to perform, if I preside at this Board in times of Peace."[53] Time was all that he required: "I flatter myself, if I have a reasonable tenure of my present situation, I shall be able to correct some of the gross abuses, which clog the wheels of the service, and if permitted to go on much longer must swallow up all the means of the Country."[54]

St. Vincent's attitude and personality had a major impact on his term in office. He believed that the Admiralty had previously lacked will and vigor. He was determined to succeed. During his career, he had often been heavy-handed, and almost always got his own way, but his assertiveness proved a double-edged sword. While the country admired him for his success, many of his own men despised him for the harsh way he treated them.[55] The first crisis he faced upon taking office seemed to indicate he would carry these tactics into politics. Dockyard workers struck for higher pay at the time of preparing for Hyde Parker's expedition to Copenhagen in March 1801. Riots ensued at Plymouth on 31 March and Sheerness on 13 April. While Addington and the rest of the cabinet seemed inclined to address the grievances of the workers, St. Vincent, who considered this action as bordering on mutiny, ordered the ringleaders to be discharged and deployed troops to drive the rest back to work. On 27 April, he ordered a tour of the dockyards and discharged workmen involved in the combination. By May, he had dismissed 340 workers.[56]

After the signing of the Preliminary Treaty, St. Vincent's first priority was to assist Addington in meeting his budget targets, by cutting naval expenditure. At the end of October 1801, Hobart directed the Admiralty to reduce the naval establishment. St. Vincent immediately ordered ships discharged, and trimmed the dockyards down to a peacetime establishment. In November, he laid off 500 laborers and 300 shipwrights from Deptford, 325 men at Woolwich Warren, and 150 coopers and yardmen from the victualing office. After the signing of the Treaty of Amiens, Hobart ordered further cuts. Addington decided to retain a larger than normal peacetime establishment, to ensure that the Royal Navy would not be caught short-handed in the event of a sudden renewal of war, but St. Vincent discharged both ships and seamen in great numbers. He reduced the naval establishment to 130,000 seamen with a projected reduction to 70,000 by the end of 1802, and a further reduction to 30,000 by the end of 1803.[57] Addington granted St. Vincent a greater degree of independence than he allowed his other ministers, and relied on the admiral's professional judgment about the strength of the establishment needed to meet Great Britain's security requirements during peace.

Addington's policy of reducing expenditure gave St. Vincent the pretext to pursue his personal goal of reforming the abuses in the dockyards. He had already begun investigating "instances of misconduct" reported at Sheerness during July 1801. By June 1802, he had decided to initiate an inquiry and ordered officials to seal and secure the yardbooks and commence a full inspection of the dockyards.[58] Almost immediately, however, St. Vincent ran up against the political issues that would hamper his crusade. Addington called an election for the summer of 1802. While he fully supported St. Vincent's principles and motives in seeking to reform abuses, he was concerned about the political implications of taking actions that might affect the interests of electors in constituencies which included dockyards. He persuaded St. Vincent to postpone the inquiry until after the election, so as not to alienate support for the government in the southwest, where there were strong naval interests.[59] When St. Vincent eventually conducted the investigations at the dockyards after the election, he discovered that the problems were worse then he had imagined. He wrote to Addington from Plymouth on 29 August that he had found "abuse to such an extent as would require many months to go thoroughly into, and the absolute necessity of a Commission of enquiry to expose them appears to the Admiralty Board here in a much stronger light than ever."[60]

His inspections of the various dockyards uncovered not only the extent of the abuses, but also the culpability of the Navy Board in covering them up. Although provided with adequate information, the board refused to investigate a number of complaints, such as one by a commissioner who complained to the board about extra payments made to workers at Sheerness. The board determined that the master shipwright was guilty of involvement, but it sheltered him from punishment. It also gave a raise in pay to a master blacksmith accused of corruption. The clerk of the cheque had failed to keep his books current and continued to pay aged and infirm workers, but the board refused to investigate. The board also failed to notice that children had been admitted as rope-makers at Woolwich. As a result of St. Vincent's investigation, the Admiralty decided to reprimand the board because "by their failure in the execution of their duty, the public has been suffered to be defrauded to a very considerable amount, and delinquencies passed unpunished."[61] Nevertheless, it was clear to the Admiralty Board that official reprimands alone would not prevent future abuses. St. Vincent did not have the authority to fire the members of the Navy Board, however, because they had been appointed by the Crown.

St. Vincent continued to press the cabinet for a parliamentary commission of inquiry to expose these abuses. A commission of inquiry would both draw greater attention to the abuses in question and have the authority to compel the production of evidence necessary to prosecute them. There was also a political reason for this policy, as St. Vincent could not hope to reform the dockyards effectively as long as the existing members of the Navy Board held their positions. He hoped that the process of an inquiry would cause many of the corrupt members to resign and leave him a free hand to appoint new members more inclined to reform.[62]

Addington and the rest of the cabinet had reservations about an inquiry. While Addington supported the principle of reform, he feared that a parliamentary inquiry might be unpopular and detri-

mental to the system of supplying naval stores. The question was ultimately reduced to one of administrative necessity versus political
expediency. St. Vincent was tenacious and eventually convinced the
cabinet to agree to establish a commission empowered to call for documents and examine witnesses on oath. The commission of inquiry
was established by Parliament in 1802, but it did not release some of
its reports until after Addington's resignation in 1804.

St. Vincent did not want to wait for the conclusion of the inquiry
to begin implementing reforms. Following the recommendations of
the report that Bentham had prepared for the previous administration, St. Vincent instituted the office of Timber Master to examine the
wood supplied by contractors. Recognizing that the navy's heavy
dependency on merchant building was expensive, he also decided to
cut costs by building ships in government dockyards. After the conclusion of peace, he abstained from making private contracts for
ships of the line because the price of timber was high. He believed
that the price would decrease and availability increase if merchants
were not competing with government for supplies. A government
study indicated that forty-six shipwrights could build a seventy-four-
gun ship in one year. He predicted that, under this system, the dockyards could build ten new ships of the line each year and the whole
fleet could be kept in repair.[63]

St. Vincent pursued reform for sound financial and administrative
reasons. Future governments, seeing the wisdom of his intentions,
implemented most of his policies, to the benefit of the Royal Navy
and the British government. Nevertheless, in the short term, there
was a price. The men who had made a fortune from the government
had no qualms about resorting to force when the Admiralty tried to
change the system that had worked to their great financial benefit. St.
Vincent gave Timber Masters the task of ensuring the quality of the
timber for building or repairing ships. Consequently, they began to
reject rotten stock that the Navy Board previously would have accepted. This enraged many timber merchants, who responded by either
raising their prices (as much as 32 percent) or refusing to sell to the
government at all.[64] There were other contractors who refused to deal

with the government. In addition, the Navy Board, appearing to side with these contractors, deliberately obstructed many of St. Vincent's reforms. He refused to yield to the contractors' demands, but the result was that navy stocks fell below the three-year supply that the Admiralty considered the customary minimum. Another problem St. Vincent created was that, having dismissed a large number of dockyard workers in peacetime, it took time to bring the dockyards back to full strength. The consequences were that the navy fell behind both in repairs and in construction of new ships. As wear and tear took a toll on active ships, there were some extraordinary delays in getting them refitted.[65] Regardless of how much the Admiralty abhorred the inefficiency and corruption, the navy could not function without the cooperation of the dockyards, contractors, and Navy Board.

St. Vincent's approach was slightly out of step with that taken by Addington in other areas of his administration. When Addington implemented retrenchment and reform, he was careful to provide for the contingency of an immediate renewal of war. St. Vincent, on the contrary, managed the navy largely on the assumption that peace would last. His reductions in naval spending were more drastic than those in the military departments, and the disruption in the dockyards weakened the ability of the navy to return quickly to a wartime establishment in the event the war resumed. Given ten years of peace, he might have overhauled the system completely and had it better prepared for the next war. The diplomatic situation, however, did not justify the assumption that peace would last that long.

The style of administration of St. Vincent and members of his staff, such as Sir Thomas Troubridge and John Markham, was particularly abrasive, and it created unnecessary and detrimental antagonism. Addington considered Troubridge and Markham as "being so violent in office as to bring discredit on the govt. He told them once (he being the Prime Minister) that even when they did things which were right they had a wrong way of doing it from habitual violence." Addington later concluded that St. Vincent, despite his abilities, was ungenerous-minded and ultimately a political liability.[66] From a parliamentary standpoint, the consequences of St. Vincent's policies and his unconciliatory approach gave the opposition considerable ammunition. The parliamentary commotion that the reforms created obscured the successful measures of the naval administration. Years later, Addington would cite the actions of the Admiralty Board as among the prominent causes of the downfall of his ministry.[67] He held St. Vincent's naval policies responsible for turning Pitt against him in the spring of 1804. One of Addington's confidants wrote:

> Nothing ever astonished or distressed Mr Addington more than Mr Pitt's sudden and unaccountable abandonment of his administration & his union with Mr Fox for the expulsion of Mr Addington—it was a proceeding discreditable to Pitt which he certainly felt to be unwarranted. Pitt could not endure the conduct of Ld St Vincent and the admiralty and it was this that determined him to force them from office even thought their fall might bring down those for whom he professed a great regard.[68]

Pitt's action raises the question of whether the damage St. Vincent's policies had done to the navy was evidence of Addington's incapacity to govern. The truth was that despite the negative implications of St. Vincent's policies, they did not substantially affect Great Britain's war effort. Upon the renewal of war in 1803, British ships of all classes still in commission far outnumbered the French. When Addington resigned one year later, the British retained this superiority. The British fleet blockading the port of Brest outnumbered the French in ships of all classes by fifty-six to forty-three and the British fleet blockading Toulon, by forty-six to sixteen.[69] The navy achieved its primary goals in terms of blockade and colonial warfare. As there was little else the navy could accomplish, the few extra ships that might have been made available if St. Vincent had been more conciliatory would not markedly have improved the British military position. A few months after resigning, Addington observed that, despite the criticisms of Pitt and other politicians: "Lord St. Vincent's System of naval Defence is highly approved of by all the Seafaring People whom I have met with, who are acquainted with the navigation of the Channel, & with the opposite Coasts of England & France; & I have good Reason for believing, that it is by no means discountenanced by the present Board of Admiralty."[70] Pitt's parliamentary strategy proved successful, however, as the eventual vindication of St. Vincent arrived too late to prevent Addington's resignation.

The Peace of Amiens gave Great Britain the breathing space it needed to recover from the strains of the war. Addington was able to restore the government finances and lower taxes. Peace brought a resumption of trade with Europe. Radicalism and social unrest subsided. The government released prisoners from jail. Thousands of soldiers and sailors went home. Fox and other aristocrats traveled to Paris to meet Bonaparte. The peace also gave Addington and St. Vincent a break from the preoccupation of foreign policy and military and naval strategy and allowed them to institute necessary reforms. As a result, Addington became extremely popular. The election that he called during the summer enabled him moderately to increase the strength of the government in the House of Commons. His halcyon days, however, would not last long. The expansion of French power on the Continent during the peace threatened British interests. By the autumn of 1802, Addington became preoccupied with foreign policy issues once again.

CHAPTER 5

The Disintegration of the
Amiens Settlement

Addington had no illusions about the durability of the Peace of Amiens. The course of the negotiations disheartened him and Hawkesbury, and the longer they interacted with French officials, the more they became convinced that Anglo-French relations would continue to be difficult. They were disappointed that they were not able to achieve better terms, but they knew that the French would not make further concessions. While they hoped that peace might last, they knew that it would probably prove merely a truce. It was a necessary truce, but, "just as they feared that Bonaparte might disregard it, they hoped that by strengthening their international position they might, when they were ready, do the same."[1]

Anglo-French antagonism persisted after the signing of the Treaty of Amiens because Bonaparte proved as frustrating for the British to deal with during peace as he had been during the war. Even before Cornwallis and Joseph Bonaparte signed the treaty, the First Consul accused the British government of directing attacks against him in the British press.[2] The authors of these articles were French émigrés whose aim was not the preservation of peace between France and Great Britain, but the restoration of the monarchy in France—a goal that they thought would be better served if the war continued. In March 1802, Talleyrand warned the British minister to France that, if the newspapers did not cease to insult the First Consul, he would direct the French newspapers to attack Addington and would employ a London newspaper to issue Bonapartist propaganda. These threats were not very effective because Addington knew that French propaganda would have little effect with the British public or on his standing in Parliament. Bonaparte's complaints did not end there, however. In May, the British minister in Paris reported that Bonaparte also objected to the way the British allowed French royalists and bishops to appear at court. Claiming that this encouraged the disaffected in France, Bonaparte demanded that the British government deport the émigrés.

The British wanted to preserve peace and develop a cordial relationship with Bonaparte and tried to conciliate him, but they would not allow him to influence the administration of British law. Hawkesbury tried to reassure the French that Addington's government had not provided any assistance to the émigrés, and pointed out that, as the offending newspaper articles did not break any British laws, he had no legal authority to deport the authors. Bonaparte rejected these reassurances. After a series of cabinet meetings, Addington decided, as a gesture of good-will to Bonaparte, to refer a specific case of an article criticizing Bonaparte to the attorney general's office for prosecution for libel. Addington also made a request, through unofficial channels, to newspapers not to publish similar articles in future.[3]

Bonaparte persisted with his complaints, claiming that there was a conspiracy of émigrés to defame the French government. He demanded that the British government suppress this conspiracy and deport all the émigrés involved, going so far as to stipulate that the more active royalists be sent to Canada and the princes of Bourbon to Warsaw.[4] The British cabinet became concerned about how seriously Bonaparte appeared to be taking these issues, and the effect this was having on Anglo-French relations. Liverpool argued that "those who were most disposed to censure the Administration for making the peace, will censure them with greater Justice, if they do not take every proper Measure to secure the Continuance of it."[5] Nevertheless, Addington could not give in to Bonaparte's demands. As he told Otto, British laws would not allow the government to control what was published in the press in the way the French government could. He could not change the laws for, "though the liberty of the press is so grossly abused, a minister would undertake a bold and fruitless task, who should attempt to introduce a bill to counteract that, which Englishmen certainly prize next to the trial by jury."[6] Otto understood the British position and tried to explain to Talleyrand that there was little that the British government could do to stifle the press, which criticized everyone.[7]

Hawkesbury believed that the hostile disposition of the French government was the result of miscommunication and of Bonaparte's ego and bad temper, rather than a deliberate policy of intimidation. He hoped that frank discussions would clarify the situation. He tried to reassure Bonaparte that the émigrés were already leaving Jersey, where they were close to the French coast, and that the British government would deport royalists and bishops involved in distributing anti-Bonaparte propaganda in France. Hawkesbury felt it essential for the future of Anglo-French relations that both governments come to a complete understanding on the issue. He believed

> that after a War in which the Passions of Men have been roused beyond all former examples, it is natural to suppose that the Distrust, Jealousy, and other hostile Feelings of Individuals should not immediately subside & under these circumstances it appears to be both the Interest and the Duty of the two Governments by a mild and temperate conduct gradually to allay these Feelings, and not on the contrary to provoke and augment them by untimely Irritation on their part, and by ascribing proceedings like those abovementioned, to causes which they have no reference.[8]

His attempt at conciliation failed, however. Talleyrand continued to insist that the British do more to resolve French grievances, and Bonaparte deferred resuming Anglo-French commerce until they complied.[9]

Disputes over trade, an important component of Anglo-French relations, contributed to the general atmosphere of mistrust and suspicion. British commercial interests expected that peace would lead to a renewal of Anglo-French trade, but Bonaparte intervened. He was determined to revive and strengthen French commerce and industry in the wake of the French Revolution, which had hampered the development of advanced methods of manufacture. Bonaparte felt that pre-war Anglo-French trade had been to Great Britain's advantage and France's detriment. And French goods sold in British markets would not compensate for the Continental markets that France would lose to British competition. The best way for him to promote the interests of French industry and trade would be by preventing British access to the markets of France, its allies and dependencies. Less than two months after signing the Treaty of Amiens, Bonaparte passed a new series of tariffs and reintroduced a law that required the seizure of all British ships of over one hundred tons entering French ports.[10]

The British government objected to Bonaparte's trade restrictions. Hawkesbury instructed the British minister in Paris to tell the French ministers that it was important for France and Great Britain to establish an agreement to cover issues of trade.[11] Not now, replied Bonaparte, though he might consider a commercial arrangement in the future. This gave him the pretext to send to London a commissioner general of commercial relations, who was really a spy instructed to gather intelligence concerning social unrest, public opinion, and British military strength. Bonaparte sent another agent to obtain a detailed description of the port of Hull, and a third to obtain similar information in Dublin.[12] Having intercepted some of these agents' correspondence and received reports of the French having seized British ships that storms had driven into French ports, Hawkesbury refused to grant official recognition to any French commercial agents.[13]

Although the disputes over the press and commercial relations soured Anglo-French relations and created tension, they were, in themselves, insufficient to provoke a renewal of war. Hobart argued,

"If we are to renew the War with France let it be for a great Political object—but nothing in my opinion can be so impolitic or so wicked as to hazard the interruption of Peace by Newspaper invectives against the Government of France."[14] Pitt made light of the situation in stating that he would remain at Walmer Castle "till the Pacificator of Europe takes it into his head to send an Army from the opposite Coast to revenge himself for some newspaper paragraph."[15] The true significance of these rather minor disputes was that they aggravated difficult Anglo-French relations and caused the British government to doubt whether diplomacy could resolve Anglo-French disputes over major strategic issues.

The first dispute of this nature arose in September, when a rebellion in Switzerland against the regime that Bonaparte had installed gave him the pretext to intervene. Ordering the rebels to desist and restore his allies to power, he threatened to send 30,000 French troops across the border.[16] Addington and Hawkesbury considered this an act of aggression and an attempt by Bonaparte to annex further territory. The expansion of French power on the Continent, unlike the press and trade disputes, was a direct threat to the interests of Great Britain and the other Great Powers.

The continued expansion of French power, after the recently negotiated peace, posed a serious problem for the British government. It was difficult to know how far to let Bonaparte push before pushing back. Addington summed up his thinking as follows:

> I do in my conscience believe that the nation anxiously wishes for the continuance of peace, but is not afraid of war—it hopes for the best, but desires to be prepared for the worst—that it will not suffer any unworthy compromise of its honour; but that it will not permit any impassioned feelings and exaggerated representations to bear down what is due to prudence. . . . I have no hesitation in confessing, that I consider war as a dreadful evil. But dreadful as is that evil, I shall never hesitate between the alternative of the sacrifice of our honour and war.[17]

At first, the Swiss crisis appeared to be the opportunity to take a strong stand against the French. Hawkesbury made a firm but mild remonstrance to Otto, intended to buy time to send a special agent to Switzerland to gather information and offer a subsidy to assist the Swiss rebels in resisting the anticipated French invasion. There was also hope that the Austrians and Russians would oppose French interference.[18] During the period of the Swiss crisis, Bonaparte also annexed Piedmont and the Duchy of Parma, giving him control of most of northern Italy, an area of strategic interest to both Austria and Russia. Addington hoped that, with the support of the other Great Powers, he would be able to stop Bonaparte. Believing that he had an opportunity to gain the upper hand, Addington suspended further restitution of colonies as required by the Treaty of Amiens until the crisis was over.[19] Unfortunately for Addington, the opportunity dissolved too quickly. The British agent he sent to Switzerland was delayed by bad weather and did not arrive until after the Swiss had capitulated to Bonaparte.[20]

Although Addington played down this affair for parliamentary and public consumption, he had seriously considered taking military action. During the height of the crisis, Addington appeared "extremely warlike."[21] Hobart proposed that the British should join other European states, if it ever happened that they declared war against the French.[22] Nelson informed Addington on 25 October that he had "only one object in view (that of giving an early and knock down blow to our Enemy and getting again the blessings of Peace)."[23] On 30 October, Addington told Hardwicke that the government was preparing for war, "with as little Bustle as is consistent with a Degree of Activity, & Exertion, & public observation has not reached all the material steps which have been taken with a View to that object."[24] Hobart directed the commander in chief to begin preparing for a French invasion.[25] On 5 November, Hawkesbury told his father, "I am inclined to think there will be war. . . . I did not think it probable that Bonaparte would have ventured to march an army into Switzerland & in that case it might not have been difficult to have come to some compromise. But this Circumstance attended with the Defiance which he had given us not to interfere in any Continental Concerns renders any accommodation extremely difficult, if not impossible."[26]

Russia and Austria refused, however, to oppose Bonaparte on Switzerland, and the sudden collapse of Swiss resistance made British military action unfeasible. Addington consulted Pitt, who advised against military action without support from Russia or Austria. But Great Britain, he said, should use the peace to increase its military strength.[27] Addington agreed, concluding that "The Question is not one of Justice, but of Discretion."[28] The cabinet met on 8 November and confirmed Addington's position.[29] It was a difficult decision, but the primary consideration of the cabinet was that, whenever war broke out, it was important that it appear that the British government had not acted rashly: in Addington's words, "We must however take Care, not only to be right, but *very* right."[30]

Addington and Hawkesbury colored their language with moral undertones, because they believed that, in order to promote British interests, it was necessary to create a perception that the moves Bonaparte made to extend his power in Europe were unethical. It would have been dangerous for Great Britain to declare war with France unless the British government had the support of British public opinion and of the other Great Powers. The British public and the governments of the other states of Europe had favored peace in 1801 and would likely have condemned the British government for provoking a war, after such a short period of peace, unless it had strong justification. If the British government could make it appear that Bonaparte's expansion of French power was deliberately flouting the principles of the peace treaties that he had signed, Great Britain could justify taking military action to defend British interests.

To renew the war, however, would require the support of Russia and Austria. Hawkesbury told Charles, Lord Whitworth, the newly appointed British ambassador to France, "it was found upon the whole prudent to adopt a lower and more pacific *Tone* than had been originally intended. . . . It would be impossible even if it were prudent to engage the Country in a War under the present circumstances on account of any of the *aggressions* which have been hitherto committed by France. Our Policy will be to endeavour to make those aggressions the Groundwork of a Defensive System conjointly with Russia and Austria for the future."[31] The British still hoped that, given time to rebuild their economies and armies, the Russians and Austrians would eventually join a diplomatic or military coalition against France. They decided in the interim to postpone military action against the French, while continuing to court Russian and Austrian support.[32]

The Swiss affair demonstrated that the treaties of peace that Great Britain and the other states of Europe had signed with Bonaparte would not deter him from expanding French power in Europe. It also placed Anglo-French relations in a state that resembled a cold war. Addington became determined to take a stronger stand against Bonaparte and to prepare for the eventual hostilities by increasing the military and naval establishments.[33] He was able to accomplish these goals because the British economy had recovered and his financial and foreign policies had restored the government finances. The president of the Board of Trade attested to the dramatic improvement in the British economy during 1802:

> The Commerce & Revenue of this Country, were never in so flourishing a Condition: the Export of British Manufactures in the Course of last year, exceeds the amount of any former year; and Mr Addington told me on Saturday, that the Taxes imposed last year, will produce £1,400,000 more than the sum for which they were given. He will take the Sinking Fund after discharging all Charges upon it, for £6,000,000; and will thereby be enabled to bear the Expense of the additional Establishments, with very little, or without any further Burden on the People.[34]

Hobart believed that this policy was the most favorable for securing peace, as "Our best security for the Continuance of Peace, until some imperious Policy drives Bona Parte [*sic*] into War at all hazards, is in the respectable Naval and Military Establishments recently voted, & the Possession of Malta, a Possession which if ever relinquished can never be regained."[35]

The question of how best to secure the neutrality of Malta, the rock upon which the Peace of Amiens would founder, had been one of the most difficult issues during the negotiations of the Preliminary

Treaty and the Treaty of Amiens. Preservation of British interests in the Mediterranean and the Near East required that the French never occupy Malta.[36] British forces that had garrisoned the island prior to the Treaty of Amiens would evacuate the island only on the condition that it remain independent of France. Although Addington insisted that "Malta forms an entirely separate Question," British policy concerning the island changed as Anglo-French relations deteriorated in 1802.[37] As late as 6 September 1802, Addington fully intended to evacuate Malta in conformity with the treaty.[38] Less than two weeks later, however, Hobart admitted privately that "for the present we have determined to take no step respecting Malta being inclined to hold it as long as we can."[39] Provisions for securing the independence of Malta had not been met: Naples, Russia, and Prussia had not fulfilled their military obligations as required by the treaty. While the French were not responsible for the delay in the arrival of the new international defense force, Malta would be vulnerable to a French invasion if the British garrison withdrew and left the island undefended.

Although the Swiss crisis initially prompted Addington to postpone further restitution of colonies as required by the Treaty of Amiens, having decided not to go to war at that time, he decided to restore all the other colonies. Hobart accordingly issued new orders to restore the colonial conquests including the Cape but not Malta.[40] The decision to retain Malta was difficult because it entailed violating the Treaty of Amiens. Addington felt, however, that he could justify the retention of Malta in the eyes of the British public and the governments of the other European powers. According to a cabinet memorandum, "As the System of Encroachment pursued by France since that period has not only added greatly & unexpectedly to the Power of France, but may lead to further Encroachments in other quarters, His Majesty thinks He is warranted in not giving up those Securities which He still possesses, and particularly that it is His Determination, in conformity to the wishes of the Inhabitants, to appropriate the Island of Malta as part of His dominions."[41] This did not mean that Addington was inflexible on this point. He was willing to consider other arrangements that would provide for adequate

British security in the Mediterranean. The future of Malta and Anglo-French relations hung in the balance during the early months of 1803, as Whitworth tried to negotiate a settlement with Talleyrand in Paris.

The British government preferred to play for time rather than bring the crisis to a head during the first few months of these negotiations. Hawkesbury asserted, "there is no precedent to govern one's conduct; but the sentiment seems to be that it is hardly possible to continue the relations of peace & amity with a power whose conduct & whose language are so professedly hostile and on occasion of this nature we might be exposed to the clamour of the public and of the Army. On the other hand it cannot be denied that the pro-crastination of hostilities even if they should ultimately be unavoidable for a few months would be very desirable."[42]

The publication of Colonel Horace Sebastiani's report in *Le moniteur* in January 1803, however, stirred Anglo-French relations into turmoil. Bonaparte had sent Sebastiani to gain intelligence on British activities in Egypt and the Eastern Mediterranean. In his report, he complained that the British not only had failed to evacuate Malta, but also had retained troops in Egypt contrary to the Treaty of Amiens. He asserted, however, that it would take only a small French force to dislodge the British from Alexandria. As *Le moniteur* was the official organ of the French government, Addington and Hawkesbury interpreted the report as a sign that Bonaparte was considering another invasion. This rendered possession of Malta even more important, as it was the only base from which the Royal Navy could effectively protect the Turks from a French attack.

The key to British policy toward Malta had always been the attitude of the Russians. The British had agreed to surrender Malta in 1801 because they knew that they would sacrifice the goodwill of Alexander I if they retained it. By the end of 1802, the attitude of the Russians toward the independence of Malta changed: they were no longer adamant that it be restored to the Knights of Malta. In fact, the Russians began to see advantages to having the British retain Malta. Alexander Vorontsov, the Russian chancellor and foreign minister, hinted to Sir John Borlase Warren, the new British ambassador to

Russia, in December 1802 that the British should retain the island. More important, in January 1803, Prince Adam Czartoryski, the new foreign minister, stated definitively that the tsar wanted Malta to remain British to prevent the French from invading again.[43] This immediately removed any constraints on British policy toward Malta.

This news appeared to be a sign that Russia might be willing to cooperate with Great Britain against France, not just on Malta but on other issues as well. On the pretext that the French were preparing to seize Egypt, Hawkesbury instructed Warren on 1 February to propose a new arrangement to the Russians. If they would not conclude a defensive alliance, would they make a more limited agreement, either public or secret, to protect the Turkish Empire against French aggression? Hawkesbury argued that an agreement ought to be concluded as quickly as possible because, owing to the great distances between London, St. Petersburg, and Constantinople, the British and the Russians could help the Turks in an emergency only if arrangements had been made ahead of time.[44] Once again the Russians declined, arguing that if France became aware of the arrangement, it would provoke a Continental war. The Russians did wish to cooperate with the British over the future of Turkey, but had calculated that the French would not risk another attack.[45]

Hawkesbury also made a simultaneous overture to the Austrians through Starhemberg. This time he did not propose a formal alliance but rather suggested that they confer secretly about France. Hawkesbury wished to find out what would have to happen before the Austrians would be prepared to declare war on France. In the words of Starhemberg, he wished to discover what would be "the last drop of water that would cause the glass to overflow."[46] But the Austrians were unsure of the answer themselves. They were certainly not prepared to risk the future of their empire to fight for British objectives on the Continent, while the British remained safe across the Channel. Austria was in no position, militarily or financially, to bear the full brunt of the French army in a Continental war. Addington and Hawkesbury, like Pitt and Grenville before them, also failed to understand that the Austrians were threatened equally by Russia. The Austrians feared that any security to be gained in Central Europe by defeating France might not compensate them for the loss of security they would suffer in Eastern Europe. They had already learned a painful lesson about how the Russians and Prussians could take advantage of Austria's involvement in a war with France. Russia and Prussia had increased their power in Eastern Europe by collaborating to seize Polish territory in 1793 without compensating Austria, in what was called the Second Partition of Poland.

Hawkesbury told the French that the British would retain Malta until they received an adequate explanation for Sebastiani's report, even though he doubted that the French would provide one. Bonaparte continued to insist that the British evacuate Malta, and Otto threatened Hawkesbury with war if they refused. In Paris on 20 February 1803, Bonaparte reprimanded Whitworth at the Tuileries. In a long and stern lecture he insisted that he would never permit Great Britain to retain Malta, and claimed, in Whitworth's words, that "of the two he had rather see us in possession of the Faubourg St. Antoine [a district of Paris] than Malta." Bonaparte asserted that the question of peace or war depended on Malta, and threatened that he would invade England, if war resumed.[47]

Addington was surprised by this threat and by Bonaparte's claim to have 480,000 troops ready for war, but he was uncertain whether Bonaparte was serious. Was he really prepared to go to war, or was he bluffing? Whitworth's dispatches and private letters did not provide a clear answer. According to Whitworth, Bonaparte had a fiery temper and was inclined to fight, but he was personally unpopular in France and French government finances were in disarray. Nevertheless, the British government believed that, even if he lacked the proper military and financial resources, Bonaparte was so unpredictable and unstable that he might still provoke a war. The exaggerated reports of the volatility of Bonaparte's personality led Hawkesbury's father to speculate rather hopefully about his health, "It is possible that Bonaparte may go mad, and may die in his Delirium."[48]

At this point in the negotiations, the French were increasing their naval and military establishments along the French and Dutch coasts of the Channel. The only prudent course for Addington was to prepare for war, while continuing to negotiate a solution for the issue of Malta. On 8 March, the king issued a proclamation in Parliament augmenting the British armed forces.[49] Addington then called out the militia and strengthened the navy by 10,000 men. This provoked Whitworth and the British minister at The Hague to complain that Addington had unnecessarily heightened Anglo-French tension. They believed that the French military and naval preparations were legitimately intended for the West Indies, where the French government was still trying to suppress the slave rebellion.[50] Addington was already aware of this, but he speculated that, if war resumed, Bonaparte would divert those military resources from the West Indies to the British Empire.[51] Concluding that the resumption of war was only a matter of time, Addington was not willing to leave British forces unprepared.

These preparations incensed Bonaparte. On 13 March, he again accosted Whitworth at the Tuileries and, flying into a rage in front of a large audience, began a long and loud diatribe against the British government and Whitworth personally. He exclaimed to all the foreign ministers that the British wanted war and he would give it to them.[52] Talleyrand later tried to control the damage by insisting that Bonaparte had merely lost his temper,[53] but this did not lessen Anglo-French tension, and, as each side became more firmly committed to its own position, the opportunities for a peaceful resolution decreased.

Hawkesbury continued to offer suggestions to resolve the impasse over Malta, but to no avail. In early March, he proposed terms for a new Anglo-French agreement that would revise the Treaty of Amiens to allow the British to occupy Malta for six years, after which they would hand it to the Maltese. In return, the British would recognize Bonaparte as the head of his new territories in northern Italy. When the French rejected that offer, he suggested new terms whereby the British would obtain the island of Lampedusa, which was close to Malta and from which the British could defend it.[54] Hawkesbury was willing to trade Malta for Lampedusa because "it is important . . . that if the effort with respect to Malta should be found desperate, the course we have proposed should be taken for the purpose of satisfying the public here that Malta is not the cause of the war, and that if the object for which we require to keep Malta can be obtained by any other means we shall be satisfied."[55]

The British attitude toward the question of peace or war hardened during the course of the negotiations. At first, they wished to delay a settlement to ensure that the country would support the war and to determine whether the Russians would agree to an alliance or some form of close diplomatic cooperation. By the middle of March, there were signs that British public opinion was turning in favor of war. Starhemberg reported to Vienna that he thought war would be extremely popular in Great Britain.[56] On 31 March, Hawkesbury demonstrated this harder line by insisting to Whitworth that there must be "some treaty or Convention by which the differences of the Two countries will be settled *or War,*" and two weeks later he concluded that the decision must be made immediately.[57]

Although the British had hoped to forge a military or diplomatic alliance with Russia prior to resuming the war, they came to the conclusion that Russians were still not ready to fight. This made the decision whether to go to war more difficult, as there were obvious military advantages to waiting until the Russians and Austrians were ready. While it would be harder for the British to fight the French on their own, they could hold back and wait for allies only as long as they could continue to hold Malta and control the timing of the resumption of war. Bonaparte had stated clearly that he would declare war if the British did not evacuate Malta.[58] Addington knew that, if the British were to fight a naval war with success, they had to strike before the French had time to prepare. In early 1803, he knew the French navy was not capable of challenging the British, and the colonial expeditions to the West and East Indies that Bonaparte had just sent would be easy pickings for the Royal Navy.

Having assumed that the British were bluffing, Bonaparte was caught off guard when Whitworth asked for his passports, signaling that Addington was about to declare war. Talleyrand then tried to delay Whitworth's departure from Paris as long as possible, but without actually agreeing to sign a treaty that would allow the British to retain Malta or Lampedusa. On 29 April, Talleyrand promised him a favorable response to Hawkesbury's latest proposal, but after a further delay, the proposal turned out to be merely to give Malta to Russia. After Whitworth had left Paris, Talleyrand sent a courier to intercept him at Calais with a proposal that the British keep Malta for ten years, during which French forces would remain in Otranto and Taranto. Addington believed that this was just another attempt to delay the British declaration of war.

Besides the obvious strategic reasons for Great Britain to declare war immediately, there were also financial considerations. In 1801, the continuation of the war had jeopardized the British economy and the government finances. In 1803, the continuance of peace threatened to do the same. The British economy in general, and the financial markets in particular, suffered from the uncertainty over whether the peace would continue. Traders and investors were waiting on diplomatic developments because they knew that war would have important economic consequences.[59] Philip Rashleigh, an influential M.P. from Cornwall, told one of Addington's supporters how the uncertainty about the peace hurt the British economy and worked to the advantage of Bonaparte: "He knows the way of ruining England by Peace as well as in War; for by keeping you on a War Establishment & uncertainty, he Prevents all the Mechanicks [*sic*] & Merchants from carrying on their business, without any risque [*sic*] to himself."[60] Once war was declared, commercial enterprises could restructure with the certainty that restructuring was absolutely necessary. The issues of military spending and the government finances were other considerations. The cold war, which had intensified as a result of the British rearmament in March, entailed a considerable expense that could be borne over the short term, but would become problematic over the long term. Hawkesbury explained to the Russians that, during the protracted negotiations preceding the declaration of war, "This Country has . . . undergone serious inconvenience from the great expense of the armament, from a long and irksome state of Suspense, and from the opportunity which has been thereby afforded to France for extending her Preparations."[61] Delaying the war further would work to the benefit of France and the detriment of Great Britain.

Addington had chosen to make the compromises necessary to secure peace in 1801, but refused to make the compromises necessary to continue peace in 1803, because the circumstances of foreign and domestic politics were different. In 1801, several important considerations weighed heavily in favor of peace. By May 1803, all of these conditions had changed. Great Britain's relations with Russia were improved. By the spring of 1803, the careful attention of Addington and Hawkesbury had rendered the Russians better disposed to the British than at any time since the formation of the Second Coalition. Even though the Russians refused their overtures of alliance, Addington could reasonably expect that the Russians might be prepared to cooperate against the French in the future. Equally important, the domestic situation was much improved, as peace and a good harvest had caused a sharp decline in both the price of bread and the incidence of food riots. Isolated disturbances still occurred, but there was no longer evidence of potentially revolutionary unrest. The revival of trade and Addington's financial policies had also restored the government finances. Peace had provided for the recovery of the British economy, as trade with Russia, Germany, and Italy had resumed, saving many commercial enterprises in Great Britain. As a result, customs and excise duties were more productive, enabling Addington to repair the government finances, and permitting them to bear the expense of a war establishment.[62] The Treasury reported in January 1803 "a very considerable improvement in the Revenue; the greatest part of which cannot reasonably be ascribed to any other cause than a progressive increase of the wealth of the Nation."[63] Addington concluded that parliamentary and popular opinion were prepared to support a war to defend Great Britain's strategic interests and that the state of the finances could bear the strains of war.[64]

Most important of all, it had become clear that Bonaparte would continue to threaten British strategic interests even during peace, and that the British could not defend those interests through diplomacy.[65] The list of his territorial acquisitions since the signing of the Preliminary Treaty in October 1801 included Louisiana, Piedmont, Parma, and the Cisalpine Republic. He had also ensured that Switzerland was effectively a puppet state of France. British political and parliamentary opinion interpreted these acquisitions as evidence that France would not cease to annex new territory until it was resisted by military force, and if Bonaparte were given the opportunity he would annex Malta. Bonaparte refused British offers to negotiate an amendment to the Treaty of Amiens and stated publicly that he would declare war if the British failed to evacuate the island. Addington would probably lose his parliamentary majority if he left Malta undefended. As evacuation was not a viable option, war appeared inevitable. Addington calculated that it would be to Great Britain's advantage to declare war rather than to wait and allow France more time to increase its naval strength before Bonaparte declared war.

This is not to imply that Bonaparte was the sole cause of Anglo-French antagonism. The aggressive manner in which the British achieved their naval, colonial, and commercial dominance antagonized France, as well as the rest of Europe and the United States. Great Britain proved no better than other Europeans states at fulfilling its international commitments. The British misrepresented the extent of the expansion of their empire: during the negotiations over the British evacuation of Malta, Hawkesbury told the French that the British had done nothing but make concessions over and over again, while keeping nothing.[66] This was not true, because Wellesley was continuing to acquire more territory in India. Otto repeatedly pointed out to Hawkesbury that British dominance and expansion in India had to be taken into account in the context of Anglo-French relations.[67] Hawkesbury tried to avoid discussing India by arguing that British gains in India did not affect the independence of France. The British wanted a balance of power to restrain France in Europe, while leaving Great Britain predominant overseas. For these reasons, Bonaparte was as suspicious of the British as they were of him.

The issue central to the breakdown of the Treaty of Amiens was one not of moral superiority but of practical self-interest. The diplomatic challenges Addington confronted with Bonaparte were not unique to Great Britain. Over the course of the Napoleonic Wars, Bonaparte posed a frustratingly difficult problem for the other Great Powers as well. Paul Schroeder, who has written the definitive history of European international history from 1760 to 1848, demonstrates the unique and crucial role that Bonaparte played in international politics during the tumultuous first fifteen years of the nineteenth century. The statesmen of Great Britain, Russia, Prussia, and Austria originally assumed that Bonaparte was like themselves: ruthless and unscrupulous but prepared to operate in accordance with the generally accepted rules of eighteenth-century European diplomacy. Given the extent of power that Bonaparte attained, they were willing to tolerate French hegemony in Europe.[68] Nevertheless, Addington and the leaders of other Great Powers, even when they genuinely did not want to fight France, found that "it was impossible to do business with Napoleon, that peace with him on his terms was more dangerous and humiliating than war."[69] Historically, the Great Powers harbored a strong sense of jealousy, suspicion, and antagonism toward each other, as well as toward France. They even fought against each other during the course of the Napoleonic Wars. It was only after repeated experience had demonstrated that they could not coexist on terms of peace with Bonaparte that they suspended their mutual animosity in order to build a grand coalition cohesive enough to defeat him. The British were merely the first to reach that conclusion.

Addington's foreign policy had a direct effect on the strength of his parliamentary majority. By early 1803, Addington realized that, if the war resumed, it would put further strains on the cabinet and his parliamentary position. He believed that the best means of strengthening the ministry to handle the increased administrative burden and parliamentary pressure was to form a coalition with Pitt. This does not mean that he was dependent on Pitt's support. Although Addington had relied heavily on Pitt's advice and assistance while he was learning the ropes, as he gained a better grasp of office and felt more comfortable in his position he consulted Pitt less. After the debates on the Treaty of Amiens, Pitt left London. In September 1802, he became so ill that he almost died. Illness kept him away from London for long periods.

Pitt's absence from Westminster during the autumn of 1802 actually had the effect of strengthening rather than weakening Addington's position, because he and his colleagues were able to demonstrate that they could stand on their own. Liverpool claimed in December 1802 that "the Character of Government is set up in the House, and with the Publick; and it is fortunate that all this has been done without the assistance or support of Mr Pitt, so that they stand now very much upon their own Ground."[70] Hawkesbury later confirmed the view that the "Government is stronger in Publick Opinion at the present moment that it has been at any Time since its formation and that in one point of view We have gained Strength even from the absence of Pitt."[71] During the time that Pitt had been out of office, his power and influence had declined considerably.[72] He still retained a large band of personal supporters, but he no longer commanded the loyalty of independent members as he had while in office. Although he remained influential, his political stock had declined when he returned to the House in the spring of 1803.

Addington still believed that the advantages to be gained by a coalition with Pitt were worth pursuing. The cabinet was not in a difficult position, but, as war loomed, it became expedient to add more weight to the ministry. Addington envisioned a coalition whereby the addition of Pitt and Dundas (who took the peerage of Viscount Melville in 1802) would strengthen the government. He was even prepared to relinquish the leadership of the government to obtain this end. This is another example of how Addington's commitment to the king and his country far outweighed any consideration about his own personal status. He was not jealous, and he did not relish power. His only concerns in pursuing a coalition with Pitt were that the terms be respectful to the king and fair to his cabinet colleagues.

To this end, he invited Pitt to discuss politics in January 1803, and broached the subject of Pitt's returning to office.[73] For Addington these discussions seemed to patch over the differences that had arisen between the two friends over the course of the previous eighteen months. He did not realize that, prior to their meeting, Pitt had made up his mind to oppose Addington's financial policies. At the end of January, Pitt concluded that, unless Addington and his colleagues changed their policies, "the task of exposing their blunders will be more disagreeable both to me and them, but must at all events be executed, both for the sake of my own character and the deep public interests involved."[74] When they discussed the subject of Pitt returning to office, Pitt's language was vague and Addington misinterpreted it. Addington got the sense that Pitt would consider serving with him under terms of equality. Later, Addington resumed the discussions by employing Melville as an intermediary. Addington proposed that he and Pitt should be on equal footing in the government as secretaries of state with a mutually acceptable third party, possibly Chatham, to act nominally as First Lord of the Treasury.

Pitt was appalled at this proposition and spoke disdainfully of it. One of his friends recounted a conversation that he had with him afterward: "'Really,' said Pitt, with a sly severity—and it was almost the only sharp thing I ever heard him say of any friend—'I had not the curiosity to ask what I was to be.'"[75] Pitt responded to Addington through Melville that it was absolutely necessary for there to be "an avowed and real Minister, possessing the chief weight in the council, and the principal place in the confidence of the king. In that respect there can be no rivalry [*sic*] or division of power. That power must rest in the person generally called the First Minister, and that Minister ought, he thinks to be the person at the head of the finances."[76] This had the effect of undermining their recent reconciliation, because it appeared to Addington that Pitt was changing his mind and would now return to office only as prime minister. Pitt's cold response dismayed Addington, but he was determined not to let his own personal feeling get in the way. If Pitt would consider joining a coalition only on the condition that he become prime minister, Addington would accept that. On 3 April, he sent another overture to Pitt, which led to a series of difficult and painful meetings. Addington had been optimistic on the eve of these meetings, but was gravely disappointed at their outcome. The attempt to cement a reconciliation between two old friends actually ended up driving them further apart.

The negotiations commenced with a misunderstanding that was evident when Pitt told Addington that he thought that his friend had, "in some respects, understood what has passed between us in a different light from that in which I viewed it, and in which I hoped it had been distinctly placed by the whole tenour of our conversations."[77] As the negotiations continued, the misunderstandings became worse. Each man misinterpreted the other to such a great extent that each felt it necessary to document his own version of what had passed. Pitt's view was that, from the start, he had declined to commit himself to any specific terms of arrangement until he had heard the wishes of the king. He explained:

> Our interview originated, as I conceive, in a strong wish expressed by yourself, that I might be induced to return to my former situation in the King's service. On this point I stated that the only ground on which I could think myself called upon to give any positive answer to such a proposition, or to say any thing that could be in any degree binding with respect to the details of any arrangement connected with it, was, that of receiving some direct previous intimation of his Majesty's wish to that effect, together with full authority to form, for *his Majesty's consideration,* a plan of arrangements in *any* manner I thought best for his service, *as well out of those who were in the former,* as *those who are in his present government.*[78]

Pitt stated that in essence he would take office only if the ministers resigned *en masse* and the king asked him to form a government granting him a clean slate to appoint new ministers at his discretion. Unwilling to negotiate with Addington the terms of an arrangement, he demanded complete control over a new government that would include some of Addington's strongest opponents and exclude most of Addington's allies.[79] He added, "As my opinion on this point cannot admit of alternation, it would be fruitless to resume our discussion, if you entertain, on your part, any idea of its proceeding on any other basis."[80]

Addington was determined that his own personal situation should not pose an impediment to an arrangement that would be in the best interests of the country. He told Pitt, "if I could justify the recommendation of it upon public grounds, the only honourable course I could pursue would be to concur in the sacrifices it would require, and to put myself entirely out of the question; *and this I should do with the utmost readiness and the most perfect satisfaction.*" He thought there was a chance that Pitt might become more flexible. "In the mean time I shall entertain a hope, that you may not feel it necessary to adhere, in its full extent, to the proposition which you have made."[81]

Although Addington remained willing to sacrifice his own position, he was not prepared to sacrifice those of his colleagues without consulting them first. While several of them had expressed the desire to have Pitt to join the government, they refused to surrender their positions if there was the possibility that their posts would be given to Grenville and his supporters. The cabinet consequently rejected Pitt's proposal. As Addington subsequently explained to him that the members of the cabinet would not consent to "new-model, reconstruct, and in part to change the government, instead of strengthening it, as had been suggested, by the union of those, who had concurred in opinion respecting its leading measures." He added that regarding the proposal to include in the cabinet men who actively opposed the government, "they could not, consistently with what appeared to them to be due to the interests of the public, and to their own characters, give their advice, that steps should be taken to carry it into effect."[82] Pitt responded that he "never had any idea of forming an accession to strengthen the present government."[83]

Pitt was angry that Addington had consulted the cabinet about their discussions. He had not presented Addington with the terms of a specific arrangement, "which it was for them to consider whether they ought to recommend to his Majesty to carry into effect."[84] Nevertheless, he stated clearly to Addington that he would include in the new government whomever he thought fit, including his former colleagues. Everyone expected Grenville and Windham to be among them. Addington raised these points with his cabinet colleagues, while they deliberated on whether to resign to facilitate Pitt's return to office. As the details of their negotiations began to become known to the public, Pitt requested that Addington show the king all of their correspondence. Addington complied. The king's response was to support Addington. He said sarcastically of Pitt, "He desires to put the Crown in commission—he carries his plan of removals so extremely far and high that it might reach me."[85]

The crux of the dispute was a fundamental difference of opinion about the formation of the new government. One explanation of the whole affair was that it "failed, solely from one point—from the proposal of including Lord Grenville and Mr. Windham in the new arrangement."[86] This is true at one level. The ministers may have agreed to resign, if Pitt had assured them that Grenville and Windham were not to be included in the new government. Indeed, Grenville was also responsible to a certain extent for exacerbating the differences between Pitt and Addington. During the negotiations, he strove to dissuade Pitt from joining Addington. He argued strenuously that the current ministers must be removed, and if Addington and Hawkesbury were to be retained they must hold only minor offices.[87] Addington noted that there appeared to be a change in Pitt's attitude after he had met with Grenville. It was at that point that Pitt demanded Addington's resignation and "the removal of Lord St. Vincent and Lord Hawkesbury from their respective offices: he also considered the removal of Lord Pelham and Lord Hobart as indispensable."[88] As the sitting prime minister, who retained the confidence of the king and the support of a majority in Parliament, Addington felt that he should have some input in the formation of the new government. This Pitt denied.

Some of Pitt's closest supporters tried to change his mind. Melville recognized that Addington had been more loyal to Pitt than Grenville had been and considered it a mistake to bring the latter into a new government. He claimed, "If you, professing to adopt a part of the present Government as Colleagues in yours, should accompany that

Robert Banks Jenkinson, Lord Hawkesbury
by Sir Thomas Lawrence
(By courtesy of the National Portrait Gallery, London)

declaration with an avowed intention of commencing your Government with a Measure distinctly degrading and hostile to every member of the present Government, it would be harsh and unjust, and I mistake greatly the general Feeling of the World, if the Public would hold you up in refusing at so critical a moment, taking the Government upon you, upon such a ground."[89] Other of Pitt's former colleagues such as Chatham, Castlereagh, and Hawkesbury also disagreed with him.[90] Pitt refused to take responsibility for the deterioration in his relationship with his former friends in the government. One of them asserted, "You have brought several persons who were your best friends, into a situation, which now brings them to the verge of hostility with you; & that you have a *duty* which you owe them. . . . You cannot, in honour, permit [them] to suffer for acting according to your declared wishes, & sacrifice them to those who apparently acted contrary to your declared wishes. . . . They therefore rendered you a great personal service, & you owe them gratitude."[91] Pitt felt that those whom he had persuaded to accept office in 1801 should not complain if he required them to sacrifice their positions.[92] Later Cornwallis concisely summarized Addington's position:

> I do not think in the negotiation in March last, that Addington, supported as he was by a large and very respectable majority in Both Houses of Parliament, and by no means unpopular with the nation at large, could have been justified in laying the King, his colleagues in office, and all his friends in Parliament, at the feet of Mr Pitt, without venturing to enquire to what degree of humiliation they were to be expected to submit, by a public declaration of his own total inability to go on with the Government.[93]

Pitt was asking more than he could reasonably expect of Addington.[94] For Addington to have resigned at that time would have been an admission of failure, and he had not failed. Quite the contrary, his policies had been ratified by a majority in Parliament and received favorably by popular opinion. Almost everyone, other than Grenville's supporters or Pitt's admirers such as Canning and his allies, approved of his performance. It was a constitutional practice that prime ministers resign only when they had lost the confidence of the king or the

William Pitt by John Hoppner

(By courtesy of the National Portrait Gallery, London)

support of Parliament. Addington had lost neither. He was prepared to contravene constitutional practice and withdraw, but only if an arrangement could be made on acceptable terms. The terms proposed by Pitt were not acceptable. The king felt that had Addington resigned, it would have undermined the authority of the Crown. Pitt's actions verged on trying to force a new set of ministers upon the king.[95]

This episode was personally devastating to Addington. Pitt had been a childhood friend and political mentor. He had regretted Pitt's resignation as much as anyone, and had agreed to take office on the assumption that he would continue to enjoy Pitt's support. There had been a time when he valued Pitt's friendship more than his own political career. Throughout their negotiations, Addington demonstrated that, in order to bring himself and Pitt together, he was prepared to make the greater sacrifice. What hurt even more than the content of the letters that Pitt wrote to him was the curt and formal tone, so different from the friendly correspondence that had passed between them over the years. Their relationship would never be the same again.

It had never been Pitt's intention to cause hard feeling. His sole concern was to sustain the reputation that he had developed as a "patriot" minister who lacked wealth, connections, or party apparatus. Pitt tried to emulate his father, whose political strength drew from his reputation as a patriotic statesman "acting disinterestedly for the national good, independent of party rancour or faction, and hostile to all forms of mismanagement resulting from the corruption and jobbery of eighteenth-century politics."[96] As a "patriot" minister the Younger Pitt required popular support to sustain his political power. Like his father, he developed a reputation for integrity, which, combined with his speaking ability, was the greatest source of his political power. He could not maintain this reputation if it appeared that he was grasping for power, especially after he had resigned on a point of principle. He felt that the only way that he could return to office and sustain his reputation was if the king and the will of the people spontaneously called on him to take the reins of power. He would not stand forward, but would acquiesce if called upon to serve.[97] This required the current ministers to resign unconditionally and the king to ask him to form a new government. Addington and the king were not willing to comply.

From a strictly parliamentary perspective, Addington was not unduly alarmed by the failure of the negotiations. He had tried to forge a coalition that would have given greater weight and strength to the government and enabled it to weather more safely the difficult storm that he saw brewing ahead. His situation was not desperate, and he merely shrugged off this lost opportunity. He regretted that he had not been able to obtain the assistance of Pitt and Melville, but the opposition remained fractured and the parliamentary position of the government remained strong. Addington demonstrated strong leadership in standing up to Pitt, but he would soon face a stronger test of his leadership.

By the middle of May 1803, Addington and Hawkesbury concluded that war was inevitable. The negotiations with the French had continued long enough to convince parliamentary and public opinion that it was not possible to resolve Anglo-French differences through diplomacy. Addington believed that this was the best time to act. On May 18, while the House of Commons was in session, Addington entered dressed in the uniform of the Woodley Cavalry, symbolizing the calling of the nation to arms. He wanted to make an impressive showing that would rally the patriotism of the House. He interrupted the proceedings to announce important news. Great Britain had declared war on France.

CHAPTER 6

Prelude to the Third Coalition

Deciding to declare war was difficult for Addington, but finding a way to win the war proved even harder. An effective foreign policy was absolutely necessary. Great Britain required Great Power allies to fight the French on the Continent. Furthermore, it was essential for the British not to provoke the enmity of the other states of Europe, as they had done with the League of Armed Neutrality during the previous war. These considerations underlay the critical role of diplomacy in the British war effort.

IN SEARCH OF NECESSARY ALLIES

Russia was the focus of British diplomacy. A month prior to the British declaration of war, the tsar, sensing that Anglo-French relations approached a crisis, sent an offer of mediation to Addington. Unfortunately, given the usual delay in communication between St. Petersburg and London, the note arrived too late.[1] The Russians were not ready for war, and a British declaration of war might be contrary to their interests. As it was vital to British foreign policy not to alienate Russia, the British wanted to demonstrate their willingness to cooperate with Russian initiatives. Addington was willing to consider specific proposals that would address British security concerns; the tsar's proposal was, however, only a vague offer to act as a channel of communication between Great Britain and France.[2] Although accepting the tsar as a go-between might have been worthwhile earlier in the year, the situation changed once the British declared war. It would be impossible for Great Britain, in Hawkesbury's words, "to suffer the Negotiation to be further continued, except on the Basis of some distinct proposition by which the present Differences might be immediately and satisfactorily adjusted."[3] Hawkesbury explained further that the British were indeed anxious for the intervention of Russia, provided that it did not require them to suspend their military activities. He stated to Simon Vorontsov:

> Your Excellency must be aware, from the communications which I have had the Honor of making to you during the course of the negotiation, that the French Government, without having ever shown a sincere Disposition to listen to the just pretensions of this Country, have manifested a considerable anxiety to defer the period of a Rupture, and have thought it material to their interests to employ every means in their power for that purpose. . . . It is clear therefore that the delay arising from any new negotiation would, in the first instance, operate to the advantage of France and to the Injury of Great Britain, whilst its ultimate success would remain extremely precarious.[4]

There was good reason to suspect that Bonaparte was trying to manipulate the Russians because he desired a suspension of hostilities not as a prelude to settlement, but to nullify the advantage gained by the British declaration of war. Nevertheless, Hawkesbury had to be able to justify refusing the tsar's offer, in order to avoid appearing unreasonable. This entailed a delicate balancing act of promoting Great Britain's strategic interest without appearing to be warmongers.

Bonaparte was also competing with the British for the good opinion of Russia and the other Great Powers. The Russians, however, did not want to appear to be committing themselves to either side for fear of antagonizing the other. As they were not yet prepared militarily or financially to fight, they preferred that the Anglo-French war be postponed or avoided altogether.[5] Therefore, the Russians persevered in their negotiations to facilitate a peaceful resolution of the Anglo-

French dispute. The tsar offered to take Malta if it would help bring the war to an end, and Simon Vorontsov and Count A. I. Morkov, the Russian ambassador in Paris, sent a series of proposals back and forth across the Channel. Bonaparte tried to appear magnanimous. On 12 June, he proposed to Morkov that, if the Russians would take Malta, he would indemnify the king of Sardinia and let the British have Lampedusa. He also conceded that the British could keep Malta, if the tsar insisted. Simon Vorontsov passed on the offer to Hawkesbury on 16 June and discussed it with him the next day. The British counter-proposal stipulated that they would accept only the state of posses-sions at the beginning of the war. Under these terms, the British would retain Malta and the French would withdraw from northern Germany, which they had invaded after Addington declared war.[6] The British were not making preconditions to avoid mediation, but to ensure that the discussions would begin from a point that would be to Great Britain's strategic advantage.

The painstaking diplomacy the British pursued with the Russians eventually produced tangible benefits. As the negotiations dragged on, both Morkov and Vorontsov appeared to become more under-standing of the British position. Vorontsov even showed Hawkesbury copies of Morkov's correspondence with Talleyrand.[7] The Russians shared British concerns about the security of Malta and the French invasion of northern Germany. They also found it frustrating to negotiate with Bonaparte. Alexander Vorontsov told Morkov, "If I am not astonished by the small overtures that have been made to you by Monsieur de Talleyrand on the subject of their latest explanations with the British, after agreeing to our offers of assistance, it is that I find in them signs of the extreme duplicity and arrogance, which characterize the French government and which make them see the actions of the principal powers of Europe themselves as the simple instruments of French will."[8]

As the Russians appeared to become more understanding of the British position, Hawkesbury began to press them to grant more effective support. Russian assistance became even more urgent because the British had already accomplished most of what they could on their own. Shortly after the war resumed, British forces recaptured most of the French colonies that Addington had returned in accordance with the Treaty of Amiens. There were no further opportunities to strike a blow at French power. The other key consideration was that a French invasion of England was becoming increasingly likely. Hawkesbury made overtures for an Anglo-Russian alliance to Simon Vorontsov in London and directly to the Russian government in St. Petersburg. In discussing the situation with Vorontsov on 11 July, Hawkesbury tried to justify the war to the Russians. It was important for the British to develop war aims agreeable to all partners. Hawkesbury emphasized that Russia was the only power strong enough to save Europe from Bonaparte and that it was in Russia's interest to do so. He claimed:

> The Emperor of Russia is placed in a Situation which may enable Him to render the most important Services to Europe. It is in consequence of His Interposition that Europe can alone expect that the Cabinets of Vienna and Berlin should suspend their ancient Jealousies; should relinquish those lesser Interests which have hitherto divided them, and which by dividing them, have left them successively at the mercy of a common Enemy. It is to him that they look for that General Concert which can alone effectually remedy those evils, which must in a great measure be ascribed to the Separate Treaties of Peace which have been so improvidently concluded by many other Powers with the French Government. . . . His Majesty trusts that the Emperor of Russia will view the causes of the present War in their true light . . . and that He will perceive, that the only hopes of Tranquillity for Europe, must be derived from a Combination of the Great Powers of the Continent, with His Imperial Majesty at their Head, who shall be steadfastly determined to make new and extraordinary efforts for the purpose of circumscribing the Power, and restraining the Ambition of the Government of France.[9]

The solution was the formation of a third coalition of Great Powers under Russian leadership, financed by British gold. The next day, Hawkesbury sent an offer to St. Petersburg through Warren, proposing that, if the Russians would lead a coalition of the Continental powers against the French, the British would bankroll it.[10]

Hawkesbury's overtures were premature, however, because the Russians were still reluctant to take sides officially in the Anglo-French conflict. The Russians, although sympathetic to the British and willing to help them to a certain extent, felt that the French had not threatened any essential Russian strategic issues, and the tsar's plans for domestic reform still required peace. The Russians also faced some important logistical problems. Russia was, like Great Britain, geographically situated on the periphery of Europe. The Russian army lacked direct territorial access to Western and Central Europe. Alexander Vorontsov had pointed out to Warren that the distance between France and Russia was so great that there was little the Russians could do to reduce French power.[11] In order to engage the French, they would have to cross Austrian or Prussian territory. The Russians had to wait until the Austrians were strong enough to reenter the war and provide the Russian army with safe passage to French territory. When Alexander Vorontsov received the formal offer of alliance on 10 August, he responded that the tsar was not yet ready to fight and still retained hope for the success of his peace proposals. He intimated that, if the French refused to cooperate, something might have to be done to protect northern Germany and the Turkish Empire (two areas the Russians considered to be within their own sphere of influence) from a French attack. The only hope that Warren held out was that "the Chancellor observed that if Bonaparte made His attack on England and failed, as every one here hoped and wished He might; that then perhaps the Courts of Vienna and Berlin might be induced to come forward with effect."[12] This was little consolation.

Addington and Hawkesbury envisioned not just an alliance with Russia but a Grand Coalition including Austria and Prussia. The traditional British approach to obtaining the support of the two German powers was to try to convince them that France was as great a threat to them as it was to Great Britain. The basic premise of this strategy, however, was false. The greatest threat to both Austria and Prussia was each other. This was why they had found it so difficult to cooperate when the war with Revolutionary France began in 1792. The theaters of Germany and Poland were far more important to Austria and Prussia than were the Netherlands or the Mediterranean, where French acquisitions threatened British interests. The plan of forging a Grand Coalition under Russian leadership was not in the interests of Austria and Prussia. A strong France was necessary to Austria and Prussia as a counterweight to the growing power of Russia. The two German powers would not fight until the French threatened areas of vital strategic interest to them.

Fortunately for the British, that is precisely what Bonaparte began to do after the war recommenced. His first move was to invade Hanover, which was an important British strategic interest because George III was also the Elector of Hanover. French troops also occupied the port of Hamburg, which was an important trade link for British goods entering northern Europe. British hopes that Bonaparte's invasion of Germany would provoke a response by the two German powers were, however, overly optimistic, given the signals that the Austrians were sending. Not only had Austria refused to oppose French intervention in Switzerland in 1802, but also, in January 1803, an Austrian official told the British minister in Vienna, Sir Arthur Paget, that Austria would require six to eight years of peace in order to restore its financial and military resources. Nevertheless, Austria would continue to play an important role in European affairs, and it was necessary to gain the Austrians' trust, even if they refused to enter the war in the short term.[13]

Addington worked diligently to gain the confidence of Starhemberg. Upon taking office, Addington tried to remove all grounds of conflict between Great Britain and Austria. The key issue of contention between them was the repayment of the loans that the Austrians had contracted with the British government during the 1790s. Under the terms of the loans, Austria was to have begun repayment within six months of the conclusion of peace, but having been virtually bankrupted by the war, the Austrians were unable to pay when the loan came due in the summer of 1801. Addington agreed to postpone collecting on the loan because he wished to maintain Austrian goodwill. He colluded with Starhemberg to provide the Austrians with a legal justification for delaying the repayments when the loan came due and did not press them to pay afterward. This carried a political price, however, as Parliament had guaranteed the loans and was committed to paying the interest.[14]

After the war resumed in May 1803, Hawkesbury raised with Starhemberg the issue of Austria's reentry into the war. Starhemberg insisted that Austrian policy was to maintain strict neutrality. If Austria became disposed to enter the war in the future, it would require a subsidy of £2 million.[15] Hawkesbury denied that the British government could afford that amount, but in July, he offered £3–400,000, if the Austrians would sign a secret convention immediately.[16] This was not enough for the Austrians. Undaunted, Hawkesbury continued to conciliate Starhemberg in London and directed Paget to court the Austrian government in Vienna. He instructed Paget to attempt to convince the Austrians that "the whole of His Majesty's conduct during the late discussion with France, has been dictated by no other motive than by His solicitude to provide for the safety of His own Dominions and in as far as his single exertions conduce to that salutary end, to promote the tranquillity and independence of the Continent, so seriously menaced by that restless spirit of ambition and aggrandizement by which the councils of France appear at present to be uniformly actuated."[17] To corroborate these assertions, Hawkesbury sent along copies of the papers presented to Parliament concerning the Anglo-French negotiations. This was important because Talleyrand also was giving the Austrians copies of documents outlining the French version of the negotiations.[18] This battle for European opinion was crucial to both sides because the disposition of these powers, even if they remained neutral, could influence the course of the war.[19]

Hawkesbury's assessment of the position of the German powers was that the Austrians had the right inclination but lacked the resources while the Prussians possessed the resources but lacked the inclination.[20] He did not realize that the Prussians had little to gain and much to lose by fighting the French. By the Treaty of Basel of 1795, France had recognized Prussian predominance in northern Germany, something Austria had always refused to do. The French inva-

sion of Hanover, however, threatened that position. Hawkesbury
hoped to take advantage, and instructed Francis Jackson, the new
minister in Berlin, to make this overture:

> If the Prussian Government should appear to be at last sensible of the
> difficulties of their own situation in consequence of the System of
> Inertness and Indifference which they have been induced to adopt—if
> they should be really disposed to make a sincere and vigourous effort
> for the defence of the North of Germany—but if you should judge it
> impracticable to secure their exertion without some promise of pecu-
> niary succours, you are authorized to make them the following offer:
> That upon the commencement of Hostilities against the French
> Armies, His Majesty will advance to them the Sum of Two Hundred
> and Fifty Thousand Pounds, and that upon the Evacuation of the Elec-
> torate of Hanover by the French Forces (for the purpose of its being
> restored to His Majesty and of the repassage of the Rhine by the
> French Army) His Majesty will make a further advance of Two Hun-
> dred and Fifty Thousand Pounds.[21]

Hawkesbury cautioned Jackson to make the offer only if the Prussians
appeared likely to accept. Unfortunately, that was not the case. Jackson
realized that the Prussians were averse to assuming the risks of engaging the French. There was hope that the Prussians might be willing to
act in future if they were assured of Russian military support. In the
meantime, Jackson chose to withhold the offer. Six months later,
Hawkesbury asserted that the offer should remain open but reiterated
that it should not be pressed unless likely to be accepted.[22]

During the remainder of 1803, Russia and Great Britain appeared
to be moving closer together, but the Russians maintained official
neutrality. Hawkesbury also continued to warn Warren "to abstain
from every thing which can have the effect of irritating the Russian
Government. It is highly desirable that all conciliatory means should
be used to bring them to a just Sense of the present situation of
Europe, and of the exertions which their own Security and Honor
must at last infallibly require from them."[23] Although he had made no
apparent progress in bringing the Russians into the war, Hawkesbury
was determined to pursue his line, as "Changes of opinion & of Men
are in such Govts frequently sudden; We should never lose sight of

this, & consequently never be discouraged in pursuit of our Ultimate object."[24]

British hopes of drawing the Russians into the war revived once again at the beginning of 1804, when Alexander Vorontsov retired owing to poor health and was replaced by Czartoryski, who favored close Anglo-Russian relations. He gave Hawkesbury's overtures serious consideration because the British were necessary allies in defending Turkey against France. He also felt that it was in Russia's interest to be considered by the British as their primary ally. Otherwise, the British might form an alliance with the Austrians. Czartoryski also estimated that Russian military and financial resources had been restored sufficiently to be ready for war if it became necessary for Russia to fight. When Warren pressed once again for Russia to join a coalition, however, Czartoryski refused. He was struggling with the dilemma of delaying Russia's entry into the war without alienating the British in the meantime. On the eve of Addington's resignation in 1804, Czartoryski continued to argue that Russia should not move until Austria and Prussia were ready.[25]

In summary, Addington and Hawkesbury worked hard to pave the way for the formation of a Grand Coalition that would fight for objectives of both Great Britain and the other Great Powers. In the end, they failed to achieve their ultimate objective because Great Britain had nothing concrete to offer its prospective allies apart from financial subsidies. Paying foreign armies to fight for British objectives on the Continent was favored by British parliamentary and public opinion because it spared the lives of British soldiers, but it gave Great Britain a poor reputation as a military ally. The British appeared to want all the benefits of winning the war against France without risking their share of the resources to fight it. The amounts of money that the British offered would cover only a small portion of the costs their prospective allies would incur if they joined the war.

British diplomacy under Addington, however, demonstrated some understanding of the strategic interests of the other Great Powers and a willingness to make compromises. This helped to develop stronger diplomatic ties between Great Britain and Russia, Austria, and Prussia, but it was not enough to cement a military coalition. The other Great Powers did not feel that the French threat to their strategic interests was great enough to justify going to war at that time. The power relationships between Russia, Austria, and Prussia complicated matters further. Russia would not act without the support of Austria. Prussia would not act without the support of Russia. And Prussia and Austria were more suspicious of each other than they were of France. They would not join the war unless their finances and military resources improved and the French threatened their interests more directly. The British had no choice but to wait upon a decisive event or change of circumstance before their plans for forming a Grand Coalition could succeed.

NEUTRAL DIPLOMACY

While Addington and Hawkesbury courted the support of the three Great Powers, they also understood the importance of developing good relations with the lesser powers: Holland, Spain, Naples, Portugal, Denmark, Sweden, and the United States. They considered these states potential allies not of Great Britain but rather of the French. Of the lesser powers, the two states with the greatest potential to provide effective support to the French war effort were Spain and Holland. Both had been Great Powers during the seventeenth century but had declined militarily to the point that they could not resist the armies of Revolutionary France. Their geographic proximity to France also enabled Bonaparte to intimidate them by sending large armies to their borders and threatening to invade. Large French forces remained stationed on Dutch soil, despite Bonaparte's agreement to withdraw as part of the Treaty of Lunéville with Austria in 1801. Spain and Holland presented great strategic value to Bonaparte because Great Britain had significant commercial and strategic interest in both the Iberian Peninsula and the Low Countries. They also possessed the largest navies after those of Great Britain and France. As they had fought with the French during the 1790s, it was important, from the British perspective, to prevent them from allying with the French again.

It would have been advantageous to Great Britain for Holland to remain neutral during the war, but Holland could not be effectively neutral while French garrisons remained on Dutch soil. On 20 May 1803, Hawkesbury instructed Robert Liston, the British minister at The Hague, to propose to the Dutch that, if the French troops withdrew and respected the neutrality of Holland, the British also would respect their neutrality. Liston was also to warn the Dutch that, if the French used Dutch territory or shipping to attack the British, they would have to take military measures against Holland. Hawkesbury hoped that the Dutch government would be able to arrange the withdrawal of French troops, but he was disappointed. In the end, Great Britain severed diplomatic ties with the Dutch because the French began arresting British subjects in Holland.[26]

British foreign policy toward Spain had two stages. The first was to encourage Spain not to provide any material assistance to the French war effort. Spain was better positioned than Holland to remain neutral: there were no French troops on Spanish soil, and Spain possessed greater military resources with which to resist the French. In the event that Bonaparte invaded Spain, the greatest concern from the British point of view was the Spanish fleet, which the Royal Navy had been monitoring since Addington declared war.[27] Hawkesbury told John Hookham Frere, the British minister at Madrid, that he supported Spanish neutrality, but that if the Spanish assisted the French war effort or allowed the French to cross their territory to attack Portugal, the British must declare war on Spain.[28] The Spanish indicated that they wished to avoid war with the British, but claimed to be in a difficult position. They tried to assist Russia in its efforts to mediate a peace settlement, but Bonaparte wanted them to assist the French war effort. He demanded that Spain either declare war on Great Britain or pay France a subsidy of 24 million livres a month. The Spanish explained to Frere that they could not afford to pay Bonaparte the amount he demanded and, therefore, they had no option but to declare war on the British, or face a French invasion. They privately indicated to Frere that the British should consider their declaration of war as merely nominal. They did not wish to engage the British fleet or interrupt Anglo-Spanish commerce. Although officially at war, they wished to avoid any actual fighting.

The Spanish declared war on 12 August 1803, but Frere remained as British minister in Madrid, as if nothing had changed. Frere's dispatches to Hawkesbury indicated that, despite the formal declaration of war, the Spanish continued to remain favorably disposed to the British. Ultimately, the Spanish declaration of war had little effect on the course of Anglo-French hostilities, until Addington left office in 1804. Hawkesbury was satisfied to let this state of affairs continue, as he explained to Frere in January 1804:

> The intelligence which had been received from the Court of Saint Petersburgh [*sic*], and from the other Courts of Europe, though it affords no certain prospect of any confederacy being formed amongst the principal Powers of the Continent, for the purpose of opposing the extravagant ambition of the present government of France, is however so far more favourable with a view to that object than any communications which have been made from the same quarters since the renewal of Hostilities that his Majesty feels additional reasons, (conformably to the system of Policy which He had already laid down) for endeavouring to preserve the relations of Peace with Spain as long as is compatible with his Honour, and a due attention to the essential interests of His Dominions.[29]

This was a compromise that suited both sides.

Great Britain also strove to maintain good relations with Denmark and Sweden. The League of Armed Neutrality (of which the two states had been a part) had seriously threatened Great Britain in 1801, and the British needed to ensure that the Danes and the Swedes did not revive the League. Although Great Britain was on friendly terms with Russia, the Danish and Swedish navies could threaten British naval and commercial interests if they joined with the French fleet. The French invasion of Hanover also heightened Denmark's strategic importance, as it would allow the French to close the Elbe and Weser rivers, important lifelines for British trade into Europe. The closures would force British merchants to find alternative routes. Hawkesbury hoped to use Denmark as one of these alternative entrepots. To this

end, in June 1803, he sent Liston, who had been recalled from The
Hague, on a special mission to Copenhagen with instructions to persuade the Danes not to ally with the French and to keep their ports
open to British shipping. Hawkesbury also instructed Liston to propose an alliance to Denmark. The terms were that the British would
agree not to make peace with the French until all of Denmark's possessions were restored, if the Danes would agree not to make peace
until the French had evacuated northern Germany.[30]

Hawkesbury did not expect the Danes to accept the alliance but
hoped that they would at least agree to remain neutral. The Danes,
alarmed by the French invasion of Hanover and fearing that their
own territory was in danger, sent 15,000 troops into Holstein.[31] They
became even more concerned in November 1803, when the French
began enforcing requisitions from Hamburg, Bremen, and Lubeck.
Their only consolation was a promise from Russia to come to their
aid if the French invaded Denmark.[32] As long as the French threatened Denmark, it was in the interest of the Danes to maintain good
relations with the British, in spite of the fact that the British navy had
attacked Copenhagen only two years before. Although the Danes
could not join a military alliance with the British, they were able to
remain neutral and keep their ports open to British shipping.

The role of Sweden was not quite as critical as that of Denmark,
but the British needed to cultivate good relations to secure access to
the Baltic and to keep the Swedish fleet neutral. Anglo-Swedish relations had remained cool during the peace, as the Swedes were late in
acceding to the Anglo-Russian Convention of 1801. The Swedes
remained attached to the principles of the Armed Neutrality, and they
were unhappy with some of the provisions of their existing trade
treaty with Great Britain. Nevertheless, they favored accommodation
with the British because they were already on poor terms with the
Russians and the French invasion of Hanover threatened their territory in Pomerania. Having heard that the Swedes favored an accommodation, Hawkesbury made some commercial, naval, and colonial concessions that improved Anglo-Swedish relations and helped lay the
groundwork for Sweden's accession to the Third Coalition in 1805.[33]

The status of the kingdom of Naples was also of interest to Great Britain because it encompassed southern portions of the Italian peninsula and the island of Sicily, which gave Naples a strategic position in the center of the Mediterranean. It was difficult, however, to persuade the kingdom of Naples to remain neutral. Although Naples was technically independent, the French had refused to remove their garrisons from Otranto and Taranto (which they occupied during the previous war) until the British had evacuated Malta. The Neapolitans also feared that a large French force would invade from the north through France's new Italian satellite states. Naples was important commercially and strategically to the British. Before the war resumed, Hawkesbury sent a special envoy to Naples to promote Anglo-Neapolitan relations. While it would be advantageous to Great Britain if Naples remained neutral, the most important consideration was that the British fleet should be on terms of equality with the French in Neapolitan ports. If the Neapolitans refused entrance to British ships of war, they must also exclude the French. The focus of British attention was the island of Sicily. Besides being the major supplier of food and water for Malta, Sicily was also an important naval base. If the French gained control of the island, it would seriously jeopardize the British position in the Mediterranean. For this reason, Hawkesbury decided that, in the event the French should receive special privileges in Naples, the British should invade Sicily and occupy the Forts of Messina.[34]

Hawkesbury's Neapolitan diplomacy was remarkably successful considering the pressures on the Neapolitan government. First, the Neapolitan government kept its ports open to British trade. This was important not only for supplying Malta, but also because many ports in Europe were closed to the British. Second, the principal advisor to the Neapolitan King Ferdinand, General Sir John Acton, cooperated fully with British representatives. He agreed to allow British forces to occupy the Forts of Messina, in the event French forces in Naples threatened Sicily. Together Acton and the British devised a plan under which the Neapolitan forces intended for Malta would be transferred to the Forts of Messina, and the British would provide financial assistance to renovate the fortifications. The Neapolitan government was able to keep the French forces at bay until 1806, at which time the British seized the island of Sicily.[35]

Bonaparte also appeared to be contemplating a military strike against Portugal and the Turkish Empire, which had been the only remaining allies of the British at the end of the previous war. Great Britain's former allies would provide little assistance in offensive operations against the French, but they at least might resist if the French attacked them. In June 1803 Hawkesbury informed the Portuguese minister in London that he expected Portugal to remain neutral. In the event the French attacked Portugal, the British were inclined to assist, but he could make no firm promises concerning men, equipment, or subsidies.[36] It was necessary to defer any plans for the defense of Portugal until it was clear whether the Portuguese themselves were prepared to resist. In July, despite the opinion of George III that it was "impossible for troops to be in a more hopeless state than the Portuguese are at present," Hobart sent a military advisor to Portugal to assess the condition of the troops. He informed the cabinet that the Portuguese were not capable of resisting the French. Recruiting for the peace establishment was poor owing to low levels of pay, and the Portuguese army suffered from poor leadership, a lack of discipline in the ranks, and low morale. The cabinet concluded that sending British forces to defend Portugal at that time would have been a waste of valuable resources.[37]

While the independence of Portugal was important for strategic reasons, the main concern was over the future of Brazil, because it was possible that Bonaparte's recent difficulties in Louisiana and St. Domingue would turn his attention toward South America. The prime consideration was ensuring that the French did not obtain control of Brazil or the Portuguese fleet. Hawkesbury accordingly suggested that the Prince Regent of Portugal sail with his fleet to Brazil "and endeavour to establish there a great, powerful and independent Empire," promising that the British navy would assist the evacuation and provide protection for the Portuguese navy.[38] This plan was resurrected five years later, when the British navy facilitated the evacuation of the Portuguese royal family to Brazil. In 1803, this was premature because the French promised not to attack the Portuguese if they paid a subsidy of one million livres. As Portugal made no territorial concessions to the French, Hawkesbury expressed no concerns to the Portuguese about the arrangement.[39]

The Turkish Empire appeared to be in less immediate danger, but the threat of a French attack on Egypt or the Morea greatly influenced the British cabinet's planning. Sebastiani's report drew attention to these threats, and fear concerning the future of the Turkish Empire was one of the most important reasons that Addington and Hawkesbury decided to keep Malta in contravention of the Treaty of Amiens. After the war resumed, it was necessary to keep the French out of Turkish territory. In that sense, it was preferable for the Turks to remain neutral, because forming an alliance with the British might provoke a French attack. A British alliance with Turkey would be possible only in the event Russia agreed to form a coalition, because the Russians could divert most of the French forces toward Central Europe and away from the Middle East.[40]

The other power that Addington and Hawkesbury had to watch closely was the United States. The focus of Anglo-American-French relations in 1803 was the territory of Louisiana. The Americans became alarmed when they discovered that Spain had ceded it to France, because the French appeared better able to establish a lasting presence. As a result, the Americans became increasingly hostile to the French and looked to the British for support. Sir Edward Thornton, the British secretary of legation in the United States, informed Hawkesbury on 3 July 1802 that President Thomas Jefferson "not only regards the cession of Louisiana and New Orleans as a certain cause of war between the two countries, but makes no scruple to say, that if the force of the United States should be unable to expel the French from those settlements, they must have recourse to the assistance of other powers, meaning unquestionably Great Britain."[41] A year later, Hawkesbury predicted that the Louisiana question was likely to facilitate closer relations between Great Britain and the United States. Thornton suggested that the British should seize the island of New

Orleans and give it to the Americans as a means of cementing stronger Anglo-American relations. This was not feasible while Great Britain and France remained at peace, but once war appeared inevitable in April 1803, Addington revived the idea and suggested it to the American minister in London, Rufus King.[42]

When the war resumed, Anglo-American relations appeared more favorable than ever, but this improvement was short-lived. Soon after the British declared war, the American government learned that James Monroe, the American minister in Paris, had successfully negotiated the purchase of the Louisiana territory. This completely transformed the nature of Anglo-American relations; as Thornton noted, "I can scarcely credit the Testimony of my own Senses in examining the Turn which Affairs have taken, and the manifest Ill-Will discovered towards us by the Government of the present moment."[43] These sudden shifts in Anglo-American relations were more apparent than real. The improvement of relations during 1802 and 1803 was based solely on common hostility to France, which resulted from the French acquisition of Louisiana. Once the question of Louisiana was resolved, Anglo-American relations merely reverted to their previous state of tension.

The Louisiana purchase proved a serious dilemma for Addington. At first, he was extremely pleased that Bonaparte had relinquished it. Addington told Sir Francis Baring, one of the directors of Baring's Bank, which was involved in the purchase, that he approved of the Franco-American treaty. Upon reflection, however, Addington began to have doubts. He soon realized that the Americans intended to pay the French with capital raised on the London stock exchange. At one point, Baring's Bank was transferring to the French government two million francs each month. This not only provided Bonaparte with much needed capital to finance the war, but also constricted the British money markets, to the detriment of British industry and the British government. In December 1803 Addington decided that he must stop these financial transactions because he expected that the French would use the money to finance an invasion of England. He instructed Baring's Bank to abandon its involvement with the financial transactions regarding the Louisiana purchase.[44] The Barings refused to comply with this request and continued to pay the money. In the end, Addington decided to do nothing about it. Although these payments assisted the French, to have overtly interfered with the transfer of Louisiana might have provoked the American government into forming a military alliance with the French. It would have placed an enormous strain on Great Britain's resources were the Americans to invade Canada. The biggest lesson of the American War of Independence had been that the British must avoid fighting the Americans and the French at the same time.

Addington and Hawkesbury's war diplomacy achieved all that it appeared possible for it to achieve. The British possessed little leverage because financial subsidies alone could not entice powers to join the war when they were not disposed to fight. Their position in the war was influenced largely by forces beyond their control. Although they achieved no stunning successes, having been dealt a very poor hand, they played it rather well.[45] They had set certain minimum objectives and achieved them. None of the Great Powers of Europe allied with the French, and most of the lesser powers remained neutral. The careful cultivation of close relations with Russia, Austria, and Sweden also laid the foundation for the Third Coalition that Pitt later carried to fruition. The delay in the entry into the war of Russia and Austria was the result of internal considerations. It is clear, however, that the Third Coalition would not have been possible in 1805 without the improvement of relations between Great Britain, Austria, Russia, and Sweden that occurred while Addington was prime minister.

Addington and Hawkesbury handled foreign diplomats with greater skill than the previous foreign secretary had done. Grenville had expected other states to consider the threat posed by expansion of French power to be as important to them as it was to the British, and to continue to fight even after their financial and military resources were exhausted and their existence as a Great Power threatened.[46] These states would fight effectively only for their own interests, and sometimes fighting a war was contrary to those interests.

Rather than pressing them to fight, Hawkesbury often encouraged them to negotiate with the French.

Foreign diplomats who worked with Addington and Hawkesbury attested to their diplomatic skills. Starhemberg explained: "I was personally at least as close in friendship with Lord Grenville and Mr Pitt, but despite their distinguished and irrefutable talents, I cannot deny that their successors are infinitely better for us. I find Mr Addington and Lord Hawkesbury less egotistical and above all less stubborn than their predecessors, who, although now out of office, are angry with us for not being at war with France."[47] He often reiterated that Addington was more reasonable toward Austria than his predecessors had been.[48] Although he had criticized Addington for signing the Treaty of Amiens, he admitted that it took great courage to declare war again after having made such sacrifices to obtain peace. From the moment Addington declared war, Starhemberg was completely satisfied with the men he thought "might be the wisest ministers to govern Great Britain in a long time."[49] Starhemberg disagreed with the proposition that Pitt should return to power and severely criticized the way the opposition attacked Addington in Parliament. Otto agreed with Starhemberg in preferring Addington and Hawkesbury to Pitt and Grenville. Otto perceived a difference in both substance and style. Addington's original determination to consolidate peace in 1801 and the respect he demonstrated toward foreign powers was a departure from Pitt's policy and practice. Otto also claimed, "All of the diplomatic corps are pleased with the dealing of Mr Addington and Lord Hawkesbury, whose manners and frankness have replaced the haughtiness of Lord Grenville and the underhanded politics of Mr Pitt." The sentiments of most of the other foreign diplomats were similar.[50] Even Simon Vorontsov, who sometimes disagreed with Hawkesbury, expressed regret that they would no longer be working together after Hawkesbury resigned in May 1804.[51]

The comments of Starhemberg and Otto on the conduct of British foreign policy argue for qualifying the criticism that the successive British governments after 1801 had learned nothing important from the previous war about forming and leading a new coalition, and were "ignorant of Europe and indifferent to its interests and its fate."[52] Addington and Hawkesbury had not yet grasped the vision of a new international system that was necessary in order to achieve a peace settlement that would conform to the interests of all of the Great Powers, but they had begun to learn some of the small lessons on the way to achieving that goal. For Great Britain to achieve security for its strategic interests in the war with France, it had to cooperate more effectively with its military allies. This required taking into account the different strategic interests of other states and finding ways of assisting them to preserve those interests in forging a joint plan of action. It was also important to recognize that there were occasions when for military, financial, or other domestic reasons, states were unable to offer the British military assistance, no matter how much the British were prepared to pay. Addington and Hawkesbury demonstrated a greater understanding of the complexity of the positions of other states and an unprecedented willingness to compromise with those states. These small steps ultimately provided the foundation for the foreign policies that their cabinet colleague Castlereagh, as foreign secretary, pursued successfully ten years later. In the short term, these policies also paved the way to the forming of the Third Coalition, which created a second front in Central Europe that diverted French troops away from the Channel coast in 1805 and gave the British a much needed breathing space. The British still had much to learn on the road to victory in 1815, but by 1804 they were beginning to steer in the right direction.

CHAPTER 7

"Once more unto the breach"

An analysis of Addington's war policies is necessary for an understanding of the nature of the parliamentary crisis in 1804 that led to his resignation. Addington's opponents claimed that he was incapable of carrying on the war and that Parliament turned once again to Pitt. A few politicians who believed that Addington had been a good peacetime minister claimed that he was ill-suited to run the war. It is interesting to note that some contemporaries had made the same criticisms of Pitt when he was prime minister. Although the political problems emerging from Addington's foreign and war policies led to his downfall, the criticism of him was not necessarily justified. Rather his policies were misconstrued, deliberately or inadvertently, by self-serving politicians trying to force his resignation.

As the British could not fight the French effectively in Europe without the help of Great Power allies, the only sensible policy was to follow the advice of one of the Royal Navy's senior admirals, George Keith Elphinstone, Viscount Keith, that "this is a War unlike any former and must be Differently treated. Defence and Security in the first Instance is the *first Duty* owed to the Kingdom after which New Scenes might open."[1] While the British fought alone, their first priority was the security of the

British Isles. Their second was to find ways to hamper the French war effort and curb French expansion through naval, colonial, and commercial warfare. Addington based his war policies on the immediate threat of a cross-channel invasion and the lack of options for striking a blow against French power until the Russians and Austrians entered the war. These concerns are evident throughout the policies concerning home defense, grand strategy, and war finance. The inescapable and overriding fact was that, owing to diplomatic, military, and geographic realities, the initiative lay with Bonaparte.[2] Considering the weaknesses inherent in Great Britain's position, Addington sought to accomplish realistic objectives.

HOME DEFENSE

The new war began where the last had ended: Bonaparte had 100,000 soldiers poised to cross the Channel. The troops that the French had intended originally for Louisiana or St. Domingue were reassigned to England, as Addington anticipated. Just as in 1801, when Addington took seriously reports of Bonaparte's military preparations along the Channel, he again expected that Bonaparte would consider an invasion of either England or Ireland. Early intelligence reports confirmed this conclusion. The French had the military and naval capacity to launch an invasion, and Bonaparte was clearly planning one.[3] Other than invading Hanover, Bonaparte did not have another means of striking a major blow against Great Britain. As long as the British lacked European allies, Bonaparte could concentrate a large force on the Channel coast without the fear of having to divert troops to another front. This time it appeared that the war between France and Great Britain would be fought across the Channel rather than in Europe or overseas.

Although the general opinion of the British and foreign governments was that Bonaparte would have to be mad to attempt an invasion, most believed him reckless enough to try.[4] Hobart told Wellesley, "This Country I can almost venture to assure you is out of the reach of Danger from Invasion but I am not sufficiently sanguine to think that no attempt will be made."[5] Addington could not afford to take the threat lightly, and Hawkesbury saw the necessity of preparing for an invasion, despite Hobart's doubts.[6] It was far from certain that the Royal Navy would defeat an invasion force at sea. As Keith pointed out, the right combination of weather conditions could disperse the Channel fleet and present a short opportunity for the French to cross safely.[7]

Addington based his defense policies squarely on the fear of an early invasion.[8] Pitt and Windham criticized him for concentrating too heavily on home defense and neglecting offensive operations. "A war that should be completely defensive, would . . . be both dishonourable and ruinous," claimed Pitt.[9] York, who as commander in chief had access to intelligence and other military information not available to Pitt and Windham, believed that the French would seize the opportunity to invade before the British were adequately prepared. He expected the French to cross the Channel by the summer of 1803. St. Vincent, for the same reason, told Keith not to leave his post at the head of the Channel fleet to come to London.[10] The only way that the British could defeat a large force of veteran French soldiers, according to York, was to meet it with an even larger British force, as soon as possible after it had landed, and before it had the opportunity to organize. Under these conditions, a massive but relatively untrained force was preferable to a small, well-trained one.

Addington's foresight in maintaining large peacetime establishments for the army paid dividends by ensuring that British forces entered the war better prepared than for other wars. The British had 132,000 regular forces, 80,000 of which were stationed at home. During the peace, Yorke, as secretary at War, had revised the laws concerning the militia and increased its ranks to 70,000, of which 50,000 were to be raised in the first instance and 20,000 as a supplementary militia. This new legislation was first implemented in March 1803, when Hobart called out the old militia in response to the French military preparations on the Dutch coast. After the renewal of war, he called out the supplementary militia in May.[11] As a result, in the first few months of the war the combined force of the regular army and militia in Great Britain was over 130,000, and this was greater than the largest army that Bonaparte could have sent across the Channel at that time.[12]

As York's defense plans required more men than the militia alone could provide, Addington brought forward several new measures. The most important was the Additional Forces Act, usually referred to as the army of reserve.[13] This provided a further 50,000 men under terms similar to the militia. Addington also introduced the Military Services Bill, which became the Defence of the Realm Act, often referred to as the Levy en Masse (the term that had been used for the implementation of a form of conscription by the French government in 1793).[14] This legislation confirmed that the king could require military service of all subjects in the event of invasion. This act served two purposes. The first was as a reserve measure to be used in case of actual invasion. The second was to provide men with an incentive to volunteer for another branch of the military forces, which would exempt them from service under the terms of this act.

The branch most successful in obtaining recruits was the volunteer force. Addington, as the commander of the Woodley Volunteer Cavalry, understood the value of the volunteers, but he was concerned about their financial costs and effectiveness as compared to the more formally organized branches of the regulars and the militia. He had disbanded many of the volunteer regiments during the Peace of Amiens and, when the war resumed, he had concerns about the expense of creating further volunteer regiments.[15] Addington overcame these qualms because York demanded a large force immediately.[16] While Hobart and Pelham had served in the militia and felt that it was a more effective force, they also appreciated the value presented by the volunteers, which could assemble a greater number of men more quickly than could the militia. Addington and his colleagues realized that the state of the emergency in 1803 did not give the government the luxury to be selective about the nature of the force it raised. They needed a large force as soon as possible. Addington's volunteer legislation provided an incentive to individuals to join because they would be exempt from being drafted for mandatory service in the militia in addition to being exempt from service under the

Defence of the Realm Act. He also provided an incentive to communities to raise large volunteer forces by suspending the Defence of the Realm Act in districts that raised a sufficient volunteer force. These inducements, combined with a massive outpouring of patriotic fervor, resulted in overwhelming numbers of offers to join the volunteers.[17] Addington spoke of the sudden growth of the volunteer system as a mutual commitment on the part of the British government and the British people: "It was a pledge on the part of the government, that they should never attempt anything hostile to the constitution. It was a pledge on the part of the people that they valued as well as understood its excellence; that they were steadily attached to it, and determined to preserve it."[18] As a result of the success of his volunteer policies, Addington gained the reputation for being "the Father of the Volunteer System."[19]

Nevertheless, Addington's volunteer policies were too successful, in certain respects. Volunteer regiments throughout the country quickly became oversubscribed. The men who joined the volunteers were exempt from having to serve in the militia or the army of reserve, making it difficult for many districts to raise their militia and army of reserve quotas. As the militia and army of reserve were better trained and organized, they would have been more effective in resisting the French. Furthermore, the government was unable to provide sufficient weapons and allowances for all the regiments offering service. At the beginning of the war, the supplies of arms were low. They were higher than usual for peacetime—twice as high as in 1801—but too low to meet the initial demand at the beginning of the war. The Ordnance Office could supply enough weapons for about 150,000 soldiers, but returns for the volunteers alone soon approached 300,000, and the total force, including those stationed in Great Britain, Ireland, and overseas, was projected at 600,000. The production of weapons was slow, as gun making did not yet employ a production line, and the ministry had difficulty procuring foreign supplies.[20]

This mass of relatively untrained men lacking proper weapons was an easy target for criticism by M.P.s, local officials, and the public. Addington and his colleagues were overwhelmed by the extent of the correspondence. The need to answer requests for arms and clarification of the laws interfered with the other work of the Home Office.[21] Toward the end of 1803, volunteer business also took up a great deal of time in Parliament. This was not because the crisis was serious, but because most M.P.s were members or commanding officers of volunteer regiments and believed themselves experts on the subject. Many blew minor grievances out of proportion as an excuse to censure Addington for his defense policies. By keeping the debate on minor questions of administration and supply, the opposition placed the ministry, which lacked a truly great orator, in an awkward position. Addington, Hobart, and Yorke introduced amendments to their military legislation to address the more serious consequences of the expansion of the volunteer forces. The subsequent criticism that they had not thought out their measures well enough in the first place was hardly justified, given that no one else had anticipated the sudden growth in the ranks of the volunteers.

While Addington's volunteer measures may have put his parliamentary majority at risk, they did not place the country in any military danger. With over 380,000 volunteers (not including 70,000 in Ireland) and a combined military force of over 615,000 in December 1803, the government had raised the largest army in British history.[22] While most of the men individually might not have been a match for Bonaparte's seasoned veterans, York had ensured that many were well-trained, and the quality of these troops improved over time. Addington's military measures had achieved their most important goal, which was to raise a large force in a short period. In the words of Cornwallis, who was the most experienced military commander at the time: "Government have [*sic*] acted properly in endeavouring only to make as much soldiers as it was possible to render a force so composed, and no man, whether civil or military, will persuade me that 300,000 men, trained as the volunteers at present are, do not add very materially to the confidence and to the actual security of this country."[23]

Even more important than the size of the defense forces was how they were deployed. Bonaparte had stationed almost 100,000 troops in the Channel ports and was building a flotilla of shallow-bottomed boats to take men, horses, artillery, and supplies to England. He had not made a final decision about where they would land, but it would have to be in a region that could feed and supply his men. The target must contain a port where heavy artillery and supplies could be unloaded.[24] York, trying to anticipate Bonaparte's strategy, based his preparations for the invasion on two assumptions: that the French would strike before British defense forces were assembled and trained, and that the French initially would attack only points of strategic importance and then follow the shortest route to London. This meant either invading the Kentish coast and marching north-west, or invading the Sussex coast and marching north. The first was the shortest route by sea, the second the shortest by land. Therefore, York felt that the best means of preparing to repel this attack was to concentrate all forces in the southeast of England as quickly as possi-ble. He informed Hobart that "with the exception of Plymouth the greater Portions of the Troops in the distant parts of England should be immediately collected in the Eastern and Southern Districts to Frustrate any attempt which may be made upon the Capital, before the full measure of intended Preparation is Effective."[25] While this would weaken the forces in the other parts of the country, York sug-gested that the volunteers and yeomanry take over police duties, and he promised to send a "Regiment of Heavy Cavalry from the Eastern district to be stationed in the manufacturing and populous Towns in the Center and North of England."[26] Local officials in these regions would complain about the loss of troops for their districts, but as the French would certainly not land in these regions, moving troops to the Southeast was in the best interests of the overall defense of the country. It was also necessary that these forces receive top priority for the limited weapons available from the Ordnance Office.[27] In many ways, a shortage of manpower and weapons in the North was unim-portant, as long as the forces in the Southeast were large and properly supplied.

As time passed, York's strategy for deploying the forces changed. At first, he knew he would have only relatively untrained volunteer and other irregular forces. They would have difficulty overcoming the French in battle, but could wear down the enemy in a strategy of guerrilla warfare: "From the first moment of a landing being made, the great object of the irregular Troops must be to Harass, alarm and Fatigue an enemy—nothing can more effectually contribute to this object than the operations of small bodies of men well acquainted with the country who will approach and fire upon the advanced Post of His army without ever engaging in serious action or hazarding themselves."[28] When the enemy advanced from the coast, these forces were to attack his flank and rear and intercept small detachments in search of food and supplies.

By the end of August, when more troops had been assembled and better trained, York became more confident in their ability to resist invasion. He then decided that the best strategy would be to meet the French on the beaches: "Short of a total Defeat perhaps the period of the Enemy's greatest weakness, would be the moment of His landing, and the time He is preparing His artillery and Stores to commence his March. . . . I should therefore look upon 2,000 additional Men which could be brought to the Beach in the first 24 Hours as of greater importance than treble the number which might join the Army at a later period of the Contest."[29]

While Addington and York were more confident about defeating an invasion, they continued to expect that the French would cross at any time. On several occasions during the autumn and winter, they received reports that the invasion was imminent or had been launched, but the reports proved false. At the end of December, a storm blew Admiral Sir William Cornwallis's squadron blockading Brest off station and it had to take refuge at Torbay. This gave the French fleet an opportunity of two days to join an invasion force, if it embarked. Upon hearing the news, Addington sent orders to the coast to prepare for an invasion. Fortunately for the British, the French did not take advantage of the opportunity. Nevertheless, as a result of these threats, Addington and York continued to take measures to buttress the defense of southern England.[30]

As early as July 1803, York had advocated constructing field fortifications, as quickly as possible, because "the Erection of such Works must be immediate with a view to their probable utility."[31] He wished them placed at "Points where a Landing threatens the most important interests of the Country," as they would provide important advantages against an enemy short of artillery.[32] In August he began pressing Addington for further funds. Although Addington was concerned about the cost at first, he eventually agreed to these requests.[33] York's priorities were first to construct substantial fortifications on the Western Heights overlooking the Port of Dover and then to build ten Martello towers along the coasts of Kent and Sussex. These towers were not built until after Addington resigned, but he and Hobart made the decision to initiate construction.[34]

Addington and York also considered other methods of retarding a French advance in the event that a landing proved successful. The Royal Engineers in 1801 first discussed plans for deterring a French advance by flooding portions of Kent and Sussex. In July 1803 York supported the plan.[35] Even if the French were able to cross these flooded territories, they would find it difficult to live off the land, as they had done in Europe. The War Office planned to remove all horses, carts, and livestock, and to destroy everything that could not be carried away. This plan changed after October 1803. York, having become more confident of the ability of his troops, decided that, as they would not be forced to retreat, they would need such stock as remained.[36]

Addington made administrative as well as military preparations for potential invasion. If the French landed in Essex, he and the king planned to move to Chelmsford, and if in Kent, to Dartford. The queen and the royal treasure would move to Worcester. The press would be censored and the books of the Bank of England stored in the Tower. Addington also prepared legislation for enforcing martial law. Expecting that an invasion would deflate paper currency, York arranged to pay the army with gold.[37]

The navy also played an important role in home defense. It was necessary to have squadrons for coastal defense in case the French evaded the British fleet in the Channel. In response to York's request for a permanent squadron to defend the Eastern District at the mouth of the Thames at Hollesley Bay, St. Vincent sent Keith's fleet with another in tow.[38] York considered the squadron insufficient, but St. Vincent opposed weakening the already stretched blockading squadrons.[39] Hobart also ordered the reestablishment of the sea fencibles, a branch of the volunteer force stationed in port towns. By February 1804, a force of over 25,000 sea fencibles had been raised.[40]

Despite incessant criticism from the opposition in Parliament, Addington and the rest of the government were confident that British forces would be able to defeat a French invasion. The British soldiers were not as skilled as the French, but an overwhelming superiority of numbers and the advantages of fighting on their own territory should have enabled them to resist. As York pointed out, "The extent of army which an Enemy may land, depends not upon His numbers at Home but upon His means of transporting them to this Country."[41] The French could embark only a limited force, some of which was bound to be lost on the voyage, and the defense plans of Addington and his colleagues appeared sufficient to handle the remainder. Hawkesbury confidently asserted that, "If they should come we are prepared to meet them & I trust the Question of Invasion will be settled for ever."[42]

GRAND STRATEGY

The difficulties Addington faced in devising an effective grand strategy were common to all of the British governments of the period. Yet many British politicians continued to believe that Great Britain was capable of making a substantial contribution to the defeat of France, if only the government would employ the correct strategy. Pitt, with all the confidence of a man who did not have to prove his claim, asserted in early 1803 that the most effective strategy was obvious: "strike in the first instance some sudden blow on any vulnerable point."[43] He did not suggest where these vulnerable points might be. After managing the war for almost a decade he had never found such a truly vulnerable point to attack. Only two British campaigns succeeded during the entire course of the French Wars: in Egypt in 1801 and the Peninsula after 1808. They succeeded because they were uniquely suited to the advantages of the British sea power, in that they occurred on the periphery of Europe far removed from the center of French power, in territory where the inhabitants opposed the French occupation.[44] In 1803, there were no French troops stationed in either Egypt or Spain or in any other theater that held out the same prospect for success. It is also important to note that the only other major amphibious operations, the invasions of North Holland in 1799 and Walcheren, Holland, in 1809, proved dramatic failures. Therefore, it was essential to weigh the risks before embarking on such expeditions.

Addington's approach to the war was both cautious and traditional. During the previous war, Pitt's cabinet colleagues Grenville and Dundas had disagreed fundamentally about how to fight. Grenville, as foreign secretary, argued that only a grand coalition of Great Powers fighting on the Continent would beat France, and that money and troops spent on colonial adventures wasted the resources required to win the battles that really mattered. Dundas, as secretary for War, felt that, because Continental allies could not be expected to fight for British objectives, it was necessary to concentrate British resources in the theaters of war where they had a chance to fight effectively. He also supported pursuing polices that strengthened the Royal Navy and the economy, to enable the country to survive a war of attrition.[45] That both men were right in their own way illustrated the British dilemma. Grenville's strategy could be effective when allies were willing to assist, but most of the time they were not. Dundas's strategy helped strengthen the British financial and strategic position but could not win the war.

Addington preferred a Continental strategy and Hawkesbury worked hard toward building a coalition. In the meantime, without the help of Great Power allies, the British had to do what they could on their own. Addington tried to improve the British position by taking the offensive in the naval and colonial spheres, where the British possessed the advantage. The three most important theaters of naval warfare were the Channel, the Mediterranean, and the Caribbean. In

March 1803, when relations with France were deteriorating rapidly, Hobart ordered impressment and began to prepare the navy for war. The Admiralty directed a squadron to gather intelligence off Cherbourg. By the end of March, Yorke claimed: "This week we shall have at least 10 sail of the Line off the Lizard, or in Cawsand Bay, & as all the Frigates are armed, a Night's time will suffice to block up all the Ports from the Texel to Brest."[46] In April the Admiralty increased the home squadron and the defense of the Thames and the Medway River in Kent, and further reinforced the Channel squadron in early May.[47]

Addington's declaring war before the French were ready gave the British a temporary advantage by enabling the Royal Navy to employ the strategy of blockade effectively.[48] To maintain command of the Channel, the Royal Navy had to contain the French fleet in port. Admiral Cornwallis sailed immediately to blockade Brest, which he accomplished within thirty-six hours. As Brest was the commercial port of the French West Indian trade and the only French harbor on the Channel coast capable of servicing a large fleet, it was the most important French port outside the Mediterranean. The Royal Navy also established blockades at Rochefort and Lorient.[49] The close blockade not only prevented French warships from joining the invasion forces but also cut France's overseas commercial lifeline. St. Vincent's blockade strategy included two lines of defense. The first sealed the ports as closely as possible, with warships and strategically placed frigates cruising the harbor. The inshore squadron of battleships remained close behind and the rest of the fleet not far away. The second line consisted of various squadrons falling back on the strategic center close to southernmost point of Cornwall, able to follow the French to Ireland or up the Channel.[50]

The Mediterranean was next in strategic importance to the Channel. During the peace, Bonaparte improved his strategic position by annexing Leghorn and Elba, signing treaties with the Barbary States, and obtaining access to the Black Sea. If he could dominate the Mediterranean, he could exclude Great Britain from trade in the Near East, capture the Russian trade, and threaten the Ottoman Empire.

After reading Sebastiani's report, which had reinforced fears that Bonaparte would sail for Egypt, Hobart sent instructions in March 1803 to the Admiralty to command the Mediterranean squadron to be on alert to prevent the French from attempting an amphibious attack on the Turkish Empire.[51] In May Nelson took command of the Mediterranean fleet with instructions to prevent the French fleet from leaving Toulon. While Cornwallis was to resume St. Vincent's policy of a close blockade of Brest, Nelson's mission was more complicated: he was not only to blockade Toulon, but also to watch Leghorn and Genoa in case the French tried to launch an invasion of Egypt from Italy. In effect, he was to blockade three ports simultaneously. Nelson was also to ensure the security of Malta, protect the king of Naples, and monitor the activities of the Spanish fleet.[52]

Hobart had also been monitoring the situation in the West Indies prior to Addington's declaration of war. By the end of March, he decided that the Royal Navy should intercept any French ships that left Dutch ports, regardless of whether they were headed for Louisiana, as the French claimed.[53] He reinforced the squadron in the Leeward Islands and ordered it to intercept any French reinforcements.[54] On 16 May, two days before the actual declaration of war, Hobart sent instructions to both the East and West Indies. He ordered Wellesley in India to capture Cochin and the Dutch islands. In the West Indies, he ordered the capture of St. Lucia and Tobago and Martinique. He also directed British troops in North America to attack St. Pierre and Miquelon. By 10 June, having received intelligence that the proprietors of Surinam, Demerara, Berbice, and Essequibo desired British protection, Hobart ordered the capture of those colonies as well.[55]

These colonial initiatives were remarkably successful, as the British recaptured St. Lucia, Tobago, St. Pierre, and Miquelon by the end of June. British West Indian forces then recaptured Demerara, Essequibo, and Berbice by the end of September, and by May 1804 had recaptured Surinam. British forces accomplished these goals without difficulty or substantial reinforcements.[56] Hobart sent only 159 troops to the West Indies in 1803, and two new regiments were sufficient to aid the force invading Surinam in 1804.[57] Of the colonies returned by the Treaty of Amiens, the British recaptured all but the Cape and Martinique prior to Addington's resignation. Martinique proved the most difficult to subdue, owing to its size and the strength of the French garrison, but having recaptured Tobago the British were able to establish an effective blockade of Martinique that prevented the French from deriving any military or commercial advantage from the island. The only remaining French possession in the West Indies was St. Domingue, which the British had never captured before. The command of the sea enjoyed by the Royal Navy, however, prevented the French from even sending reinforcements to subdue the slave rebellion on the island. Although Addington knew that he could not defeat Bonaparte through colonial warfare, this strategy improved the security of British colonies, provided opportunities for the expansion of British commerce, and deprived France of many of its most important overseas strategic and commercial bases. These victories were also valuable for morale.

The effective use of blockade by the Royal Navy also hampered Bonaparte's war effort on the Continent. The French advance through northern Germany to attack Hanover gave them control of the Elbe and Weser rivers, from which they excluded British shipping. In June and July the British responded with a blockade of these rivers.[58] In an attempt to increase the economic pressure on France, in September Hobart directed a squadron in the Channel to blockade the port of Havre de Grace to sever its communication link to Paris.[59] The British blockades, particularly at Brest, effectively interrupted French and foreign trade and bottled up the French navy, preventing it from attacking the Royal Navy or even practicing maneuvers.[60] Nevertheless, they did not seriously harm the French economy because the French were able to draw upon the resources of the Continent. The British deprived the French of luxury items such as sugar, coffee, and spices, but this had only a marginal effect on the French war effort.[61]

Addington also considered the option of a major amphibious operation. As he had raised a sufficient defense force by the autumn of 1803, he planned to have 20,000 men available for an offensive operation either in Europe or South America in the event that they could be deployed effectively. On 4 September, he claimed that "The Time is not, I trust, very remote, when we shall find ourselves in such a State, as to admit of the Application of a large Force to other Purposes than those of mere Defence, & of domestic Security." By April 1804, Yorke, who had succeeded Pelham as home secretary the previous summer, suspended the army of reserve legislation in order to enable the regular army to recruit greater numbers. The question was to determine where an amphibious force could effectively be deployed. Hobart favored capturing the Portuguese and Spanish colonies in South America. Hobart had suggested such a plan as early as July 1801, but Addington and Hawkesbury ruled it out, because it would undermine their foreign policy objectives in relation to Spain and Portugal. The cabinet also considered plans for Continental expeditions that foreshadowed the Walcheren invasion of 1809 and the Peninsular campaign. The chances of success in Holland appeared slight, however, with a large French force on the Channel coast, and a Peninsular campaign would not be feasible until the French army invaded Portugal. Addington ultimately decided not to deploy the force because there were no opportunities for which the prospects of success would have justified the risk that such a venture would have entailed.[62]

There was criticism of Addington for not sending a force of 30–40,000 to southern Italy, but this criticism was questionable.[63] Besides the obvious logistical problems, it is also doubtful whether the British could have succeeded in that theater. The king of Naples did not want British troops on his soil, because they would undermine his authority and act as a magnet for a large French counterinvasion. Even after the French actually invaded, he was reluctant to allow British troops to secure possession of Sicily because it might give the French incentive to retain a larger force in Naples. In Italian territory already controlled by France, it is unclear whether the local population would have preferred British troops to French. Addington and Hawkesbury clearly remembered that after the French invaded Holland, a large portion of the Dutch population had demonstrated that they preferred a French occupation to the restoration of the old Dutch regime. When the British and Russians invaded Holland in 1799 to drive the French out, few of the Dutch gave them any assistance.

Addington was not deliberately avoiding an offensive war in order to entice Bonaparte into a showdown on the Channel.[64] He seriously considered using his force of 20,000 for an offensive operation, if he could only find a theater where such an operation could have a reasonable chance of achieving a worthwhile strategic objective. Unfortunately for Addington, the course of the war did not provide him with the occasion to use this force effectively. One historian has described Addington's war policies as "unspectacular," but that was because Great Britain had no opportunity for achieving a significant military or naval victory.[65] A more effective war strategy was beyond the means of the British government at that juncture. A few years later, when conditions on the Continent had changed substantially, the British would have the option of planning and conducting an effective operation. The Peninsular campaign played an important auxiliary role to the allied offensive in Central Europe. But in 1803 and 1804, as at most points during the war, Addington faced a "dearth of strategic options."[66]

WAR FINANCE

The system of parliamentary-backed public finance was crucial to the ability of the British to wage war.[67] But while it assisted the government in enduring long wars, the system placed restraints on how the British waged war, restraints that did not apply to more autocratic states. Bonaparte raised a large army by conscription and supplied it by sequestering the property of internal enemies of the state, exacting payments from conquered and client states, and having his troops live off the land in the states that they invaded. The tsar of Russia had millions of serfs at his disposal and conscripted the Russian aristocracy to provide men and supplies for the Russian war effort. These options were not available to Great Britain because, as a parliamentary state, the government was limited by Parliament, which controlled the raising of troops and financial resources. War supplies had to be met by loans and taxes sanctioned by Parliament. This meant that the government had to use measures that a majority in both houses of Parliament would support. M.P.s were reluctant to approve the formation of large armies, which they believed posed a threat to the traditional freedoms of British subjects. They also opposed excessive taxation, even in wartime. Therefore, Parliament had the power to limit the war effort through its control of the government purse.

Addington's decision to negotiate peace in 1801 was largely influenced by his belief that the poor state of government finances would not permit him to continue the war. Financial reform and the respite granted by the peace improved the finances to the point at which the option of declaring war was viable, but the cumulative debt remained large, and the Treasury required greater sources of revenue to continue the war for an extended period. When the war resumed, Addington realized that he had to introduce important new financial measures to fight it.

The health of the Treasury required a careful balancing of loans and taxes. Addington abolished the income tax in 1802 for political reasons and made up the deficiency through an extraordinarily large loan. The financial necessities of war, however, required a change in policy. Addington realized that it was important to raise sufficient war taxes to avoid the necessity of a large loan. A memorandum on the financial measures of the ministry declared that in 1803 "It was proposed by a System of War Taxes to raise a Sum for the service of the year so considerable as to supersede the necessity of borrowing any sum materially exceeding that which would be applicable to the reduction of the public debt."[68]

Addington's concern was that if the government met the demands of war by borrowing, the national debt would become unmanageable. He believed that raising, at the beginning of the war, as much money as possible through war taxes, it would decrease the long-term burden. Another consideration was that large loans drove up interests rates, which hurt British trade and government revenue. In devising his first war budget, Addington calculated that the nation could afford £10–12 million in war taxes, but that he could not raise the Customs and Excise beyond £8 million. In order to make up the shortfall, Addington decided to reintroduce the income tax.[69]

The income tax that Pitt first introduced in 1799 presented both political and administrative problems. First, some taxpayers considered the requirement to declare aggregate income to be an invasion of privacy. Men involved in trade and commerce, in particular, strongly objected to making their total worth public. Second, relying on the individual to submit an honest assessment of his own income, without adequate means of ensuring accuracy, gave him the opportunity to defraud the government. Pitt's tax consequently failed to deliver the revenue that he had anticipated. Basing his projections on a total national income of £100 million, Pitt estimated that a tax of 10 percent would yield £10 million, but in three years it failed to reach an annual yield of £6.25 million.[70]

Addington was adept at financial matters, having studied them for years before he took office. During a debate in the Commons in 1798 he had displayed a sound understanding of the history of taxation. His study of legislation during the reign of William and Mary (another time when England was at war with France) gave him the inspiration for his reforms.[71] When abolishing Pitt's tax in 1802, Addington knew that it would require substantial modification were it to be reintroduced in the event of war. Consequently, when he reintroduced the tax as part of his budget for 1803, he redressed the two most important flaws of Pitt's original tax. To eliminate the concern about the invasion of privacy, he abolished the requirement for declaring aggregate income. In its place, he divided income into five categories that were calculated separately: (1) property; (2) trade or profession; (3) investments in government stock; (4) salaries of government offices; and (5) all other income. The most fundamental reform, however, was to require that the tax be collected at the source, rather than from the taxpayer. Renters deducted the tax from the rent paid to the landlord; employers deducted the tax from wages paid to employees; and the bank deducted the tax from interest paid to bond- and shareholders. Individuals made no declarations of their total income and the opportunities for evading the tax were severely curtailed.

Having calculated that these reforms would make the tax more efficient, Addington tried to make it less unpopular by cutting the rate from 10 percent to 5. In his original proposal, he set the same rate on all schedules, but to make it fairer to the poor—who did not own land or stock—he exempted all incomes below £60 per year, and arranged a sliding scale for those between £60 and £150. Based on his original proposals, Addington projected that his tax would raise £4.5 million. Even after some modifications that reduced the yield, it actually produced £4.7 million, which was only 20 percent below the yield of Pitt's tax that had been set at twice the rate.[72]

Addington's income tax reforms were tremendously successful. Revenue from the tax allowed him to avoid further increasing the customs and excise and other war taxes. Future ministries recognized the value of these reforms. Even Pitt did not substantially alter the tax when he returned to power in 1804. Ultimately, the income tax proved vital to the ability of the British to survive the war in later years, and without it they would not have been able to afford the large financial subsidies they granted to their Continental allies in 1813 and 1814.

After declaring war in May 1803, Addington and his colleagues spent most of their time and energy raising a large force for home defense, and it was these policies in particular that provoked the parliamentary assault that would ultimately wear down Addington's majority in both houses of Parliament.[73] Addington's parliamentary opposition justified itself on the grounds that he was less capable of providing for the proper defense of the country than Pitt or other leading politicians would have been. Previous and subsequent experience proved, however, that no one was more adept than Addington. For example, Pitt abolished the army of reserve in 1804, replacing it with a Permanent Additional Forces Act that raised only 13,000 men in two years. This drew the remark from the Speaker of the House of Commons in 1805 that it was hard to justify Pitt's hostility to Addington's policies, when his own measures proved even less effective.[74]

After Windham took the War Office in 1806, he dismantled the volunteers and revised the Defence of the Realm Act with measures that M.P.s found confusing and the generals found difficult to implement. Windham clearly demonstrated that while he could find fault with Addington's measures, he could not devise more effective policies himself.[75] Yet the partisan rhetoric of Addington's enemies obscured the real achievements of his policies. Richard Glover, in his comprehensive study of British defense policies during the Napoleonic Wars, was the first historian to penetrate the rhetoric and provide an accurate assessment of what Addington had really accomplished: "The mesmerism of brilliant oratory by men who were all outside this cabinet blinded contemporaries to the merits of those within it and seems still to exercise at least a portion of its spell over historians of later generations. All told, then, Addington had a bad press. Yet his war policy may be judged worthy of no small praise."[76] Although there were imperfections in some of Addington's policies, they were largely irrelevant in the larger context. The British could not achieve security for their interests, even with the assistance of Great Power allies, until they together had developed a vision of peace terms and a new international system that would meet the security interests of all the Great Powers, including France.[77] While Castlereagh would eventually grasp this vision, it would take ten more years of observing the war and the course of European diplomacy. In the meantime, Addington's war policies met all the short-term objectives capable of achievement given the limitations of Great Britain's strategic position.

CHAPTER 8

The Downfall of Addington

*T*he *declaration of war* and the military and naval policies that Addington pursued did not immediately affect his parliamentary position. His majorities in both houses remained strong. Some independent members thought that Addington was leading the government effectively during the war. William Douglas, the fourth duke of Queensberry, a powerful Scottish peer, rejected the idea of Pitt replacing Addington: "I am for no changes. Government is wise, prudent, and dispassionate; with perfect ability to determine what is fit to be done, and to defend it. . . . If Mr Addington can't get us out of the Scrape I believe the thing can't be done."[1] A friend of Lord Nelson wrote in January 1804, "I cannot tell you how happy it makes me to see Mr Addington pursuing a Career so interesting and important, with such peculiar dignity and Success. . . . The more I hear of him the more I like him, & every Act of his Government gives me greater Cause of Admiration & Satisfaction."[2] The declaration of war proved very popular and was supported by many in Parliament who had opposed the previous war. Yet, within a year, Addington's government appeared to be on the verge of being defeated, raising the question of why his parliamentary support decreased so suddenly at this particular time.

The answer lies not in the policies that the government implemented but in the character, skill, and personal agenda of five key men: Grenville, Fox, Pitt, Melville, and Addington. Gradually, between the summer of 1803 and the spring of 1804, Grenville, Fox, and finally Pitt and Melville decided to oppose Addington, forcing him to resign so that they could take office themselves. They did not describe their objective in these terms. They claimed that the government ought to be formed of a union of the men with the greatest talents and abilities. Agreeing among themselves that they were such men, no doubt they honestly believed that they could govern more effectively than Addington and his colleagues and that their attempts to drive him from office were in the national interest. It was ironic that when Grenville, Fox, Pitt, and Melville finally got the opportunity to govern, they proved no more effective than Addington.

The reason that they ultimately succeeded in forcing Addington to resign lay in his character. Addington was an astute and effective politician and an able administrator. Unfortunately for him, the key to longevity in office was not the ability to govern, but the ability to manage parliament. The survival of an administration depended on whether it could sustain a parliamentary majority. The question was essentially one of numbers. The prime minister had to employ a variety of different strategies to ensure that a majority of both the Commons and the Lords would continue to support him. Certain functions of this job Addington performed well. These proved sufficient to keep him in office for three years, but when his opponents began to attack him on all sides, he lacked the aggressiveness and ruthlessness to fight them on their own terms. Ultimately, Addington's character and temperament prevented him from being able to manage parliament effectively in the circumstances of the spring of 1804.

THE REVIVAL OF OPPOSITION

Addington did not face a strong opposition until March 1804, but the seeds of one had been sown long before. It all began with Grenville. Although he had defended the new ministers during the war in 1801, he went into systematic opposition after they signed the Preliminary Treaty, because the terms did not address the war aims that he had pursued while in office. He claimed that his opposition to Addington was solely on the issue of the terms of the peace, but he and his colleagues opposed the government on almost every important issue thereafter. Grenville denied that he had any personal motives for this opposition. He declared that his only political objective was to facilitate Pitt's return to office. Behind the scenes, however, his brothers were already planning a new ministry and discussing the distribution of offices among themselves and their friends. During the period of Pitt's retirement, Grenville was actually moving further away from his cousin both politically and personally, to the extent that some of Pitt's friends accused Grenville of having ambitions to displace him. According to one them, "from the period of the peace of Amiens he began to *set up for himself,* and to endeavour to collect as many as he could detach from Pitt on that question into a body of which he should be the leader and oracle, and I have no doubt that he considered himself from that period as the leader of a distinct party."[3]

For two and a half years, Grenville and his allies, for all their sound and fury, had signified little. Between October 1801 and December 1803, few M.P.s beyond their immediate patronage voted with them. The Grenvilles were actually extremely unpopular, because they epitomized the corrupt professional politicians the independent country gentlemen so despised.[4] Hawkesbury's father, who had been a cabinet colleague of Grenville, claimed that the members of his party were "so self important & troublesome, that it is better to have them as Enemies than Friends."[5] Tierney suggested that Grenville's opposition worked to Addington's advantage: "Mr Addington is daily acquiring additional strength & popularity. Seriously, the violence of the new opposition (the Grenvilles, Canning ect [*sic*]) has wrought wonders in his favor."[6] As late as August 1803, they had failed to put a dent in Addington's parliamentary majority. Canning lamented, "I see no reason now why A[ddington]'s administration should not hobble on, & outlast the Country."[7]

The peace that alienated Grenville gained Addington the support of the Foxite Whigs. As the Whigs greatly outnumbered Grenville's party, Addington's majorities actually increased. Nevertheless, Fox's support was not solid, and lasted only as long as Addington was able to maintain the peace. Once he had declared war, it did not matter to Fox whether Addington or Pitt were in office, because they were both, in Fox's opinion, puppets of the king. Fox was unable, however, to take all of the Whigs back into opposition, because many Whigs considered themselves to be primarily allies of the Prince of Wales, rather than followers of Fox. They had become estranged from Fox during the peace, and several were moving closer to Addington. Tierney, who had tried to negotiate a coalition in 1801, continued to support Addington and accepted the office of treasurer of the navy in May 1803. Sheridan was also on good terms with Addington and supported him in the Commons with his votes and debating skill. Erskine admired Addington personally and on several occasions entertained an offer of office. These men were less concerned than Fox was about the issue of the king's power to choose ministers, and they drew an important distinction between Addington and Pitt. For them the greatest evil that could befall the country was for Pitt to return to office. They were also unsympathetic to Fox's opposition to the war. They believed that Addington had made the right decision. Even Grey felt unable to oppose the resumption of the war, and had to content himself with criticizing the manner in which Addington and Hawkesbury had conducted the negotiations with France.[8]

Addington's parliamentary majority remained solid through the end of 1803. The division lists demonstrate that he retained the support of some of the Whigs and most of the members who had backed Pitt.[9] Only the small followings of Grenville and Windham, on one hand, and that of Fox, on the other, provided any sustained opposition, and the two groups voted for different reasons and were often on different sides of issues. Addington was not concerned about these two groups in opposition because he believed that Grenville and Fox would never join forces.[10] In many ways, Grenville was an even greater adversary of Fox than Pitt was. Since 1791, Grenville had been the strongest spokesman for Pitt's ministry in the Lords, and Fox its strongest critic in the Commons. They were poles apart on issues such as the powers of the king, the repression of social unrest, and the prosecution of the war (which Grenville had supported more strongly than had Pitt). After Pitt resigned, Grenville supported Addington, while Fox opposed him, until the preliminaries of peace were announced, when Grenville and Fox switched sides. They did not find themselves in agreement until Addington resumed the war. Even then, they criticized Addington for opposite reasons: Fox for resuming the war; Grenville for not fighting it vigorously enough. Although unexpected political alliances had been formed in the past, they required some community of interest or principles. In 1794, the Portland Whigs joined Pitt, their longtime adversary, because they all agreed on a vigorous prosecution of the war and the need to suppress social unrest. Grenville and Fox, on the contrary, had nothing in common but their opposition to Addington and support for Catholic Emancipation.[11] If, as they claimed, their object was not to obtain office for themselves, it was not clear what could have formed the basis of an alliance between them.

Nevertheless, an alliance is precisely what happened. Realizing that his own small numbers and those of his allies were having little effect in Parliament, Grenville tried without success to convince Pitt to join him in outright opposition. He began to notice that Fox was speaking out strongly against Addington, particularly on the volunteer legislation. Grenville made a last unsuccessful attempt to win over Pitt on 9 and 10 January 1804. He then decided to look for assistance elsewhere.[12] His brother, Thomas Grenville (who was a natural intermediary because he was a close friend of Fox), proposed to meet Fox to discuss cooperation against Addington. Fox proved willing, and by the end of the month he and Grenville had agreed on two fundamental points. The first was that Addington should be forced to resign. From Grenville's point of view "A declared and regular opposition to the present Government was now more than ever an indispensable public Duty."[13] Fox concurred: "Let us first get rid of the Doctor is my principle of action."[14] Their second point of agreement was that the new government should include the greatest political weight and talents in the country.[15] What this really meant was that Pitt should include friends of both Grenville and Fox in the ministry that would replace Addington's. When Grenville stated that the new government should not be based on a principle of exclusion, he meant that it should not exclude Fox, but that it should exclude Addington and all of his colleagues.

This sudden political elopement provoked a generally negative reaction. Cornwallis considered Fox's alliance with Grenville to be unethical.[16] Addington was more surprised than alarmed, because Fox and Grenville were both unpopular and unlikely to gather a large following. Nevertheless, as Hobart acknowledged, "although the arrangement does not appear a good one for forming an administration, it seems admirably calculated for annoying his Majesty's present ministers."[17] Pitt thought that, as there was little prospect that they would achieve very large divisions, their action was foolish and possibly dangerous.[18]

Pitt's attitude was important, as he ultimately held the key to Addington's future: he possessed the largest personal following in Parliament and the potential to sway many of the independent members in the Commons. When Addington met with the king and Pitt for the first time after Pitt's resignation, the king had said that "if we three but stick together, all will go well."[19] This proved prescient. The king never wavered in his support for Addington. In October 1803 he offered to make Addington a Knight of the Garter. Addington declined the offer, as he had done before, but the king remained determined to show Addington a mark of esteem. Pitt, however, had begun to drift away from Addington almost from the start. At first it had been gradual, but by the termination of the coalition negotiations in April 1803, the gap had become insurmountable. Pitt's position became difficult as he remained torn between the commitments that he had made to Addington and the king, on one side, and to his closest friends and colleagues, who pleaded with him to betray Addington and return to office, on the other.

Pitt and Addington were always well disposed to one another. It was the actions of others that created the political and emotional gulf between them. The two parties most responsible were Canning and Hiley Addington. Canning's animosity toward Addington increased as time passed. Although he rationalized his opposition on the grounds of policy and constitutional principle,[20] at heart his opposition to Addington was based on personality. He worked tirelessly to destroy Pitt's relationship with Addington by keeping them apart physically, exaggerating Addington's defects, taking his comments out of context, and accusing him falsely of slighting Pitt. With the help of Grenville and others, Canning gradually succeeded.

Addington's brother Hiley actually did more than anyone else to assist Canning. Hiley was the Addingtonian version of Canning, with all of the vanity, animosity, and duplicity, but without any of the wit. Hiley was a marked contrast to his brother. Where Addington was personable, forthright, mild, considerate, polite, and understanding, Hiley was unfriendly, dishonest, hot-tempered, selfish, acrimonious, and jealous. Addington maintained a strong fraternal bond with Hiley ever since they were children, but he often found him difficult to manage. Hiley was overly ambitious, but Addington recognized his brother's administrative limitations and was unwilling to promote him to the level that he desired. Although Hiley was disappointed at not receiving higher office, he was extremely protective of Addington, particularly when it came to attacks on his honor. Like Canning, he picked on minor slights to his mentor and blew them out of proportion. His greatest mistake, however, was to provoke a propaganda battle with Canning, which caught both Addington and Pitt in the middle.[21] This culminated in a pamphlet war during late 1803 and early 1804, with one side attacking Pitt and the other Addington. Although the authors of the pamphlets were anonymous, it was clear that Hiley and Canning were behind them. Suspicion arose on both sides that Addington and Pitt were more directly involved. Pitt certainly blamed Addington for the attacks against him.[22] In September, Pitt was still so bitter that he refused to speak to any members of the cabinet, and although Castlereagh tried to assure him that Addington was not responsible for the pamphlets, he refused to believe it.[23]

Nevertheless, having declined Addington's offer to join the ministry, Pitt also refused to go into overt opposition. The problem was that, while he was waiting for Addington to resign, there was no sign that either the king or the majority of M.P.s wanted a change in government. Therefore, he decided to attack some, but not all, of Addington's policies in an attempt to demonstrate to the king that his ministers were supposedly incapable.[24] In Pitt's first speech after Addington declared war, he gave one of his best performances ever. He demonstrated a firm and committed support for the war, but without any direct reference to the man who had initiated it. He intended it to appear as covert criticism. His first overt attack on Addington took place in June 1803. After disingenuously assuring Addington of his support,[25] he arranged for an M.P. named Colonel Peter Bold Patten to move a motion of censure on the ministers. Pitt then rose to move the orders of the day, in order to appear to rescue the ministers from such a censure, while depriving them of the chance to defend themselves. His intention was to "evince to the public that . . . he was at liberty to remove them [the ministers] if he pleased."[26] The scheme backfired, however, as Addington and his colleagues opposed Pitt's motion with a vociferous debate and won the vote by a large majority. Pitt then left the House and the government defeated Patten's motion by an even larger majority.

Hawkesbury and Liverpool were completely baffled by Pitt's action. Hawkesbury thought the only reasonable explanation was that "He has been worked upon by such of his personal Friends as are Enemies to the present Govt until his mind is compleatly [*sic*] unhinged—his Health has certainly suffered most seriously—he looks dreadfully & his Physician says that his nerves have been compleatly shook by a state of agitation & uncertainly in wh[ich] he has been kept."[27] Liverpool believed that the whole affair had severely hurt Pitt's reputation.[28] The true significance of this episode was that Pitt was now an enemy of Addington. Years later Addington wrote, "Mr Pitt's amendment on Patten's motion was an act of explicit hostility: it was universally so considered & from that time his opposition never relaxed whenever it could be shown."[29] At the time, Addington spoke truthfully when he said, "I have not had a happy hour since the coolness arose between Mr P[itt] & me, & I would take sixty steps towards a reconciliation if I thought he would take one,"[30] but Pitt would not.

Addington's majority remained unshaken until January 1804.[31] Although the opposition had become more active, it had not yet become effective. According to James Harris, first Earl of Malmesbury (who was a diarist, retired diplomat, and confidant of Canning, Grenville, and Pitt), party spirit ran high: "The debates in the House of Commons grew more long, and more contested, and none of the measures of Government, for the volunteers, or indeed for any other purpose, were allowed to pass unnoticed or unopposed."[32] At that point, Pitt realized how ambiguous his position appeared and felt that he had to make it clear. The crux of his problem was that he was undecided about what he should do.[33] He wanted Addington to resign but did not want to be seen as actively having forced him to. Pitt's primary objective was to maintain his "Character," but it was difficult to see how best to achieve this goal, given the sticky situation in which he found himself.[34] His policy of supporting Addington in general, while hoping to weaken his majority by pointing out his mistakes, was not working.[35] His attack on the volunteer system in late January did not have the effect that he had hoped, as Addington's majority remained firm.[36] Yet he refused to join Grenville and Fox in opposition, leaving Hobart to declare confidently, "Neither Mr Fox's principles nor Lord Grenville's manners are popular; and Mr Pitt, standing aloof with a Catholic millstone about his neck will not be an object to attract a large body of political speculators."[37] Subsequent events would demonstrate that Hobart was mistaken.

The importance of the king's political role arose once again when he suffered another attack of porphyria in February 1804. As with the two previous occasions in 1788 and 1801, the government hoped that the king would recover soon, while the Prince of Wales planned for a regency. Although the doctor's reports were promising, the prince demanded to speak with both Addington and Pitt about new arrangements, and this created considerable political uncertainty. Everyone assumed that the Prince of Wales, if granted the full powers of a regent, would dismiss Addington and ask Fox to form a government. Within a few weeks, the king recovered, but concern persisted about his ability to handle the normal load of government business, and the political future remained uncertain. Pitt's plan for supplanting Addington depended on his being able to persuade the king to dismiss the ministry.

Pitt attempted to achieve this goal through an overt public attack in Parliament and a covert approach behind Addington's back. Eldon, who was one of the most influential ministers in Addington's cabinet, met secretly with Pitt on 5 March. Eldon had never considered himself as attached to Addington. The purpose of his visit with Pitt was to facilitate Pitt's return to power. By assisting Pitt at this junction, Eldon improved his chance of remaining in office after the change of government. When they met again three weeks later, Eldon informed Pitt that most of the cabinet wished that he would resume office.[38] According to Eldon, they desired Pitt to replace Addington as prime minister and they were prepared to resign their positions, but only on the condition that Addington would be retained in some other office. When Pitt refused, Eldon indicated that the cabinet would not give Addington up. Nevertheless, this encouraged Pitt to commence a concerted parliamentary assault on Addington's position, because he assumed that many M.P.s, including some of the current ministers, wanted him to take office.

In February, Pitt had told Malmesbury that "he would never make the turning out of this Administration the object of his endeavours," but from the middle of March he was conspiring with Melville to do just that. Pitt's plan consisted of two stages. The first was to organize a sustained parliamentary assault on all aspects of government policy. The second was to explain his sentiments to the king once he had recovered from his illness. Pitt began his assault on 15 March with a comprehensive attack on St. Vincent's naval policies and a call for government papers on the navy to be laid before the House. He questioned "whether the preparations which have been made by his Majesty's ministers, in the direction of naval affairs, have been commensurate to the magnitude of the crisis in which we are placed."

Many observers considered Pitt's attack to have been factious rather than a sincere expression of alarm at the state of the navy. Even Pitt's most recent biographer admits that many of Pitt's criticisms of Addington's naval and military policies were misconceived, exaggerated, and unfair. Liverpool later stated that Pitt did not disagree fundamentally with these or other of Addington's policies, but "in order to destroy the . . . Government pretended to do so." This might explain why Pitt made such a poor case against St. Vincent. He asserted that the best mode of defense against invasion was to deploy small gunboats in shallow waters, but Addington's supporters were able to convince the Commons that St. Vincent's policy of close blockade of the French ports was the best means of defense. Pitt lost the debate, but the ministerial majority was only seventy-one, which was forty to fifty votes lower than expected.[39]

Pitt then attacked Addington's measures for home defense, and the government majority continued to decrease. This was a result not so much of the force of the arguments as of parliamentary management. On one of Addington's flanks, Pitt and Melville worked hard gathering their supporters for votes in both houses. Melville's role was particularly important because he had long been Pitt's strongest political lieutenant and his influence on Scottish electoral patronage was considerable. On 29 March, Pitt ordered Melville to bring out the Scottish vote and by 4 April he requested a statement of its strength. On another flank, the Whigs were also pulling together. After Fox joined Grenville, many of the members close to the Prince of Wales, including Sheridan and Erskine, continued to support Addington and tried to convince the prince to support him as well. Thereafter, the duchess of Devonshire, who had been involved in the negotiations that led to the Grenville-Fox alliance, employed both her charm and her famous Devonshire House hospitality to bring the friends of the Prince of Wales back together with Fox.[40] The duchess also arranged for an overture from the prince to Pitt. Pitt then planned for a new government that would exclude Addington and Fox, but include Moira and members of the party of the Prince of Wales. By the middle of April, Pitt realized that Addington was taking serious alarm, and he organized his attacks to have the greatest effect in Parliament. On 18 April, Pitt decided to delay his motion on the Army of Reserve Suspension Bill until more of his supporters had arrived in Westminster so that his division would be larger. Privately he predicted that the issue would be settled within two weeks.[41] Once Pitt had finally determined to destroy Addington's position in Parliament, he was able to arrange his own accession to office in a short time. The key to his success lay in parliamentary management, a skill that he and Melville had mastered, but Addington had not.

PARLIAMENTARY MANAGEMENT

As Addington resigned because he was on the verge of losing his parliamentary majority, it is important to understand why he lost support. The mere fact that Grenville, Fox, and Pitt entered systematic opposition did not necessarily mean that they would be able to muster enough votes to defeat Addington. The government had withstood the parliamentary attacks of Grenville and his colleagues for over two years, and those of Fox since the war resumed. Pitt had difficulty denting Addington's majority on the votes on a series of issues, but Addington's support was not solid. The central issue was parliamentary management. In the words of John Robinson, an expert election strategist who had managed the government interest in the election of 1784, "great abilities alone, or the greatest, will not lead men nor can Englishmen be drove, but that address, temper and management must be called in to aid."[42] The peculiar nature of the unreformed political system rendered parliamentary management both complex and precarious.

Addington retained the complete confidence of the king and remained popular in the country.[43] He could count on the king's friends, but he did not have a strong following of his own. Finding himself in the unexpected position of forming a government, he did not place a priority on gathering together men who would be loyal solely to him. Instead, he relied on the help of Pitt and the king to persuade the best men available to take office. This was sensible at the time because without the help of these two men he probably would not have been able to fill all of the offices. Nevertheless, those whom Pitt and the king persuaded to accept office retained mixed loyalties. This was not unusual for eighteenth-century ministries, but combined with the rest of Addington's problems it undermined his position.

The lack of sufficient landed magnates with control over many parliamentary seats was also a deficiency in Addington's cabinet. The issue of magnates was not a management issue per se, in that they were not a reflection on the skills or abilities of the prime minister. Nevertheless, including magnates in an administration made parliamentary management easier. Addington did win the support of a few peers, such as George Boscowan, third Viscount Falmouth, and Francis Basset, first Baron De Dunstanville, who controlled many seats in Cornwall. In addition to the few seats Portland controlled, Pelham was related to the duke of Newcastle, who controlled the votes of four or five in the Lords.[44] Nevertheless, they could not match the patronage of the magnates who eventually opposed Addington. His parliamentary majority would have been more solid, if he had had the security that control over parliamentary seats could have brought to his ministry. It was also dangerous to have such parliamentary strength harnessed by the opposition. Initially, Addington's strong parliamentary position made it seem as if the lack of magnates did not matter, but in the long run it proved a serious deficiency. The greatest advantage presented by the magnates was that they could ensure solid parliamentary support in times of crisis. Their clients would almost always vote with them regardless of the course of the debate. This is precisely what Addington needed in the spring of 1804.

The management of elections was also important. Although elections did not directly determine the fates of governments, they did provide an opportunity for ministers to strengthen their position in Parliament. Addington called an election in the summer of 1802 but failed to build his own power base in Parliament. The reason was that, like the king, he personally abhorred spending public money to buy parliamentary seats.[45] He also realized that political corruption was one of the most persistent complaints of radical and opposition critics of the system of government. He was not a political animal by nature. He found many aspects of the political system distasteful and did his best to avoid or ignore them. He wanted his government to be successful and popular, but he disdained increasing his own personal following through what he considered to be unsavory methods, such as using government money to purchase elections.[46] This attitude, though it attested to the strength of his character, was a serious liability for a prime minister.

Addington seemed completely satisfied with the results of the election, but he should not have been. He was short-sighted in believing that he did not need to consolidate his support. He wasted an excellent opportunity to obtain more loyal supporters, who could have given him the strength to weather tougher times. Instead of taking control of the management of elections, he remained almost aloof, allowing Pitt's friends Rose and Melville (both of whom he mistook to be his friends as well) to secure control of many seats. Melville personally controlled at least twenty-six members elected in Scotland in 1802.[47] As a result, Melville and his Scottish allies continued to exercise more power in Scotland than the government did.[48] A shrewder politician would have seen the rift that was growing and have prepared for the possibility that Pitt and his allies might change sides, no matter how unlikely that appeared at the time. Addington was not that canny. He was naive to expect that pledges and friendships would endure. Hardwicke stated that Addington's greatest fault was his fear of giving offence. In this way, he helped sow the seeds of his own parliamentary misfortune.[49]

Addington also failed to manage government patronage to ensure his own personal support. In exercising government patronage, the prime minister had to find a way to share power with his ministers without alienating them, as some had accepted office precisely for the patronage that it entailed. Addington gave too much control to his colleagues. He granted virtually unlimited control of naval patronage to St. Vincent.[50] He also left control of the Foreign Office appointments in Hawkesbury's hands. This proved to have been a mistake on at least one occasion. Hawkesbury appointed Charles Arbuthnot as under-secretary, not knowing that Arbuthnot secretly held him in utter contempt. Addington also appears to have left the distribution of minor offices to his brother Hiley and to his brother-in-law Bragge.[51]

Addington retained control of several areas of patronage, but he did not always exercise that power strategically. He managed appointments to the church jointly with the king. Addington also played a large role in Irish patronage. He made all the appointments that were directly under the control of the British government—Lord Lieutenant, chief secretary, chancellor of the Exchequer, and Lord Chancellor—but also had a say in those under the control of the Irish government. While Hardwicke and Pelham fought for control of the Irish appointments, Addington usually supported the former. His overriding principle in Irish appointments was to honor all promises made to ensure the passage of the Act of Union. This had the effect of decreasing the scope for building loyal support, but he was fortunate that most Irish M.P.s chose to support him anyway.[52]

Addington failed to make maximum use of the patronage at his disposal to increase his support among placemen. Two examples illustrate this point. When the clerkship of the Pells became vacant, he gave it to his son Harry. This was a mistake because it was a coveted prize that could have been used to attract further support for the ministry. Addington also seriously mismanaged the offices of joint paymaster of the forces and surveyor of the royal woods and forests. In first forming his administration Addington sought to include Glenbervie, who refused several times to take the Board of Control and only agreed in the end to accept the joint paymastership. A year later, Hiley, who was dissatisfied with the office of secretary of the Treasury, pressed his brother to give him something better. He sought cabinet office but Addington silenced him with the joint paymastership.[53] To facilitate this move, Addington had to shuffle Glenbervie over to surveyor of the woods against his will. When the affair had ended, Addington lost considerable goodwill from Glenbervie without completely pleasing Hiley.

Addington's greatest personal deficiency was that he could not match the debating skill of the most prominent speakers in the House of Commons. He spoke well on occasion but he could not consistently deliver eloquent and witty speeches that could compete with Pitt, Fox, or Canning, and he did not think quickly enough on his feet to parry successfully the attacks of the opposition. He lacked not only the speaking style of Pitt, but also his predecessor's great sense of timing, which was the key to a great performance. On a number of occasions, Addington's timing proved most unfortunate. The best example was when he entered the House of Commons to declare war. He wore the uniform of the Woodley cavalry because he wanted to make an impressive showing that would rally the patriotism of the House. When he entered everyone noticed the uniform. Unfortunately, at that very moment the members were debating a medical bill. Some M.P.s found it amusing that "the Doctor" would make a dramatic entrance during the debate on the subject of medicine. This spoiled the entire effect. The opportunity to demonstrate inspired leadership turned instantly into a humorous anecdote for his opponents to exploit. It was symptomatic of the misfortune that he suffered throughout his term as leader of the House of Commons.

Addington required the support of talented debaters in his cabinet to make up for his deficiency. Originally, Glenbervie had predicted that, if the ministry could weather the initial storm, men of talent would join it, but unfortunately for Addington this did not happen. Although a great weight of talents lay beyond government control and many able speakers were restless for office, he was unable to recruit them. When opportunities to make changes arose, he took advantage of only a few of them. The most successful was to bring in Castlereagh, who was an able administrator and possessed some speaking ability. Spencer Perceval, whom Addington promoted to the non-cabinet post of attorney general, quickly developed into an effective speaker. A vacancy in the position of treasurer of the navy in September 1801 gave Addington an opportunity to bring in greater strength, as it was a popular post, but the best candidate that he could find was Bragge.

When Addington's overtures to Pitt failed, he tried to recruit

Melville, Sheridan, and Erskine, but to no avail. His only success was to persuade Tierney to take office as treasurer of the navy in May 1803.[54] He needed Tierney's help in the Commons, as he had decided to promote Hawkesbury to the Lords to take over the leadership from Pelham. Addington had decided to move Pelham, a troublesome colleague who proved a bitter disappointment in debate and management of government supporters in the Lords. Addington was able to persuade Pelham to exchange the Home Office for the less important office of the chancellor of the duchy of Lancaster. Addington then promoted Yorke to the Home Office and Bragge to fill Yorke's place as secretary at War. Yorke soon regretted the move, however, and pointed out that Addington should have used the office to bring in greater strength to the government, rather than merely shuffling the existing ministers. In Addington's defense, it is doubtful whether any of the men of talent would have been willing to take the office without requiring him to make sacrifices that he would have found unacceptable.[55]

Addington also suffered from problems created by insufficient loyalty among some of his cabinet colleagues. St. Vincent and Pelham were independent. Some of the rest of the cabinet had initially been followers of Pitt, and when Pitt began to separate himself from Addington, several gradually lost faith in Addington's abilities. As early as November 1802, Eldon wanted Pitt to replace Addington. Portland and York also admitted that they preferred the former government. The failure of the series of negotiations between Pitt and Addington in 1803 disheartened Hobart and Yorke.[56] Hawkesbury and Liverpool were two of Addington's most loyal supporters. Both were more optimistic than Yorke about their prospects for remaining in office, and held Pitt responsible for breaking faith with Addington. Nevertheless, they were more concerned with saving their own political careers than with remaining loyal to Addington.

The consequence of Addington's shortcomings as a parliamentary manager was that, when the crunch occurred in 1804, he lacked talented debaters to defend his policies and sustain the votes of the independent members who had supported him up until then. Although

Addington's and Hawkesbury's performances were improving, and Perceval and Castlereagh were emerging as talented speakers, there was no one to match the rhetoric and eloquence of Pitt and Fox. Tierney had talent, but, as treasurer of the navy without a seat in the cabinet, he was not in the best position to defend ministerial policy. Many M.P.s did not bother to examine the details of government policy and did not appreciate the insurmountable constraints that limited the options available to government. Eloquent members of the opposition were able to convince these M.P.s that Addington and his colleagues were mismanaging the war. Style mattered more than substance to these men.

Addington and Castlereagh also alienated some of the support of an important independent interest: the East India Company. The government was caught in the middle of a struggle between the Court of Directors in London and Governor-General Wellesley in India. Addington and Castlereagh had difficulty playing the role of mediators, and were able to satisfy Wellesley but not the Court. Twenty-three East India members deserted Addington as a result. This left the ministry with the support of only thirteen by April 1804, while the opposition had increased its total to at least fifty-six.[57] The loss of this support proved crucial.

Addington failed to get out the vote not only at election time but also for critical divisions in Parliament. The strong division against Pitt on Patten's motion in June 1803 had helped to keep Addington's majority solid for several months thereafter. He failed to ensure equally strong divisions, however, once Pitt decided to enter systematic opposition in March 1804. The problem was not so much winning over the support of the undecided or members of the opposition, as retaining the votes of traditional government supporters. In describing the division on Pitt's motion against St. Vincent on 15 March, Yorke noted that about fifty "of our *Friends* went away and would not vote."[58] Yorke also admitted that the government did a poor job of whipping for the division on 17 April.[59] While Pitt and Melville had been organizing their support since the end of March, the government did not begin to canvass for votes until a few days before the important divisions. Hawkesbury's carelessness actually led to a defeat in the Lords on a minor motion in April.

On the opposition side, Pitt and Melville demonstrated the importance of effective political management. Pitt had learned, over the course of seventeen years in office, effective strategies for ensuring parliamentary support. He made careful preparations prior to debates. He canvassed for opinion and lobbied in advance of introducing measures. He focused on winning the support of the more active M.P.s who were effective at influencing the votes of others. He arranged for key supporters to be appointed to parliamentary committees. Outside of Parliament, he built political ties through social intercourse at White's Club and the soirees hosted by Jane, the duchess of Gordon. When Pitt was prime minister, he had even employed Addington as smoother of personal relations with backbench M.P.s.[60]

Most important of all, he had Melville at his right hand. Melville for many years had been the most powerful man in Scotland. There had been a power vacuum in Scotland in the mid-eighteenth century, and he used the patronage at his disposal to increase his personal power. Largely as a result of his influence, Scotland, which had one-sixth the population of England, received one-quarter of government pensions and one-third of the sinecures. The support that this engendered, combined with a masterful control of elections in Scotland, gave him control of thirty-two seats compared to four for Addington and three for the Whigs after the 1802 election. By the end of 1803, he had more power in Scotland than the government had.[61] One of Addington's Scottish allies informed him that "it is still almost universally believed that Lord Melville and his friends enjoy the patronage of this country; the consequence of which is that in fact they still possess the whole of the power and influence attached to it. There is no County Meeting where they do not rule, there is no Public Meeting which they do not give the tone."[62] This was partly Addington's fault. He had largely deferred to Melville and his nephew William Dundas in the administration of Scotland and India, which increased their power. He then alienated Melville when he meddled in the elections for a few constituencies in Scotland and made changes to the list of Scottish pensions that Melville had drawn up. Addington also enraged Melville by objecting to the latter's corrupt methods and announcing an intention to manage Scotland more fairly and impartially. Melville consequently delivered the support of Scotland for Pitt's assault on Addington in March and April 1804. Melville "zealously whipped the Scottish members who, as Moira noted, obediently flocked southwards to deliver 'a thundering blow against Addington.'"[63]

The strength of the opposition increased dramatically during the month after Pitt declared open hostility to the government. Addington's failure to act earlier meant that the opposition began to gather momentum. The run on Addington's majority resembled a run on a bank, with supporters rushing to withdraw their political capital and invest it with Pitt, whose stock appeared to be rising.

Addington foresaw a parliamentary defeat on the horizon and nursed a strong distaste for the unsavory aspects of parliamentary politics. The loss of the support of Parliament provided him with an honorable pretext for resignation. Had he resigned any earlier, as Pitt suggested, it would have been insulting to the dignity of the office and the king. Defeat was now imminent. He could resign like a chess player facing an irrecoverable position. He sent an overture to Pitt through Castlereagh to discuss the best means of carrying on the government. Addington offered to resign if Pitt would give him assurance that he was not committed to bringing Fox and Grenville into office. Pitt remain steadfast in his refusal to discuss the matter with anyone but the king. On 22 April, hoping to speed up a change in the government, he wrote a letter to the king outlining his political views and presented it to Eldon. The Lord Chancellor did not deliver the letter until 27 April, as he wished to wait until after the debates in the Commons of 23 and 25 April and until the king had held his first council meeting since the onset of his latest illness.[64]

It was just prior to the decisive divisions that the Prince of Wales pressed Sheridan and Erskine to withdraw their support from Addington. In a division in the Commons on 23 April, the government majority dropped to fifty-two and Yorke declared that the game was up.[65] Two days later the majority dropped to thirty-nine. Hawkesbury tried to rally support for the vote in the Lords on a motion scheduled for 30 April proposed by George Granville, the second marquess of Stafford, on the defense of the country, but by then it was too late. Addington estimated that at best he could hope for a majority of ten. The opposition had a detailed lists of peers and their anticipated votes that projected for the government a majority of only thirteen.[66]

The votes in the Commons and Lords were equally conclusive.[67] On 26 April, Addington, without consulting his colleagues, went to the king and informed him of the necessity of resigning.[68] The king tried to dissuade him, offering to dissolve Parliament and to call a new election, but Addington refused. Addington then asked the king to consult Eldon about approaching Pitt to form a new government, unaware that Eldon had already done so two months earlier. Eldon showed the king Pitt's letter on 27 April, and two days later Addington met his cabinet and announced his intention to resign. On 30 April, Hawkesbury rose in the Lords and requested the postponement of Stafford's motion owing to important new developments, which everyone understood to mean that Addington was about to resign. A few hours later, Fox asked Addington privately in the Commons if this were so, which he affirmed. The House then dispersed amidst somber silence.[69]

Pitt, Grenville, and Fox had finally succeeded in overthrowing the government. Although Grenville and Fox were the first to enter systematic opposition, it was Pitt who gave the opposition the strength needed to threaten Addington's parliamentary majority. As Starhemberg pointed out, the resignation of the government was not "as a result of the general voice of the country," as some people assumed, "but solely of some prominent persons' exaggerated enthusiasm for Mr Pitt and the common wish of individuals from all parties to give themselves an opportunity to obtain any office whatsoever."[70]

Despite the decline in Addington's parliamentary majority, there were political observers in addition to the king who believed that

Addington should remain in office and fight the opposition. One of these was Warren Hastings. He met with Addington on 5 May and recorded the substance of their discussion in a memorandum. As he was not politically allied to anyone, he felt that he could accurately reflect public opinion. He claimed that despite what had happened in Parliament, public support for Addington was growing.

> The People see and know, that an ample, sufficient and well distributed provision has been made for their defence against the threatened invasion; they see resources called forth, for which no one gave this country credit; they are pleased with the economy of the public expenditure; they have proclaimed a spirit of zeal and unanimity, which they certainly neither showed, nor felt, during the last war nor during the late administration; they have not been intimidated by the power of arbitrary arrest, and endless imprisonments; and even your enemies admit your integrity, while they profligately sneer at it.

Despite Addington's lack of eloquence in parliamentary debate the public saw him as "prompt in reply, candid in explanation, and your mind stored with all the knowledge that can qualify you to discharge the arduous duties of your station." Hastings concluded by pressing Addington that he owed it to his king and country to remain in office.[71]

Hastings was not the only observer who regretted Addington's resignation. Addington would later receive a deluge of letters, including some from people he had never met, reflecting similar sentiments. Nevertheless, Addington's resolution was fixed. Five days later, on 10 May 1804, Addington returned the seals of office to the king. As a reward for service, the king offered Addington an earldom, the Garter, an annuity and a pension for Mrs. Addington of any amount that Addington desired. Addington declined them all.[72]

The collapse of the Addington ministry was the result of the combination of two factors. The first was the creation of a formidable opposition once Pitt joined Grenville and Fox to force the king to replace Addington. They concentrated their attacks on Addington's war policies for best effect, even though there was little substance to their criticisms. Addington could rightly ridicule them as "one man objecting to too great an extension of one part of our force, another lamenting any attempt at its diminution; some recommending a greater and some a lesser addition to the regular army, and others who differ as to that particular species of naval force we should employ; some preferring a large number of small vessels, and some a small number of large vessels."[73] On the contrary, Addington and his colleagues presented a thoughtful and reasonable response to the military challenges that they faced. Years later, Grey declared that Addington's "Military measures were the only ones which had hitherto produced any speedy or large augmentation of our army."[74] Starhemberg praised Addington for "the energy that he was able to inspire in the Nation in the present crisis, possibly the most important in which Great Britain has yet ever found itself."[75]

Nevertheless, criticism of the ministry had an important impact on Parliament owing to the debating skill of the opposition and high expectations that M.P.s held for Great Britain's performance in the war. Addington and his colleagues should have been able to parry these attacks and weather the political storm, but Addington handicapped himself by refusing to fight other politicians on their terms with all the traditional weapons of government at his disposal. If provoking an election and engaging Pitt in a bitter fight for control of seats was the only way that he could remain in office, then he was not interested. His failure was a failure of political will: he had no stomach for the kind of political fight that he faced in 1804, and was not prepared to pay the personal costs necessary to remain prime minister in those unsavory circumstances. He could face tough policy decisions, but he could not face the personal acrimony and underhandedness involved in a prolonged parliamentary struggle.

Lord Holland and others thought that Addington resigned to prevent the political crisis from causing a relapse in the king's health.[76] Addington told the Speaker of the House of Commons that the king dreaded the prospect of a defeat in Parliament because he feared it would drive him mad again. There was more to Addington's decision, however, than mere concern for the king. It seems evident that

Addington no longer wished to be prime minister. His last few weeks in office were miserable. Looking back on the year, he described it as "gloomy in almost all respects & to me the most painful of my life."[77] Pitt had long been Addington's most valued friend, and the loss of that friendship was more devastating than the political attacks in Parliament. Addington had not sought office in the first place. Leaving it was actually a great relief to him, even though the process was humiliating and created considerable personal ill-will. The most valid criticisms of Henry Addington as prime minister center on his lack of political determination. He was not willing to pay the price to remain in office when the situation in Parliament became tough. He was a natural conciliator, not well-suited to adversarial politics. He did not possess the killer instinct necessary for longevity in the office of prime minister.

Henry Addington's Legacy

istorians have often treated Addington's ministry as merely an interlude between the two Pitt ministries, but developments while Addington was in office had an important impact on the future of British politics. The most significant consequence was the emergence of Addington as a formidable parliamentary force. During his time in office, he gradually built a following that, by 1804, had grown to between forty and sixty-eight, second only to Pitt's.[1] Addington's influence over these men derived from his character and personality. They found him to be amicable and courteous. He was loyal to his friends and devoted to the king. For a man who had obtained the highest office, he was remarkably humble and self-effacing. Over the course of his political career he repeatedly refused offers of cabinet posts, sinecures, peerages, honors, and other financial and material rewards of the kind that many politicians coveted. He was not a social climber. Addington enjoyed the respect of the independent country gentlemen who did not respect other political leaders. Some of them looked to him as the most prominent politician who best represented their temperament and sentiments.

Ironically, Addington gained the support of many of his followers after he resigned as prime minister. Most of his supporters, both within and outside the cabinet, had originally been supporters of Pitt. While Pitt had supported Addington, there was no need for them to distinguish where their primary loyalty lay. It was only after Pitt made public his intention to drive Addington from office that they felt a need to choose. Many observers, including some of Pitt's former supporters, were disgusted at the manner in which he openly attacked Addington for the purpose of forcing his resignation. Addington received a deluge of letters consoling him for how unfairly he had been treated.[2] An anonymous observer from Yorkshire wrote to one of Addington's friends, "A grosser instance of political chicane, if not profligacy is not to be found in the Annals of our history. The dignified retreat of your friend has added no small lustre to his character and I trust a day will come when the duplicity of a certain great man will meet its reward. In this part of the country even the most violent partizans [*sic*] are displeased with the means by which the late administration was displaced."[3] The result was that some of Pitt's former supporters joined Addington out of contempt for the former and sympathy for the latter. Yorke was one of the cabinet ministers who originally had indicated that he wanted Pitt to replace Addington. He was so sickened, however, by the manner in which Pitt and his allies had forced Addington's resignation that he not only refused to support the new ministry, but also joined Addington in opposition. He said of joining Pitt, "I have determined to have nothing to do with it. 1. Because from the Part I have taken in arranging the measures of *Defence,* I cannot consent to eat my words; & 2ndly because I foresee nothing like the confidence or comfort [which he had enjoyed with Addington], *now,* in the society of Pitt & his associates."[4] Hobart and St. Vincent also joined Addington's party. Nelson was another who became closer to Addington after his resignation. On the night before he left on his last naval mission in 1805, he ate what would be his last meal in England at Addington's home and, using his finger soaked in red wine, drew out on Addington's tablecloth the plan of attack on the Franco-Spanish fleet that he would employ in the Battle of Trafalgar.[5] Addington also retained the support of some minor magnates. As a whole, this group was not remarkably talented or influential, but their major asset was their cohesiveness and loyalty. Addington could consistently count on the support of over half of this group on every division. Even those who disliked his policies or denigrated his talents admitted that he was an important political force. As a result of the precarious balance of political parties that emerged in Parliament after 1804, the way that Addington voted on individual issues played a key role in the survival of subsequent ministries. When on certain issues Addington voted with Fox and Grenville in opposition to Pitt, together they threatened Pitt's majority.

Addington never actively sought personal political support. His party formed spontaneously of its own accord for a variety of reasons. Once it had formed, however, he worked hard to keep it together. Addington proved to be the quintessential patron because he always put the interests of his friends before his own. His loyal band of supporters made him attractive to prime ministers who needed to shore up their support in Parliament. Whenever he negotiated joining government, he expressed no interest in office for himself, as long as his friends were adequately provided for.[6] The ministers who sought his support insisted, however, that he be included in the cabinet, in order to ensure that his supporters would remain loyal to the government. The price that prime ministers paid for Addington's support was cabinet offices for a few of his friends and minor offices for several others.[7] Nevertheless, Addington was discerning in proposing offices for his friends. He was careful to evaluate their strengths and weaknesses and suggest offices to which they were suited. He would attempt to secure cabinet posts for those who were qualified. He would suggest only lesser offices for his brother Hiley and friends he knew did not have the skills necessary for cabinet office.

Although Canning unfairly censured Addington for the patronage of his relations, this was in fact an established administrative practice. Pitt's brother and cousin were in his cabinet. Most of the great Whig families (who were related by marriage to one another) also included their relatives in their administrations. In the context of the unreformed political system, it was good for party unity and for the efficient administration of business for ministers to work with their relations. One of the best examples is the added strength that Foreign Secretary Wellesley enjoyed in implementing his Spanish diplomacy during the Peninsular War, as a result of having one brother, Arthur, Viscount Wellington, as commander in chief of the British forces in the Peninsula and another, Henry Wellesley, as the British envoy to Spain.[8] Compared with many other ministers, Addington's dispensation of patronage to his relations was restrained.

Addington's rise to the status of one of the most powerful men in Parliament corresponded with the breakup of traditional parliamentary alliances that occurred during his term in office. For the seventeen years prior to 1801, British politics had been characterized by the greatest ministerial stability for more than forty years. Over the course of his long first term, Pitt had solidified his position in Parliament and consolidated executive power in the hands of Dundas, Grenville, and himself. After his resignation in 1801, however, the nature of parliamentary politics changed completely. The next twelve years were characterized by ministerial instability and political uncertainty, which resulted in the forming of six different ministries. After 1804, governments were constantly conscious of the fragility of their parliamentary majorities and were defeated on several occasions.

The most important consequence of Addington's term as prime minister was the eventual split between Pitt and Grenville. They had already begun to grow apart during their last years in government together, but their first fundamental divergence of policy was over the Preliminary Treaty, the Treaty of Amiens, and the support that Pitt continued to give Addington afterward. While Grenville strove to build the nucleus of a new opposition, Pitt rejected any formal commitments. As a result of Pitt's refusal to join him, Grenville made a pact with Fox to oust Addington and establish a broad-based ministry. This alliance grew into a firm political commitment. When the king refused to allow Fox into Pitt's second ministry, Grenville refused to serve without Fox. Grenville then entered systematic opposition with the Foxites and most of the former members of the Portland Whigs. Together these three groups formed a new and stronger

Whig party that, after forming a government in 1806–7, presented a formidable opposition to the ministries led by Portland, Perceval, and the second earl of Liverpool after 1807.

As a result of his split with Grenville, Pitt's second ministry was merely a shadow of his first. Deprived of his former foreign secretary, First Lord of the Admiralty, and secretary at War, he was left constructing a ministry out of his closest friends and some of Addington's ministers—Hawkesbury, Castlereagh, Eldon, Portland, Westmorland, and Chatham—whom he reappointed just after having forced their prime minister's resignation. Liverpool, whose son was a member of both ministries, claimed that "If We compare the Individuals of which the late administration was composed, with those of the present, We shall find the present much weaker than the preceding one, except in the single Case of Mr Pitt."[9] Admiral Sir Charles Morice Pole indicated that parliamentary opinion agreed with Liverpool: "The Politicians still assert that Mr Pitt hath not been more successful in recruiting Members of Parliament, than in encreasing [sic] the Force of the country, or in successful enterprises against the Enemy."[10] Pitt had justified his opposition to Addington on the premise that the difficulties facing the country required a stronger and more effective government, but the ministry that he was able to form was hardly a significant improvement. Despite his great reputation, Pitt was unable to bring into office with him any politicians of substance, other than Melville, and his majority in the Commons was no larger than Addington's at the time of his resignation.[11]

Having failed to include Grenville and the Whigs in his government, Pitt desperately required additional support in Parliament. For this reason he invited Addington to join his ministry in December 1804. The king also played an important role in reconciling Pitt and Addington. Still fond of Addington, the king had desired for some time that he join Pitt's government. Aware that Addington harbored bad feeling toward Pitt, the king waited for sufficient time to elapse to let tempers cool before engaging Hawkesbury as an intermediary. Hawkesbury succeeded in establishing a basis for negotiations and facilitated a meeting between Addington and Pitt at Christmas 1804 that led to a reconciliation. The deal they struck required Addington to accept a peerage despite his usual objections. Pitt felt there would be difficulties if Addington remained in the Commons because of all that had passed between them over the previous two years. Addington complied by taking the title Viscount Sidmouth and the post of Lord President of the Council.

The Pitt-Addington alliance was, however, doomed from the start. Some of Addington's friends had reservations about Addington joining Pitt's government. "It is necessity alone which hath forced the Minister to this proposition,"said Admiral Pole. "I cannot help feeling much regret at all these arrangements, as I am confident they have been provided by the Envy & Jealousy of Mr Pitt who now wishes to entail on Addington the odium of supporting Measures, the very reverse of those adopted by his administration."[12] These comments proved prescient. Events that had occurred when Addington had been prime minister precipitated Addington's eventual resignation from Pitt's government. St. Vincent's controversial commission of inquiry uncovered abuses for which Melville, as treasurer of the navy many years before, had been responsible. This gave the opposition the opportunity to propose a motion in the Commons to impeach him. Pitt expected that Addington's followers, as members of the government, would support Melville. Nevertheless, some of them harbored resentment against Pitt for his vociferous attacks on St. Vincent's reforms and Melville for commandeering the Scottish parliamentary troops against Addington in 1804. Faced with the choice of upholding the reputation of St. Vincent, who had remained loyal to Addington, or defending Melville, who had betrayed him, many chose the former. Melville lost the vote and resigned as First Lord of the Admiralty. Piqued that so many Addingtonians voted against Melville, Pitt broke a promise to Addington that the next cabinet vacancy would be given to Hobart. Pitt instead appointed Charles Middleton, Lord Barham, who was a friend of Melville. He also reneged on promises to find posts for Hiley Addington and another of Addington's friends. Addington could forgive Pitt for betraying him in 1804, but he could not stomach Pitt betraying his friends in 1805. He resigned in September 1805. Pitt's ministry hobbled on until his death four months later. It was ironic that the composition of Pitt's ministry during the early months of 1805 was precisely along the lines that Addington had envisioned when negotiating with Pitt in April 1803. A ministry led by Pitt with Melville, Hawkesbury, Castlereagh, Eldon, Hobart, and himself was just what Addington intended. Instead, Pitt's inflexibility and unwillingness to negotiate cost him an opportunity in 1803 of achieving a government that would have been stronger than the one he formed in 1804. It also cost Melville's career.

The strength and loyalty of Addington's following also made him very attractive to the Whig leaders, despite their previously marked differences on policy. During the last months of Pitt's life, Fox and the Prince of Wales pushed for a coalition with the Addingtonians rather than the Pittites. Lord Holland explained, "The disunited rump of Mr Pitt's Ministry were no party whereas Lord Sidmouth's friends . . . formed a compact body and . . . were more respectable than the clerks and secretaries of Mr Pitt's and Lord Melville's school. . . . *It will stop up all the earths* was Mr Fox's expression to me."[13] After Pitt's death, the king set aside his personal animosity to Fox and asked Grenville to form a Whig government. Grenville and Fox then required the security of the support of the solid block of Addingtonians. The Whigs had the talent and the weight but lacked numbers, and the inclusion of Addington as Lord Privy Seal ensured a ministerial majority in Parliament. The king also played an important role in Addington's inclusion. Although he abandoned his veto of Fox, the king still distrusted the Whigs and desired the inclusion of Addington, a close personal friend who shared many of his political views.

While Addington's term as prime minister had raised his political stock, his experience serving in Pitt's and Grenville's ministries tarnished his reputation and led to a decrease in the number of his supporters. His decision to abandon Pitt in 1805 and join the Whigs in 1806 diminished his reputation in the eyes of the independent country gentlemen. Grenville called an election in 1806 that cost the Addingtonians almost twenty seats. Grenville and the Whigs soon fell out with the king over the issue of Catholic Emancipation and were replaced by a group of Pitt's supporters under the leadership of Portland. The new government called another election in 1807 that returned to Addington most of the seats he had lost the year before, giving him the largest following in Parliament independent of the king's friends or the patronage of the prime minister.[14] Nevertheless, many members of the Portland cabinet, particularly Canning, refused to forgive Addington for abandoning Pitt and joining the Whigs. Although the government desperately required additional support in the Commons and would have welcomed the assistance of the Addingtonians, it was not possible at that time to include Addington in the cabinet.

The importance of Addington and his supporters became even more clear after Spencer Perceval (who had been attorney general under Addington) succeeded Portland in 1809. His ministry was extremely weak. Although he could not invite Addington to join the cabinet, he tried to recruit Bragge and Vansittart, each of whom he offered the position of chancellor of the Exchequer, but they would not accept unless Addington joined the cabinet as well.[15] The strength of the Addingtonians was apparent in the Commons in January 1810: when they voted with the government on a motion concerning the Peninsular War, the government majority was ninety-six; but when they voted against the government on a motion critical of a failed British invasion of Walcheren in Holland in 1809, the government lost by nine votes. For most of the period between 1807 and 1812, Addington and his followers assumed a nonaligned position, voting with the government on policies that they supported. Ministerial changes under the regency of 1811 led eventually to Addington's return to government. The king had another attack of porphyria from which he did not recover. The prince regent tried to form a stronger government that would include members of both the government and the opposition. The failure of these negotiations resulted in resignations from Perceval's cabinet in 1812. Perceval responded by appointing Castlereagh to the vacant post of foreign secretary and turning to Addington to shore up the ministerial benches as Lord President of the Council. It made sense at that time to strengthen the government by reuniting the remaining Pittites and Addingtonians who held similar political views.

Shortly after Addington joined the government Perceval was assassinated by a merchant whose business the war had ruined. After the failure of another round of negotiations to form a new government, the responsibility of prime minister fell upon Lord Hawkesbury, Addington's former foreign secretary, who had succeeded his father as the second earl of Liverpool in 1808. The personnel in the cabinet that Liverpool assembled closely resembled Addington's cabinet. Recognizing the talent for administration that Addington had demonstrated as prime minister, Liverpool appointed him to the important office of home secretary. He also appointed to the cabinet Vansittart and Bragge, indicating how important it was to Liverpool to retain Addington's support. Liverpool's cabinet also included Castlereagh, Hobart, Eldon, and Westmorland, who had all served under Addington. Liverpool's government lasted fifteen years, surviving a number of domestic and diplomatic challenges during the remaining years of the war and the first years of the postwar period. The Addingtonians gradually retired from the cabinet after 1822. Over the years, many members of Addington's original cabinet developed into able administrators. Their experience of office under Addington was a springboard to their careers. These men held important offices in the cabinet for most of their lives. The success of their political careers attests to the importance of Addington's term as prime minister on the twenty years of British politics that followed.

Addington's legacy can also be measured in terms of his policies. The most significant was the signing of the Treaty of Amiens. Contemporaries and historians criticized the terms but recognized that the peace provided a necessary breathing space for the recovery of the British economy and the armed forces. Even Windham, who had originally opposed the treaty, came around to this point of view. In 1809, he confessed to Addington that he had "for some time wished to tell you, that I am thoroughly convinced, if it had not been for the peace of Amiens this country could never have maintained the struggle to the present period." Windham acknowledged that the British public would not have accepted the high levels of wartime taxation had not the experience of the peace demonstrated that it was impossible to remain at peace on any terms with Bonaparte.[16] There was insufficient evidence to justify this conclusion in 1801, but the course of Anglo-French diplomacy during the peace had provided ample proof by 1803. The experience of negotiating the treaty and subsequent French policies demonstrated that British interests would not remain secure until Bonaparte had been decisively defeated. Even Fox, who strongly opposed the war, came to this conclusion after his experience as foreign secretary in 1806. Subsequent ministries saw no choice but to continue the war, even in the face of dire strategic and economic circumstances.

The style of British diplomacy under Addington influenced Castlereagh in forming the Final Coalition with Russia, Prussia, and Austria in 1813–14. Continental allies would fight effectively only when fighting was clearly in their interests. Addington's negotiations with the Russians, Austrians, and Prussians from 1801 to 1804 demonstrated that he understood the prospective allies' positions and tried to find means by which British and allied war aims could be satisfied together. British security depended on cooperating with the Continental powers, requiring the British to sacrifice some of their minor interests. This was the secret to the success of Castlereagh, Prince Clemens von Metternich, and Tsar Alexander I, who nine years later devised a war strategy and peace settlement that would secure the vital interests of all parties.[17]

Future ministries also followed up on a number of specific policies that Addington initiated. With the formation of the Third Coalition in 1805, Pitt brought to fruition the attempts to build a Continental alliance around Russia. Pitt also executed the proposal to build a series of Martello towers across the south coast of England. The decisions of the Portland ministry to fight the French in Portugal and Spain and provide a fleet to escort the king of Portugal to Brazil were strategies that Addington's cabinet had originally proposed. Addington also demonstrated managerial skill in making several lasting administrative changes. His removal of government offices from the Civil List remained permanent. Addington also transferred responsibility for colonial administration from the Home Office to the War Office. Expecting that the Home Office would acquire more business as a result of the Union with Ireland, Addington felt that transferring the colonies to the War Office would be advantageous in spreading the work more equitably. This would also ensure that the war secretary would retain administrative responsibilities in peacetime. Addington and his colleagues initiated a number of reforms that were implemented by future governments. Despite the political crisis caused by the commission of inquiry into the Royal Navy, future governments adopted most of St. Vincent's naval reforms. St. Vincent's immediate successors reversed his policies, but once the reports of the commission of inquiry were placed before Parliament, Grenville's cabinet successfully re-implemented them. Naval administration was thereafter more rational and efficient. Although Pitt and Windham largely dismantled Addington's militia and volunteer legislation, Castlereagh used them as the basis for his successful military reforms, which proved crucial to winning the Peninsular War.

Addington's experience in office also illustrates the pervading influence of the king in British politics and administration. By the late 1790s, it had appeared that Pitt, who originally owed his position to the power of the king, had entrenched himself in office so securely that he no longer required continuing royal support. The king's ability to block Catholic Emancipation, however, undermined that idea. The appointment of Addington as the king's personal choice was another expression of the power of the king. The parliamentary instability that followed Addington's appointment provided greater scope for the power and influence of the king and the prince regent.

In a broader perspective, Addington's term in office proved an important link in the development of the financial and military power structure of Great Britain.[18] During the eighteenth century, the British government grew into one of the largest and most efficient in Europe, primarily through the development of a robust system of taxation to meet the growing demands of war. Addington's revision of the income tax was a critical component in enabling the considerable increase in government spending that occurred over the course of the Napoleonic Wars.[19] Pitt's income tax, as revised by Addington, remained in place until 1816. Prime Minister Sir Robert Peel revived it again in 1842, and by the end of the nineteenth century, it had become a critical source of revenue. Although there were amendments to the tax, it retained the system of schedules and the principle of taxation at the source that Addington introduced. Addington's innovation of reviewing the state of the economy during the budget speech in 1802 emphasized the strong connections between the fate of the economy and the government finances. It also set a precedent that all subsequent chancellors of the Exchequer have followed, and the detailed budget speech has become a key feature of sessions of the legislature in countries that follow the British parliamentary system.

One of the key components in the formation of the British national identity during the eighteenth and early-nineteenth centuries was the transforming of Great Britain to the "Nation in Arms," in which Addington played an important role. Addington's declaration of war and his manpower policies increased popular participation in, and identification with, the war against Bonaparte to an unprecedented level. Popular support for the war in 1803 appeared as strong as it had been for peace in 1801. Addington had taken a gamble in entrusting weapons to such a large number of people from all regions and social classes, but the gamble paid off. They did not use the weapons to revolt, and his policies helped to foster a sense of British nationalism that crossed class lines. The determination to fight Bonaparte—the common enemy—brought together people from all levels of British society.[20]

When Addington became home secretary in 1812, he took the same approach to dealing with social unrest during difficult economic times as he had taken when he had been prime minister. In dealing with riots and sedition, he employed the legislative and legal framework that Pitt originally had developed, but only in particular circumstances where evidence convinced him that the threat to order was serious. He was less aggressive in resorting to repressive measures than many local officials desired him to be. He demonstrated this in 1819 in his approach to a series of large public meetings on the subject of parliamentary reform that culminated in a tragedy known as the Peterloo Massacre. Prior to a planned mass meeting at St. Peter's Fields in Manchester, Addington had sent instructions to the local magistrates not to disperse the crowd unless it became violent. The magistrates acted in defiance of his orders, and sent in a regiment of volunteers to arrest the speaker.[21] The result was that eleven people were killed and more than four hundred wounded. When Addington discovered the details of the massacre, he realized that, even though the magistrates had disobeyed his instructions, any attempt to censure them would have a detrimental effect on the administration of order by local officials across the country. In his mind, the only course of action was to commend the magistrates at Manchester, even though the public of would transfer blame to his shoulders. Addington did not hesitate to accept responsibility for the errors of his subordinates, even though they had acted contrary to his instructions, and this style of leadership inspired the loyalty of his followers.

Addington's term in office provided a crucial link in a long chain of developments in diplomacy, military strategy, social policy, financial affairs, and parliamentary politics. The subsequent history of British politics in the early nineteenth century cannot properly be understood without reference to the important effects of Addington's policies and the political consequences that occurred as a result of them. The history of Addington's ministry also places the years of the French Revolutionary and Napoleonic Wars into better perspective and underlines the most important characteristics of the unreformed political system. Addington's term as prime minister was the product of the peculiar and complicated world of late-eighteenth- and early-nineteenth-century British politics, and illustrates many of the interesting features of that era.

Addington possessed some of the qualities of a great prime minister, but was deficient in certain respects. He was not a brilliant parliamentarian, but he was an able administrator and a sound policy-

maker. He demonstrated courage, boldness, and fortitude. He withstood insults, abuse, and ridicule without responding in kind. He had
an enormous capacity for forgiveness, as he demonstrated by reconciling with Pitt in 1804 and again in 1806. He also initiated a reconciliation with Canning in 1812. This was the more remarkable given that
even Canning recognized he was himself the most to blame for their
estrangement.[22] Addington never sought scapegoats for his own mistakes, but rather shouldered the blame for the mistakes of others. His
loyalty to his king, his country, and his friends took priority over his
own personal considerations. He was not interested in power, titles, or
financial rewards for their own sake, but only as a means to serve his
king, country, and friends. Having accepted office reluctantly, he did
not regret having to resign. He was hurt, however, that men he had
long considered close personal friends were treating him as if he was
their political enemy.

Addington was by nature too sentimental ever to have become a
truly great prime minister. Philip Henry, the fifth Earl Stanhope, Pitt's
nineteenth-century biographer who had known Addington, stated,
"During the whole of his long career he was most justly esteemed and
beloved in all the relations of private life."[23] Addington would have
been pleased to have had that for his epitaph. After a battle with
influenza, Addington died on 15 February 1844, aged 86, at White
Lodge, his house in Richmond Park, surrounded by loving friends
and family. He knew that he would never receive a public funeral like
Nelson, Pitt, or Fox, but only a small service for friends and family at
his local parish church in Mortlake. Looking back over the course of
his life, he would not have had it any other way.

Abbreviations

Add. MSS	British Library, Additional Manuscripts
Adm.	Admiralty Office Records, Public Record Office
AE	Correspondance Politique, Archives du Ministère des Affaires Etrangères, Paris
AKV	Count Semen de Vorontsov, *Arkhiv kniazia Vorontsova*, ed. P. I. Bartenev, 40 vols. (Moscow, 1870–97)
Aspinall	*The Later Correspondence of George III*, ed. Arthur Aspinall, 5 vols. (Cambridge: Cambridge University Press, 1961–70)
Colchester Diary	*The Diary and Correspondence of Charles Abbot, Lord Colchester, Speaker of the House of Commons 1802–1817*, ed. Charles, Lord Colchester, 3 vols. (London, 1861)
Dropmore Papers	William Lord Grenville, *Historical Manuscripts Commission: Report on the Manuscripts of J. B. Fortescue, esq. Preserved at Dropmore*, 10 vols. (London: Historical Manuscripts Commission, 1892–1927)
FO	Foreign Office Records, Public Record Office
Glenbervie Diaries	Lord Glenbervie, *The Diaries of Sylvester Douglas, Lord Glenbervie*, ed. Francis Bickley, 2 vols. (London: Constable, 1928)
HHStA	Haus-, Hof-, und Staatsarchiv, Vienna
HO	Home Office Archives, Public Record Office
Malmesbury Diaries	Earl of Malmesbury, *The Diaries and Correspondence of James Harris, First Earl of Malmesbury*, ed. third Earl of Malmesbury, 4 vols. (London, 1844)

MS Loan	British Library, Manuscripts Loan
Parliamentary Debates	*Hansard's Parliamentary Debates from the Year 1803 to the Present Time, Published under the Super-intendence of T. C. Hansard.* first series, 41 vols. (London, 1803–20)
Parliamentary History	*Parliamentary History of England: From the Earliest Period to the Year 1803,* 36 vols. (London, 1806–20)
Pellew	George Pellew, *The Life and Correspondence of the Right Honourable Henry Addington, First Viscount Sidmouth,* 3 vols. (London, 1847)
PRO	Public Record Office
SIRIO	*Sbornik Imperatorskogo Russkogo istoricheskogo obshchestva,* 140 vols. (St. Petersburg, 1867–1916)
Stanhope	Philip Henry, Earl Stanhope, *Life of Pitt,* 3 vols. (3rd ed. London, 1879). Note: this edition is in three volumes, and therefore the page numbers will differ from other editions that are in four volumes.
VPR	A. L. Narochnitskii et al., ed., *Vneshniaia politika Rossii XIX i nachala XX veka: Dokumenty rossiiskogo ministerstva inostrannykh del,* first series, 15 vols. (Moscow: Komissiia po izdaniiu diplo matich-eskikh dokumentov, 1960)
Ziegler	Philip Ziegler, *Addington: The Life of Henry Addington, First Viscount Sidmouth, 1757–1844* (London: Collins, 1965)

Notes

INTRODUCTION

1. During the period of 1801–4, a few individuals received peerages that resulted in changes in their names. I have noted the change of name in the text, and used the later name in subsequent references. Henry Addington received a peerage in 1805, but for the purposes of the epilogue, I have continued to use the name Addington.

2. George Pretyman Tomline, *Memoirs of the Life of William Pitt,* 4 vols. (London, 1821); *Malmesbury Diaries;* Henry Richard, Lord Holland, *Memoirs of the Whig Party during My Time,* ed. Henry Edward, Lord Holland, 2 vols. (London, 1852); Lord John Russell, *Memorials and Correspondence of Charles James Fox,* 4 vols. (London, 1853–7); Duke of Buckingham and Chandos, *Memoirs of the Court and Cabinets of George III,* 4 vols. (London, 1853–55); William Windham, *The Diary of the Rt. Hon. William Windham, 1784 to 1810,* ed. Mrs. Henry Baring, 4 vols. (London, 1866); John Holland Rose, *William Pitt and the Great War* (London: G. Bell & Sons, 1911); Arthur Bryant, *The Years of Endurance, 1793–1802* (London: Collins, 1942) and *The Years of Victory 1802–1812* (London: Collins, 1945); John Fortescue, *The County Lieutenancies and the Army, 1803–1814* (London: Macmillan, 1909).

3. L. G. Mitchell, *Charles James Fox* (Oxford: Oxford University Press, 1992); Amanda Foreman, *Georgiana: The Duchess of Devonshire* (London: Harper Collins, 1998).

4. Christopher Hibbert, *George III: A Personal History* (London: Viking, 1998), 8–32.

5. C. Northcote Parkinson, *War in the Eastern Seas, 1793–1815* (London: George Allen & Unwin, 1954), 152–55.

6. *Glenbervie Diaries,* 1:60; Charles John Fedorak, "The Royal Navy and British Amphibious Operations during the Revolutionary and Napoleonic Wars, 1793–1815," *Military Affairs* 52 (1988): 144–45.

7. A. B. Rodger, *The War of the Second Coalition: A Strategic Commentary* (Oxford: Clarendon Press, 1964), 277; John Holland Rose, "The Struggle with Revolutionary France, 1793–1801" and "The Contest with Napoleon, 1802–1812," in *The Cambridge History of British Foreign Policy,* ed. A. Ward and G. P. Gooch (Cambridge: Cambridge University Press, 1922), 1:304; Paul Langford, *The Eighteenth Century, 1688–1815* (London: A. & C. Black, 1976); Paul Kennedy, *The Rise and Fall of British Naval Mastery*

(London: Allen Lane, 1976), 133–43; Ian R. Christie, *Wars and Revolutions: Britain, 1760–1815* (London: Edward Arnold, 1982), 258; J. Steven Watson, *The Reign of George III, 1760–1815* (Oxford: Clarendon Press, 1960), 403.

8. Ole Feldbaek, *Denmark and the Armed Neutrality, 1800–1801* (Copenhagen: Akademisk Forlag, 1980), 17–54.

9. S. Vorontsov to A. Vorontsov, 22 Mar. 1801, *AKV,* 10:89; Roderick E. McGrew, *Paul I of Russia, 1754–1801* (Oxford: Clarendon Press, 1992), 316.

10. Jeremy Black, *Britain as a Military Power, 1688–1815* (London: UCL Press, 1999), 267; John Brewer, *The Sinews of Power: War, Money and the English State 1688–1783* (London: Unwin Hyman, 1989), 167–217.

11. Charles John Fedorak, "Maritime versus Continental Strategy: Britain and the Defeat of Napoleon," *Proceedings of the Consortium on Revolutionary Europe, 1750–1850* 20 (1989): 176–82.

12. Gerald Newman, *The Rise of English Nationalism: A Cultural History, 1740–1830* (London: Weidenfield & Nicolson, 1987), 63, 75.

13. Linda Colley, *Britons: Forging the Nation, 1707–1837* (New Haven, Conn.: Vintage, 1992), 5.

14. Jeremy Black, *Natural and Necessary Enemies: Anglo-French Relations in the Eighteenth Century* (London: Duckworth, 1986), 181.

15. Newman, *Rise of English Nationalism,* 63–122; Colley, *Britons,* 88–90; Black, *Natural and Necessary Enemies,* 133; John Brewer, *The Pleasures of the Imagination: English Culture in the Eighteenth Century* (Chicago: University of Chicago Press, 1997), 82–86.

16. Black, *Natural and Necessary Enemies,* 102–3.

17. *Annual Register 1801,* "History of Europe," 117; Clive Emsley, *British Society and the French Wars, 1793–1815* (London: Macmillan, 1979), 65–90; Watson, *Reign of George III,* 406–9.

18. For regional and national studies of unrest see John Bohstedt, *Riots and Community Politics in England and Wales, 1790–1810* (Cambridge, Mass.: Harvard University Press, 1983); Alan Booth, "Food Riots in the North West of England, 1790–1801," *Past and Present* 78 (1977): 84–107; Andrew Charlesworth, ed., *An Atlas of Rural Protest in Britain, 1548–1900,* (London: Croon Helm, 1982); Marianne Elliott, *Partners in Revolution: The United Irishmen and France* (London: Yale University Press, 1982); J. Ann Hone, *For the Cause of Truth: Radicalism in London, 1796–1821* (Oxford: Clarendon Press, 1983); George Rudé, *Hanoverian London, 1714–1808* (London: Secker and Warburg, 1971); John Stevenson, "Food Riots in England, 1792–1818," in *Popular Protest and Public Order,* ed. R. Quinault and J. Stevenson (London: George Allen & Unwin, 1974), 33–69; E. P. Thompson, *The Making of the English Working Class* (Harmondsworth: Penguin, 1982); Roger Wells, *Dearth and Distress in Yorkshire, 1793–1802* (York: Borthwick Institute of Historical Research, 1977), *Insurrection: The British Experience, 1795–1803* (Gloucester: Alan Sutton, 1983), and *Wretched Faces: Famine in Wartime England, 1793–1801* (London: Alan Sutton, 1988).

19. George Rose, *The Diaries and Correspondence of Rt. Hon. George Rose,* ed. L. V. Harcourt, 2 vols. (London, 1860), 1:285.

20. Thompson, *Making of the English Working Class,* 519.

21. Wells, *Insurrection,* 183–4.

22. Watson, *Reign of George III,* 407.

23. Wells, *Insurrection,* 178–80.

24. Ibid., 183; Emsley, *British Society,* 86.

25. Watson, *Reign of George III,* 407; Henry MacLeod, *The Theory and Practice of Banking,* 2 vols. (London, 1876), 1:465, 2:2.

26. Arthur Gayer, W. W. Rostow, and A. J. Schwartz, *The Growth of the British Economy, 1790–1850* (Oxford: Clarendon Press, 1953), 145.

27. *Glenbervie Diaries,* 1:151, 204; Yorke to Abbott, 18 Aug. 1801, PRO 30/9/120, fos. 3–6; *Times,* 7 Feb. 1801.

28. Sidmouth Papers 152M/c1801/OM34; *Parliamentary History,* 36:1279; N. G. Cox, "Aspects of British Radicalism: The Suppression and Re-emergence of the Constitutional Democratic Tradition, 1795–1809" (Ph.D. diss., University of Cambridge, 1971), 29; Wells, *Insurrection,* 184–87.

29. Thompson, *Making of the English Working Class,* 517; A. D. Harvey, *Britain in the Early Nineteenth Century* (New York: St. Martin's Press, 1978), 78.

30. Viscount Castlereagh, *Memoirs and Correspondence of Robert Stewart, Viscount Castlereagh,* ed. Marquess of Londonderry, 12 vols. (London, 1848–54), 3:377.

31. J. R. Western, "The Volunteer Movement as an Anti-Revolutionary Force, 1793–1801," *English Historical Review* 71 (1956): 603–4.

32. Wells, *Insurrection;* Ian R. Christie, *Stress and Stability in Late Eighteenth-Century Britain: Reflections on the British Avoidance of Revolution* (Oxford: Clarendon Press, 1984).

33. Add. MSS 19696.

34. Add. MSS 39901 f. 62b.

35. Pellew, 1:30.

36. Pitt to Addington, 4 Jan. 1786, quoted in Pellew, 1:40.

37. Pellew, 1:63.

38. Charlotte Addington to Dr. Addington, 4 May 1787, quoted in Pellew, 1:47.

39. Ziegler, 57.

40. *Glenbervie Diaries,* 1:332.

41. Michael Duffy, *The Younger Pitt* (London: Longman, 2000), 114.

42. Foreman, *Georgiana,* 342–43.

43. Lord Hatherton, "Extracts from Lord Hatherton's Diary", ed. A. Aspinall, *Parliamentary Affairs* 17 (1964): 383.

44. J. A. Manning, *Lives of the Speakers of the House of Commons* (London, 1851), 467.

45. Quoted in Manning, *Lives,* 469.

46. Robert Southey, *Letters from England,* ed. Jack Simmons (London: Cresset, 1951), 71–74.

CHAPTER 1

1. Charles John Fedorak, "Catholic Emancipation and the Resignation of William Pitt in 1801," *Albion* 24 (1992): 49–64.

2. "State of the Cabinet 1800," Add. MSS 40102, fos. 79–81.

3. Hibbert, *George III,* 8–32.

4. The king to Pitt, 18 June 1800, Aspinall, 3:363.

5. Fedorak, "Catholic Emancipation," 56.

6. Pellew, 1:108.

7. Ziegler, 66.

8. Pitt to Chatham, 5 Feb. 1801, Edward, Lord Ashbourne, *Pitt: Some Chapters of His Life and Times* (London, 1898), 311.

9. *Glenbervie Diaries,* 1:150, 189–90.

10. Dundas to Pitt, 7 Feb. 1801, in John Holland Rose, *William Pitt and the Great War,* 440–41, also quoted in Aspinall, 3:488n.

11. The king to Pitt, 22 Apr. 1797, Aspinall, 2:566.

12. Ziegler, 55.

13. Ziegler, 94–95.

14. Stanhope, 2:292–95; *Colchester Diary,* 1:222–23, 230, 233; *Glenbervie Diaries,* 1:160–61, 278, 333; Pellew, 1:285–88, 230; Addington to Simcoe, 23 Feb. 1801, Pellew, 1:331; Mrs. Bragge to Mrs. Goodenough, 5 Feb. 1801, Pellew, 1:297.

15. Yorke to Mrs Hardwicke, 11 Feb. 1801, Yorke MS Eng. lett. c. 60, fos. 3–4; Memorandum 1801, Hobart Papers, D/MH/H/War/B7; Memorandum on Speakership, Redesdale Papers, D2002/X11; Earl of St. Vincent, *Letters of Admiral of the Fleet, the Earl of St. Vincent, 1801–1804,* ed. David. B. Smith, 2 vols. (London: Navy Records Society, 1922–27), 1:14; George Rose, *The Diaries and Correspondence of Rt. Hon. George Rose,* 1:299; *Glenbervie Diaries,* 1:295.

16. Hobart to Dundas, 14 Feb. 1801, Melville Castle Muniments, GD 51/1/62; *Colchester Diary,* 1:230.

17. Glenbervie Manuscript Diary, 4: 14 Feb. 1801; *Glenbervie Diaries,* 1:179, 222; J.-M. Alter, "The Early Life and Political Career of Robert Banks Jenkinson, Second Earl of Liverpool, 1790–1812" (Ph.D. diss., University College Wales, Aberystwyth, 1988), 53–136; Patrick Polden, "Domestic Policies of the Addington Administration, 1801–1804" (Ph.D. diss., University of Reading, 1975), 72; Judith Brown, "The Early Career of Robert Banks Jenkinson, Second Earl of Liverpool, 1790–1812: The Making of the Arch Mediocrity" (Ph.D. diss., University of Delaware, 1980), 106; *Parliamentary History,* 35:1113.

18. Pellew, 1:300n; Charles B. Arthur, *The Remaking of the English Navy by Admiral St. Vincent—Key to Victory over Napoleon: The Great Unclaimed Naval Revolution,*

1795–1805 (London: University Press of America, 1986), iv; The king to Addington, 9 Feb. 1801, Aspinall, 3:494; Addington to the king, 9 Feb. 1801, Aspinall, 3:491–93; John R. Breihan, "The Addington Party and the Navy in British Politics, 1801–1806," in *New Aspects of Naval History*, ed. Craig L. Symonds (Annapolis: Naval Institute Press, 1981), 164–65.

19. Glenbervie Manuscript Diary, 4: 10, 19, and 20 Feb. 1801; *Malmesbury Diaries,* 4:8; Aspinall, 3:505n; Lord William Auckland, *The Journal and Correspondence of William, Lord Auckland,* ed. G. Hogge, 4 vols. (London, 1861), 4:128; Memorandum 1801, Hobart Papers, D/MH/H/War/B7.

20. York to his mother, 11 Feb. 1801, Yorke MS. Eng. lett. c. 60, fos. 3–4, also quoted in Aspinall, 3:525n.

21. Duffy, *The Younger Pitt,* 118 and 122.

22. Hatherton, "Extracts from Lord Hatherton's Diary," 384.

23. Horace Twiss, *The Public and Private Life of Lord Chancellor Eldon, with Selections from his Correspondence,* 3 vols. (London, 1844), 1:138, 367; *Glenbervie Diaries,* 1:201; George Rose, *The Diaries and Correspondence of Rt. Hon. George Rose,* 1:310.

24. Glenbervie Manuscript Diary, 4: 14 and 16 Feb. 1801 and 5: 17 Mar. 1801; *Malmesbury Diaries,* 4:6; *Glenbervie Diaries,* 1:164; Aspinall, 3:499n.

25. Stanhope, 2:415.

26. Cooke to Castlereagh, 7 Mar. 1801, *Castlereagh Correspondence,* (London, 1848–54), 4:78.

27. *Colchester Diary,* 1:248.

28. Otto to Talleyrand, 1 brumaire X (23 Oct. 1801), AE Angleterre/597. In the references to the French diplomatic correspondence, I have noted the dates according to the Revolutionary calendar and provided their equivalents from the Gregorian calendar in parentheses.

29. John Lord Campbell, *Lives of the Lord Chancellors and Keepers of the Great Seal of England*, 10 vols. (4th ed., London, 1857), 9:218.

30. Chatham to Pitt, 6 Feb. 1801, Chatham Papers, PRO 30/8/122/2, fos. 151–52.

31. Wellesley to Pitt, 6 Oct. 1801, Chatham Papers, PRO 30/8/188/1; Wellesley to Grenville, 21 Oct. 1801, *Dropmore Papers,* 7:63–64.

32. Ziegler, 11.

33. Harvey, *Britain in the Early Nineteenth Century,* 122–23; Ziegler, 103, Watson, *Reign of George III,* 404.

34. Cooke to Castlereagh, 9 Feb. 1801, *Castlereagh Correspondence,* 4:28.

35. Leveson Gower to his mother, 13 Feb. 1801, Earl Granville Leveson Gower, *Lord Granville Leveson Gower: Private Correspondence, 1781–1821,* ed. Castalia, Countess Granville, 2 vols. (London: John Murray, 1916), 1:296.

36. Yorke to his mother, 11 Feb. 1801, Yorke MS Eng. lett. c. 60, fos. 3–4.

37. Liverpool to Hawkesbury, 1 June 1803, Add. MSS 38236, fo. 259.

38. Ziegler, 110.

39. Robin Reilly, *William Pitt the Younger* (New York: Putnam, 1979), 392.

40. Lady Elizabeth Holland, *The Journal of Elizabeth, Lady Holland 1791–1811*, ed. Earl of Ilchester, 2 vols. (London: Longman, 1908), 2:130.

41. *Glenbervie Diaries*, 1:160; Grenville to Carysfort, 17 Feb. 1801, *Dropmore Papers*, 6:450.

42. *Glenbervie Diaries*, 1:174.

CHAPTER 2

1. T. Grenville to Grenville, 9 Oct. 1800, *Dropmore Papers*, 6:343–44.

2. For a broad survey of parliamentary and public opinion about the war, see Emma Vincent MacLeod, *A War of Ideas: British Attitudes to the Wars against Revolutionary France, 1792–1802* (Aldershot: Ashgate, 1998).

3. *Annual Register 1801*, "History of Europe," 117.

4. Addington to Pitt, 8 Oct. 1797, Chatham Papers PRO 30/8/140.

5. Pellew, 2:2n.

6. Addington to Hiley Addington, 13 Sept. 1800, Sidmouth Papers 152M/c1800 /OZ48.

7. Pitt to Rose, 25 Oct. 1800, Add. MSS 42772, fos. 124; George Rose, *The Diaries and Correspondence of Rt. Hon. George Rose*, 1:279, 282.; Pellew, 1:266–67.

8. Sidmouth Papers 152M/c1800/OG8–23.

9. Addington to Hiley Addington, 1 Sept. and 4 Oct. 1800, Sidmouth Papers 152M/c1800/F8 and F10; Sidmouth Papers 152M/c1800/OG22.

10. "Coup d'oeil politique sur l'Angleterre" in Otto to Talleyrand, 4 floréal IX (24 Apr. 1801), AE Angleterre/595; same to same, 7 fructidor IX (25 Aug. 1801), AE Angleterre/595.

11. H. M. Bowman, *Preliminary Stages of the Peace of Amiens* (Toronto: University Library, 1901), 68.

12. Hawkesbury to Carysfort, 10 Mar. 1801, FO 64/60; Drummond to Grenville, 9 and 20 Jan. 1801, FO 22/40; Hawkesbury to the Lord Commissioners of the Admiralty, 23 Feb. 1801, enclosed in Hawkesbury to Drummond, 25 Feb. 1801, FO 211/6.

13. Starhemberg to Colloredo, 21 Oct. 1803, HHStA England/144; Karl Roider, *Baron Thugut and Austria's Response to the French Revolution* (Princeton: Princeton University Press, 1987), 292–93.

14. A. D. Harvey, "European Attitudes to Britain during the French Revolution and Napoleonic Era," *History* 63 (1978): 356–65; Michael Duffy, *Soldiers, Sugar, and Seapower: The British Expedition to the West Indies and the War against Revolutionary France* (Oxford: Clarendon Press, 1987), 377–78, and "British Diplomacy and the French Wars, 1789–1815," in *Britain and the French Revolution, 1789–1815*, ed. H. T. Dickinson (London: Macmillan, 1989), 137; Harold C. Deutch, *The Genesis of Napoleonic Imperialism* (Cambridge, Mass.: Harvard University Press, 1938), 25.

15. Hawkesbury to Grenville, 15 Feb. 1801, Add. MSS 58936, fos. 7–8.

16. Hawkesbury to Drummond, 25 Feb. 1801 and enclosure, FO 22/40; Hawkesbury to the Lord Commissioners of the Admiralty, 23 Feb. 1801, enclosed in Hawkesbury to Drummond, 25 Feb. 1801, FO 211/6.

17. Feldbaek, *Denmark and the Armed Neutrality,* 102–65.

18. Hawkesbury to Drummond, 25 Feb. 1801, FO 22/40.

19. An account of the naval battle can be found in Roger C. Anderson, *Naval Wars in the Baltic during the Sailing Ship Epoch, 1522–1850* (London: C. Gilbert-Wood, 1910), 302–12, and Feldbaek, *Denmark and the Armed Neutrality,* 144–65.

20. Ole Feldbaek, "The Anglo-Russian Rapprochement of 1801: A Prelude to the Peace of Amiens," *Scandinavian Journal of History* 3 (1978): 208.

21. Starhemberg to Colloredo, 19 Mar. 1801, HHStA England/142; Charles John Fedorak, "In Search of a Necessary Ally: Addington, Hawkesbury, and Russia, 1801–1804," *International History Review* 13 (1991): 221–45.

22. H. M. Scott, "Great Britain, Poland and the Russian Alliance, 1763–1767," *Historical Journal* 19 (1976): 53–74; Michael Roberts, *Splendid Isolation, 1763–1780* (The Stenton Lecture of 1969; University of Reading, 1970) and "Great Britain, Denmark and Russia, 1763–1770," in *Studies in Diplomatic History,* ed. Ragnhild Hatton and M. S. Anderson (London: Longman, 1970); M. S. Anderson, *Britain's Discovery of Russia, 1553–1815* (London: Macmillan, 1958) and *Europe in the Eighteenth Century, 1713–1783* (London: Macmillan, 1961).

23. J. J. Kenny, "Lord Whitworth and the Conspiracy against Tsar Paul I: The New Evidence of the Kent Archives," *Slavic Review* 36 (1977): 205–19.

24. Hawkesbury to Carysfort, 24 Mar. 1801, FO 63/60.

25. Alexander I to S. Vorontsov, 2 May 1801, *AKV,* 10:257; *Czartoryski Memoirs,* 1:280; Patricia Kennedy Grimsted, *The Foreign Ministers of Alexander I: Political Attitudes and the Conduct of Russian Diplomacy, 1801–1825* (Los Angeles: University of California Press, 1969); Constantin de Grunwald, *Trois siècles de diplomatie russe* (Paris: Calmann-Levy, 1945), 142. In the references to the Russian diplomatic correspondence, I have noted the dates according to the Gregorian calendar, even though Russia continued to follow the Julian calendar, which was twelve days behind.

26. S. Vorontsov to A. Vorontsov, 16 Apr. 1801, *AKV* 10:93–94; Alexander I to S. Vorontsov, 6 April 1801, *AKV,* 10:252; Pahlen to Hawkesbury, 20 Mar. 1801, FO 65/48; Hawkesbury to Pahlen, 19 Apr. 1801, FO 65/48.

27. Hugh Ragsdale, *Detente in the Napoleonic Era* (Lawrence, Kansas: Regents Press, 1980), 101–2; Edward Ingram, *In Defence of British India: Great Britain in the Middle East, 1775–1842* (London: Frank Cass, 1984), 69.

28. Alexander I to Krudener, 9 Apr. 1801, and same to Pahlen, 20 Apr. 1801, *VPR* 1:13, 16–17; Alexander I to S. Vorontsov, 6 Apr. and 2 May 1801, *AKV* 10:252, 255, 257; Nelson to Addington, 27 May 1801, Sidmouth Papers 152M/c1801/ON6.

29. A copy of the terms of the treaty is in *Parliamentary History* 36:18–25.

30. St. Helens to Hawkesbury, 18 June 1801, FO 65/48.

31. St. Helens to Hawkesbury, 18 June 1801, FO 65/48; Adam Gielgud, *Memoirs of Prince Adam Czartoryski and His Correspondence with Alexander I* (London, 1888), 1:272.

32. Hawkesbury to St. Helens, 11 Dec. 1801, Fitzherbert Papers 239M/0630.

33. Roider, *Baron Thugut*; Paul W. Schroeder, "The Collapse of the Second Coalition," *Journal of Modern History* 59 (1987): 248–50; Michael Duffy, "British War Policy: The Austrian Alliance, 1793–1801" (D.Phil. diss., University of Oxford, 1971).

34. Liverpool to Glenbervie, 25 Feb. 1802, Add. MSS 38311, fo. 121; Hawkesbury to Warren, 11 Sept. 1802, FO 65/51.

35. Hawkesbury to Carysfort, 8 May 1801, FO 64/61; Hawkesbury to St. Helens, 19 May 1801, FO 65/48; Addington to S. Vorontsov, 13 July 1801, Sidmouth Papers 152M/c1801/OF26; Starhemberg to Colloredo, 1 July 1803, HHStA England/144.

36. Starhemberg to Colloredo, 24 July 1801, HHStA England/142. All of the original French, Austrian, and Russian correspondence is in French. I have translated all of the quotations into English.

37. Henry Kissinger, *A World Restored: The Politics of Conservatism in a Revolutionary Period* (New York: Grosset & Dunlap, 1964); Enno E. Kraehe, *Metternich's German Policy* (Princeton: Princeton University Press, 1983); Schroeder, "Collapse of the Second Coalition," 249ff.

38. "Du système politique de l'empire de Russie," 28 July 1801, *VPR*, 1:65–66; Instruction to Morkov, 9 July 1801, *SIRIO*, 70:214; Grimsted, *Foreign Ministers of Alexander I*, 66–103.

39. Alexander I to S. Vorontsov, 12 Nov. 1801, *AKV*, 10:300.

40. "Du système politique," *VPR*, 1:63.

41. Addington to the king with a cabinet minute, 19 Mar. 1801, Aspinall, 3:512.

42. Otto to Talleyrand, 30 ventôse IX (21 Mar. 1801), AE, Angleterre/594; *The Times*, 23 June, 2 July, and 2 Oct. 1801.

43. Otto to Hawkesbury, 2 Apr. 1801, FO 27/66; Otto to Talleyrand, 13 germinal IX (3 Apr. 1801), AE Angleterre/594. For the importance of the role of Egypt in the negotiations see Charles John Fedorak, "The French Capitulation in Egypt and the Preliminary Anglo-French Treaty of Peace in October 1801: A Note," *International History Review* 15 (1993): 525–34.

44. Otto was only partially correct, as there were in fact two critical issues in the negotiations, the other being Malta.

45. Note of discussion, 2 Apr. 1801, FO 27/66.

46. Hawkesbury to St. Helens, 5 May 1801, FO 65/48; Hawkesbury to Elgin, 19 May 1801, FO 78/31.

47. Duffy, *Soldiers, Sugar, and Seapower*, 359ff.

48. Otto to Talleyrand, 3 germinal IX (24 Mar. 1801), AE Angleterre/594; HO 42/61; HO 43/12; Wells, *Insurrection*, 210–11.

49. Note of Hawkesbury delivered 14 Apr. 1801, FO 27/66.

50. Starhemberg to Colloredo, 1 May 1801, HHStA England/142.

51. Otto to Talleyrand, 4 and 7 floréal IX (24 and 27 Apr. 1801), AE Angleterre/595.

52. Hawkesbury to Minto, 24 Apr. 1801, FO 7/63.

53. Edward Ingram, "British Policy towards Persia and the Defence of British India, 1798–1807" (Ph.D. diss., London School of Economics, 1968), 221.

54. Hawkesbury to Otto, 6 June 1801, FO 27/66; Otto to Talleyrand, 17 prairial IX (6 June 1801), AE Angleterre/595.

55. Otto to Hawkesbury, 26 July 1801, FO 27/66.

56. St. Vincent to O'Hara, 21 June 1801, Add. MSS 31169, fos. 28–29; *Glenbervie Diaries,* 1:267; Liverpool to Hervey, 27 July 1801, Hervey Papers 941/56/8; Memorandum on War with France, Add. MSS 33120, fos. 110–12; St. Vincent to Lutwidge and Græme, 24 July 1801, Add. MSS 31169, fos. 30, 32; Hervey to Liverpool, 27 July 1801, Add. MSS 38235, fo. 156.

57. Otto to Talleyrand, 17 thermidor IX (5 Aug. 1801), AE Angleterre/595; Hawkesbury to Otto, 5 Aug. 1801, FO 27/66.

58. *Glenbervie Diaries,* 1:268.

59. Otto to Hawkesbury, 11 Aug. 1801, FO 27/66.

60. Otto to Talleyrand, 25 thermidor IX (13 Aug. 1801), AE Angleterre/595.

61. Otto to Talleyrand, 25 thermidor and 7 fructidor IX (13 and 25 Aug. 1801), AE Angleterre/595.

62. Note to Otto, 23 July 1801, Napoleon I, *Correspondance de Napoléon Ier: publiée par ordre de l'Empereur Napoléon III,* 32 vols. (Paris, 1858–70), 7:259; Otto to Hawkesbury, 19 Sept. 1801, FO 27/66; Otto to Talleyrand, 2 jour complémentaire (19 Sept. 1801), AE Angleterre/595.

63. Bonaparte to Talleyrand, 17 Sep. 1801, Napoleon I, *Letters and Documents of Napoleon, 1769–1822,* ed. John Howard (London: Cresset, 1961), 500–2.

64. Addington to Hiley Addington, 29 Aug. 1801, Sidmouth Papers 152M/C1801/OZ134; St. Vincent to Nelson, 14 Aug. 1801, Add. MSS 31169, fo. 36; Pelham to Addington, 23 Sept. 1801, Add. MSS 33120, fos. 41–51; *Glenbervie Diaries,* 1:253.

65. Holland, *Memoirs of the Whig Party,* 1:184–86; *Malmesbury Diaries,* 4:53; Pellew, 2:55; Yorke to Abbot, 18 Aug. 1801, PRO 30/9/120, fos. 3–6.

66. *Glenbervie Diaries,* 1:251, 262, 295; Starhemberg to Colloredo, 25 Sept. 1801, HHStA England/142; Ziegler, 123; John Holland Rose, *William Pitt and the Great War,* 468.

67. Otto to Talleyrand, 6 vendémiaire X (28 Sept. 1801), AE Angleterre/596; same to same, 7 nivôse X (28 Dec. 1801), AE Angleterre/597; Hawkesbury to Otto, 30 Sept. 1801, FO 27/66.

68. *Glenbervie Diaries,* 1:255; Starhemberg to Colloredo, 25 Aug. 1801, HHStA England/142.

69. *Parliamentary History* 36:26–28.

CHAPTER 3

1. Mrs. Ord to Mrs. Goodenough, 12 Oct. 1801, Sidmouth Papers 152M/c1801/F14.

2. Otto to Talleyrand, 21 vendémiaire X (13 Oct. 1801), AE Angleterre/596; Starhemberg to Colloredo, 13 Oct. 1801, HHStA England/142.

3. Eldon to Addington, [Oct. 1801], Sidmouth Papers 152M/c1801/OZ95.

4. *Glenbervie Diaries,* 1:268.

5. *Parliamentary History,* 36:57–72.

6. Pitt to Bathurst, 18 Oct. 1801, Earl Henry Bathurst, *Historical Manuscripts Commission: Report on the Manuscripts of the Seventh Earl Bathurst* (London: Historical Manuscripts Commission, 1923), 26; Pitt to Mulgrave, 2 Oct. 1801, Stanhope, 3:28; Pitt to Grenville, 5 Oct. 1801, *Dropmore Papers,* 7:49–50; Pitt to Canning, 26 Oct. 1801, Canning Papers 30.

7. Rose to Addington, 4 Oct. 1801, Sidmouth Papers 152M/c1801/OP48.

8. Bathurst to Addington, 4 Oct. 1801, Ryder to Addington, 2 Oct. 1801, and Canning to Hiley Addington, 2 Oct. 1801, Sidmouth Papers 152M/c1801/OP54, 61, and 75.

9. Grenville to Carysfort, 6 Feb. 1801, *Dropmore Papers,* 6:437.

10. *Glenbervie Diaries,* 1:268–69.

11. Grenville to Addington, 14 Oct. 1801, Pellew, 1:459–60.

12. Grenville to Dundas, 5 Nov. 1801, Melville Castle Muniments, GD 51/1/556/15; Pitt to Grenville, 9 Oct. 1801, *Dropmore Papers,* 7:55–56.

13. Bathurst to Grenville, 21 Oct. 1801, Add. MSS 69067, fo. 164; Montrose to Grenville, 18 Oct. 1801, Add. MSS 69067, fo. 162–64; Camden to Grenville, 9 Oct. 1801, Add. MSS 69067, fo. 156.

14. *Parliamentary History,* 36:159–91.

15. Addington to Windham, 1 Oct. 1801, Add. MSS 37880, fo. 160.

16. Windham to Addington, 1 Oct. 1801, Add. MSS 37880, fo. 171.

17. *Parliamentary History,* 36:14.

18. Ibid., 49.

19. Dundas to Pitt, 6 Oct. 1801, Melville Castle Muniments, GD 51/1/64/2; Dundas to Hope, 23 Dec. 1801, Hope of Luffness Muniments, GD 364/1/1135/2/1.

20. Bathurst to Pitt, 16 Oct. 1801, Chatham Papers PRO 30/8/112/1, fos. 40–42; Camden to Grenville, 9 Oct. 1801, Pratt Papers U840/C23/2; Camden to Spencer, 9 Oct. 1801, Althorp Papers GD 42; Keith Feiling, *The Second Tory Party, 1714–1832* (London: Macmillan, 1938), 226.

21. *Parliamentary History,* 36:72–83.

22. E. A. Smith, *Lord Grey, 1764–1845* (Oxford: Clarendon Press, 1990), 83.

23. Yorke to Hardwicke, 27 Oct. 1801, Add. MSS 35701, fos. 126–29; E. A. Smith, *Lord Grey,* 87.

24. Tierney to Grey, 22 Oct. 1801, Grey Papers.

25. Addington to Windham, 25 Oct. 1801, Add. MSS 37880, fo. 117.

26. Erskine to Bond, 28 Dec. 1801, Sidmouth Papers 152M/1801/Z149a.

27. Tierney to Moira, n. d., Tierney Papers 30M70/52G; H. K. Olphin, *George Tierney* (London: G. Allen & Unwin, 1934), 75–76; Moira to Tierney, 18 Nov. 1801, and Bute to Tierney, 18 Nov. 1801, Tierney Papers 31M70/52c and 13c; Moira to Addington, 9 Nov. 1801, Sidmouth Papers 152M/c1801/OZ41; Grey to Tierney, 24 Dec. 1801, Tierney Papers 31M70/33b; E. A. Smith, *Lord Grey,* 79; Tierney to Grey, 19 Dec. 1801, Jan. and Feb. 1802, Grey Papers.

28. Addington to Hiley Addington, 27 Nov. 1801, Sidmouth Papers 152M/c1801/OZ142.

29. Otto to Talleyrand, 9 vendémiaire IX (1 Oct. 1801), AE Angleterre/596.

30. Hawkesbury to Liverpool, 15 Nov. 1801, Add. MSS 38235, fo. 300.

31. Hawkesbury to the king, 5 Oct. 1801, Aspinall, 3:615.

32. Tierney to Grey, 9 Oct. 1801, Grey Papers; Rufus King to secretary of state, 9 Oct. 1801, Charles R. King, *The Life and Correspondence of Rufus King,* 6 vols. (New York, 1896), 3:523; Franklin Wickwire and Mary Wickwire, *Cornwallis: The Imperial Years* (Chapel Hill: University of North Carolina Press, 1980), 257.

33. Hawkesbury to Cornwallis, 7 and 8 Nov. 1801, FO 27/59.

34. Cornwallis to Hawkesbury, 20 Nov. 1801, FO 27/59.

35. Cornwallis to Hawkesbury, 3 Dec. 1801, FO 27/59.

36. Cornwallis to Hawkesbury, 6 Dec. 1801, FO 27/59.

37. Hawkesbury to Cornwallis, 16 and 17 Dec. 1801, FO 27/59.

38. Hawkesbury to Cornwallis, 17 Dec. 1801, Cornwallis Papers PRO 30/11/266, fos. 3–4. The Dutch representative arrived at Amiens on 7 December, but the Spanish had not appointed one.

39. Merry to Jackson, 21 Dec. 1801, Jackson Papers FO 353/76.

40. Joseph Bonaparte to Talleyrand, 3 nivôse X and 16 pluviôse X (24 Dec. 1801 and 5 Feb. 1802), AE Angleterre/598 and 599; Joseph Bonaparte to Bonaparte, 12 and 17 Mar. 1802, Joseph Bonaparte, *Mémoires et correspondance politique et militaire du Roi Joseph,* pub. par le Baron Du Casse, 9 vols. (Paris, 1856), 1:227, 231.

41. Merry to Jackson, 30 Dec. 1801, Jackson Papers FO 353/76.

42. Cornwallis to Hawkesbury, 30 Dec. 1801, FO 27/59.

43. Addington to the Prince of Wales, 23 Jan. 1802, George, Prince of Wales, *The Correspondence of George, Prince of Wales, 1770–1812,* ed. Arthur Aspinall, 8 vols. (London: Cassell, 1963–71), 4:254; Hawkesbury to Cornwallis, 10 Jan. 1802, Cornwallis Papers PRO 30/11/267, fos. 11–12; Starhemberg to Colloredo, 15 Jan. 1802, HHStA England/143.

44. Hawkesbury to Cornwallis, 12 Feb. 1802, Cornwallis Papers PRO 30/11/267, fo. 15.

45. Starhemberg to Colloredo, 29 Jan. 1802, HHStA England/143.

46. Hobart to Clephane, Feb. 1802, WO 6/55; Hobart to Admiralty, 12 Feb. and 4 Mar. 1802, WO 6/149.

47. Yorke to Hardwicke, 23 Feb. and 2 Mar. 1802, Add. MSS 35701, fos. 252–55, 261–70; Starhemberg to Colloredo, 23 Feb. 1802, HHStA England/143.

48. Hawkesbury to Cornwallis, 16 Feb. 1802, FO 27/60.

49. Cornwallis to Hawkesbury, 10 Mar. 1802, FO 27/60.

50. Hawkesbury to Cornwallis, 14 Mar. 1802, FO 27/60.

51. Bonaparte to Lucien Bonaparte, 1 Dec. 1801, Napoleon I, *Lettres inédites de Napoléon,* ed. Leon Lecestre, 2 vols. (Paris, 1897), 1:35; Bonaparte to Joseph Bonaparte, 29 Dec. 1801, *Mémoires et correspondance du Roi Joseph,* 1:215; Bonaparte to Joseph Bonaparte, 8 Mar. 1802, Napoleon, *Letters and Documents of Napoleon,* 513; Bonaparte to Joseph Bonaparte, 11 Mar. 1802, *Mémoires et correspondance du Roi Joseph,* 1:221; Otto to Talleyrand, 25 nivôse X (15 Jan. 1802), AE Angleterre/597; Joseph Bonaparte to Bonaparte, 17 Mar. 1802, *Mémoires et correspondance du Roi Joseph,* 1:231; Bonaparte to Talleyrand, 9 and 12 Mar. 1802, Napoleon, *Correspondance de Napoléon Ier,* 7:517, 519.

52. Cornwallis to Hawkesbury, 17 Mar. 1802, FO 27/60.

53. Addington to Cornwallis, 22 Mar. 1802, Cornwallis Papers PRO 30/11/267, fo. 21.

54. Desmond Gregory, *Malta, Britain, and the European Powers, 1793–1815* (Madison, N.J.: Fairleigh Dickinson University Press, 1996), 120–21.

55. Otto to Talleyrand, 14 ventôse X (5 Mar. 1802), AE Angleterre/597.

CHAPTER 4

1. Polden, "Domestic Policies," 141.

2. Ziegler, 148.

3. Pellew, 2:58.

4. Ibid.; *Malmesbury Diaries,* 4:70.

5. B. E. V. Sabine, *A History of Income Tax* (London: George Allen & Unwin, 1966), 34; Arthur Farnsworth, *Addington, Author of the Modern Income Tax* (London: Stevens & Sons, 1951), 34; Edwin R. A. Seligman, *The Income Tax: A Study of the History, Theory and Practice of Income Tax at Home and Abroad* (New York: Macmillan, 1911), 115.

6. Yorke to Hardwicke, 30 Mar. 1802, Add. MSS 35701, fos. 279–80.

7. *Parliamentary History,* 36:447–48.

8. Sidmouth Papers 152M/c1802/OM6.

9. *Parliamentary History,* 36:446.

10. Pellew, 2:65; Watson, *Reign of George III,* 412.

11. Breihan, "Addington Party," 163–89; Philip Harling, *The Waning of "Old Corruption": The Politics of Economical Reform in Britain, 1779–1846* (Oxford: Clarendon Press, 1996), 80–82; Pellew, 2:62–63; *Parliamentary History,* 36:322, 372–82; D. K. Keir, *The Constitutional History of Modern Britain since 1485,* 7th ed. (London: Adam & Charles Black, 1964), 387.

12. Pellew, 2:59–60; Sidmouth Papers 152M/c1802/OT1.

13. *Parliamentary History,* 36:447; Sidmouth Papers 152M/c1802/OT5.

14. *Parliamentary History,* 36:458–59.

15. Henry MacLeod, *Theory and Practice,* 2:4–6; *Parliamentary History,* 36:542–46;

P. K. O'Brien, "English Government Revenue, 1793–1815: A Study in Fiscal and Financial Policy in the Wars against France" (D.Phil. diss., University of Oxford, 1967), 218; Edwin Cannan, *The Paper Pound of 1797–1821* (London: P. S. King and Son, 1919), 70.

16. Canning to Frere, 11 Apr. 1802, Add. MSS 38833, fo. 104.

17. Ziegler, 161.

18. Otto to Talleyrand, 16 germinal X (6 Apr. 1802), AE Angleterre/597.

19. Mary Anne Addington's Notes, Sidmouth Papers, Box 51 Public Office 2.

20. *Colchester Diary,* 1:412.

21. Stanhope, 3:86.

22. Addington to the king, 30 Nov. 1802, Aspinall, 4:64.

23. *Parliamentary History,* 36:1122.

24. Rose to Tomline, 24 Dec. 1802, John Holland Rose, *William Pitt and the Great War,* 481; Polden, "Domestic Policies," 160.

25. Pellew, 2:103–4; *Parliamentary History,* 36:1124–25.

26. Steele to Pitt, 5 Feb. 1803, Cambridge University Library, Pitt Papers 6958/2925.

27. Castlereagh to Wellesley, 17 Dec. 1802, Marquess Richard Wellesley, *Despatches, Minutes and Correspondence of the Marquess Wellesley,* ed. Montgomery Martin, 5 vols. (London, 1837), 3:96. The position of president of the Board of Control normally was not a cabinet office, but Addington thought highly of Castlereagh and wanted him in the cabinet. Abbot also claimed that the funds had risen nearly 5 percent in one day, *Colchester Diary,* 1:412.

28. Liverpool to Addington, 15 Dec. 1802, Sidmouth Papers 152M/c1802/OZ46.

29. Yorke to Hardwicke, 20 Dec. 1802, Add. MSS 35702, fos. 68–71.

30. Farquhar to Addington, 12 Dec. 1802, Sidmouth Papers 152M/c1802/OZ103.

31. Minto to Lady Minto, 14 Dec. 1802, Earl of Minto, *Life and Letters of Gilbert Elliot, First Earl of Minto, from 1751–1806,* ed. countess of Minto, 3 vols. (London, 1874), 3:263; Georgiana, duchess of Devonshire, to Lady Elizabeth Foster, [17 Dec. 1802], Chatsworth Papers, Fifth Duke's Group 1677.

32. Harling, *Waning,* 30–80.

33. Harling, *Waning,* 80–82.

34. Pellew, 2:99–100.

35. Hone, *For the Cause of Truth, 100–1. Wells,* Insurrection, 219–25; Thompson, *Making of the English Working Class,* 520; J. L. Baxter and F. K. Donnelly, "The Revolutionary Underground in the West Riding: Myth or Reality," *Past and Present* 64 (1974): 129; J. R. Dinwiddy, "The 'Black Lamp' in Yorkshire, 1801–1802," *Past and Present* 64 (1974): 113–23.

36. Pelham to the Mayor of Leeds, 8 Aug. 1801, HO 43/13; Pelham to Fitzwilliam, 19 Aug. 1801, HO 43/13.

37. HO 42/65; Polden, "Domestic Policies," 213; Emsley, *British Society,* 96.

38. Fitzwilliam to Pelham, 20 July 1802, HO 42/65.

39. Pelham to Reed, 2 Sept. 1802, HO 42/66.

40. Charles Oman, *The Unfortunate Colonel Despard and Other Stories* (London: E. Arnold & Co., 1922), 2–21.

41. Memorandum on the Despard Conspiracy, HO 42/66.

42. Notes of a Speech, Feb. 1803, Add. MSS 49176, fo. 50.

43. Andréossy to Talleyrand, 4 frimaire XI (25 Nov. 1802), AE Angleterre/600.

44. Fox to Grey, 28 Feb. 1803, Add. MSS 47565, fo. 73.

45. Southey, *Letters from England, 373.*

46. Hardwicke to Addington, 21 July 1803, Sidmouth Papers 152M/c1803/OZ289; Hardwicke to Pelham, 24 July 1803, HO 100/112; Hardwicke to Yorke, 24 July 1803, and 5 Aug. 1803, Add. MSS 35702, fos. 240–41, 289–91; Pelham to the king, 28 July 1803, Aspinall, 4:115; Wickham Papers 38M49/1/45/26 and 48/4; Add. MSS 38239, fos. 77–8; account of Emmet's Rebellion by William Wickham, 5 Dec. 1803, Sidmouth Papers 152M/c1803/OL12.

47. Holland, *Memoirs of the Whig Party,* 1:183, 2:214 quoted in Ziegler, 153.

48. Southey, *Letters from England,* 71–74.

49. W. V. Anson, *Life of John Jervis, Admiral Lord St. Vincent* (London: Murray, 1913), 285; Roger Morriss, *The Royal Dockyards during the Revolutionary and Napoleonic Wars* (Leicester: Leicester University Press, 1983), 189–93; Breihan, "Addington Party," 166.

50. E. P. Brenton, *Life and Correspondence of John, Earl of St. Vincent,* (London, 1838), 2:159–60; Harvey, *Britain in the Early Nineteenth Century,* 128–30.

51. Bernard Pool, *Navy Board Contracts, 1660–1832: Contract Administration under the Navy Board* (London: Longman, 1966), 118–21; O. A. Sherrard, *A Life of Lord St. Vincent* (London: G. Allen & Unwin, 1933), 188.

52. Sherrard, *Life of Lord St. Vincent,* 189.

53. St. Vincent to Collingwood, 15 Mar. 1801, Add. MSS 31158, fo. 21.

54. St. Vincent to Fanshaw, 25 Feb. 1801, Add. MSS 31170, fo. 18.

55. Breihan, "Addington Party," 164.

56. Roger Morriss, "Labour Relations in the Royal Naval Dockyards, 1801–5," *Mariner's Mirror* 63 (1976): 38–40; Sherrard, *Life of Lord St. Vincent,* 174; Breihan, "Addington Party," 167.

57. Hobart to Admiralty, 27 Oct. 1801, and 5 Apr. 1802, Adm. 1/4188 and 4189; Emsley, *British Society,* 95; Watson, *Reign of George III,* 412.

58. Board Minutes, 7 July 1801, Adm. 3/145; St. Vincent, *Letters of Admiral of the Fleet,* 2:1–7.

59. St. Vincent to Grey, 6 Aug. 1801, *Letters of St. Vincent,* 2:191.

60. St. Vincent to Addington, 29 Aug. 1802, Add. MSS 31169, fo. 125.

61. Board Minutes, 16 Oct. 1802, Adm. 3/127.

62. Morriss, *Royal Dockyards,* 150; William Marsden, *A Brief Memoir of the Life and Writings of the Late William Marsden written by Himself with Notes from His Correspondence,* ed. Mrs. E. W. Marsden (London, 1838), 103n.

63. Morriss, *Royal Dockyards,* 29.

64. Memorandum on timber and building ships by contract, Sidmouth Papers 152M/c1804/ON21.

65. Keith to Pitt, 10 Mar. 1804, Chatham Papers PRO 30/8/149/1, fos. 37–38.

66. Martin Memoirs, 10 Sept. 1840, Add. MSS 41378, fo. 61.

67. Pellew, 2:260–61.

68. Martin Memoirs, 15 Sep. 1840, Add. MSS 41378, fo. 63.

69. Abstract of British and Enemy Ships and Vessels, 13 May 1804, Sidmouth Papers 152M/c1804/ON18.

70. Addington to Bragge, 4 Sept. 1804, Sidmouth Papers 152M/c1804/OZ130.

CHAPTER 5

1. Edward Ingram, "The Geopolitics of the First British Expedition to Egypt—IV: Occupation and Withdrawal, 1801–3," *Middle Eastern Studies* 31 (1995): 317–46.

2. For a thorough examination of the issue of control of the press in the context of Anglo-French relations and the renewal of war, see Simon Burrows, "Culture and Misperception: The Law and the Press in the Outbreak of War in 1803," *International History Review* 18 (1996): 793–818.

3. Jackson to Hawkesbury, 4 Mar. 1802, FO 27/61; Merry to Hawkesbury, 4 June 1802, FO 27/62; Hawkesbury to Merry, 10 June 1802, FO 27/62; Otto to Hawkesbury, 25 July 1802, FO 27/66; Hawkesbury to Merry, 13 Aug. 1802, Sackville Papers U269/0200/1; Sidmouth Papers 152M/c1802/OZ126.

4. Otto to Hawkesbury, 17 Aug. 1802, FO 27/66.

5. Liverpool to Hawkesbury, 18 Aug. 1802, MS Loan 72/51, fo. 39.

6. Addington to Otto, 15 Aug. 1802, quoted in Burrows, "Culture and Misperception," 817.

7. Otto to Talleyrand, 11 vendémiaire XI (3 Oct. 1802), AE Angleterre/600.

8. Hawkesbury to Merry, 28 Aug. 1802, FO 27/63.

9. Merry to Hawkesbury, 5 Sept. 1802, FO 27/64.

10. Deutch, *Genesis,* 97–98; Albert Sorel, *L'Europe et la Révolution française,* 8 vols. (Paris: E. Plon, Nourrit et cie, 1949), 6:211–12; Martin Philippson, "La Paix d'Amiens et la politique générale de Napoléon Ier," *Revue historique* 75 (1901): 303–4.

11. Hawkesbury to Merry, 20 May 1802, FO 27/62.

12. P. Coquelle, "Les responsabilités de la rupture de la Paix d'Amiens en 1803," *Revue d'histoire diplomatique* 16 (1902): 274–78; Pellew, 2:164.

13. Hawkesbury to Otto, 18 Sept. 1802, FO 27/66; Conrad Gill, "The Relations between England and France in 1802," *English Historical Review* 24 (1909): 75.

14. Hobart to Auckland, 11 Aug. 1802, Add. MSS 34455, fo. 513.

15. Pitt to Addington, 5 Sept. 1802, Sidmouth Papers 152M/c1802/OZ186.

16. Bonaparte to Talleyrand, 23 Sept. 1802, Napoleon I, *Napoleon's Letters,* ed. J. M. Thompson (London: J. M. Dent and Sons, 1954), 98.

17. *Parliamentary History*, 36:986.

18. Cabinet Minute, n.d. 1802, Add. MSS 38357, fo. 185; Yorke to Hardwicke, 30 Oct. 1802, Add. MSS 35702, fo. 34; Hervey to Liverpool, 9 Oct. 1802, MS Loan 72/13, fo. 21; Hobart to Wellesley, 14 Nov. 1802, Marquess Richard Wellesley, *The Wellesley Papers*, ed. L. S. Benjamin, 2 vols. (London: Herbert Jenkins, 1914), 158–59.

19. Addington to Hobart, 13 Oct. 1802, Hobart Papers D/MH/H/War/B52; Hobart to Dundas, Wellesley, and Grinfield, 17 Oct. 1802, WO 6/183.

20. Merry to Hawkesbury, 17 Oct. 1802, FO 27/64.

21. Camden to Bathurst, 24 Oct. 1802, *HMC Bathurst*, 30.

22. Hobart to Addington, 28 Oct. 1802, Hobart Papers D/MH/H/War/B55.

23. Nelson to Addington, 25 Oct. 1802, Sidmouth Papers 152M/c1802/ON7.

24. Addington to Hardwicke, 30 Oct. 1802, Add. MSS, 35706, fos. 75–77.

25. Hobart to York, 17 Oct. 1802, Hobart Papers D/MH/H/War/C48.

26. Hawkesbury to Liverpool, 5 Nov. 1802, Add. MSS 38236, fo. 205.

27. Pitt to Addington, 10 Nov. 1802, Sidmouth Papers 152M/c1802/OZ193. An inaccurate copy of this letter is in Pellew, 2:86.

28. Addington to Pitt, 12 Nov. 1802, Dacres Adams Papers 30/58/4/86.

29. Hawkesbury to Liverpool, 9 Nov. 1802, Add. MSS 38236, fo. 220; Hobart to Wellesley, 14 Nov. 1802, Wellesley, *Wellesley Papers*, 1:158–59.

30. Addington to Hiley Addington, 4 Nov. 1802, Sidmouth Papers 152M/c1802/F1; *Malmesbury Diaries*, 4:210; Hobart to Wellesley, 14 Nov. 1802, Wellesley, *Wellesley Papers*, 1:161.

31. Hawkesbury to Whitworth, 25 Nov. 1802, Whitworth Papers FO 323/4, also quoted in H. Beeley, "A Project of Alliance with Russia in 1802," *English Historical Review* 49 (1934): 502n.

32. Hawkesbury to Liverpool, 11 Nov. 1802, MS Loan 72/55, fo. 8; Yorke to Hardwicke, 22 Nov. 1802, Add. MSS 35702, fo. 57.

33. Memorandum on the Treaty of Amiens, 1802, Castlereagh Papers D3030/1728.

34. Liverpool to Whitworth, 13 Dec. 1802, Whitworth Papers FO 323/4.

35. Hobart to Hawkesbury, 21 Dec. 1802, Hobart Papers D/MH/H/War/B60.

36. Ingram, "Geopolitics," 334–40.

37. Addington to Pitt, 12 Nov. 1802, Dacres Adams Papers 30/58/4/86.

38. Hobart to Admiralty, 6 Sept. 1802, WO 6/49.

39. Hobart to Auckland, 16 Sept. 1802, Add. MSS 34455, fo. 521.

40. Hobart to Grinfield, 15 Nov. 1802, same to Wellesley, 16 Nov. 1802, same to Dundas, 16 Nov. 1802, and same to Stuart, 26 Nov. 1802, WO 6/183.

41. Cabinet Memorandum, 6 Nov. 1802, Add. MSS 38357, fos. 203–25; Hawkesbury to Liverpool, 9 Nov. 1802, Add. MSS 38236, fos. 216–21.

42. Hawkesbury to Liverpool, 6 Feb. 1803, MS Loan 72/55, fos. 17–18.

43. Warren to Hawkesbury, 10 Dec. 1802, FO 65/51; same to same, 20 Jan. 1803, FO 65/52.

44. Hawkesbury to Warren, 1 Feb. 1803, FO 65/52.

45. A. Vorontsov to Warren, 21 Mar. 1803, and S. Vorontsov to Alexander I, 25 Mar. 1803, *VPR,* 1:393, 399; Warren to Hawkesbury, 25 Mar. 1803, FO 65/52; A. Vorontsov to Morkov, 5 Jan. 1803, *SIRIO,* 70:616.

46. Starhemberg to Colloredo, 8 Feb. 1803, HHStA England/144.

47. Hawkesbury to Whitworth, 9 Feb. 1803, Whitworth Papers FO 323/4; Otto to Hawkesbury, 24 Feb. 1803, MS Loan 72/43, fo. 66; Whitworth to Hawkesbury, 21 Feb. 1803, Oscar Browning, ed., *England and Napoleon in 1803: Being the dispatches of Lord Whitworth and others, now first printed from the originals in the Record Office,* (London, 1887), 78–85.

48. Liverpool to Hervey, n. d., Hervey Papers 941/56/8.

49. *Parliamentary History,* 36:1162–63.

50. Whitworth to Hawkesbury, 17 Mar. 1803, MS Loan 72/18, fo. 89; Liston to Hawkesbury, 15 Mar. 1803, FO 37/61.

51. Hawkesbury to Whitworth, 7 Mar. 1803, Whitworth Papers FO 323/4; Yorke to Hardwicke, 8 Mar. 1803, Add. MSS 35702, fos. 135–36.

52. Whitworth to Hawkesbury, 14 Mar. 1803, *England and Napoleon,* 115–17.

53. Whitworth to Hawkesbury, 17 Mar. 1803, FO 27/67.

54. Hawkesbury to Whitworth, 7 May 1803, *England and Napoleon,* 224–26; Andréossy to Talleyrand, 17 floréal XI (7 May 1803), AE Angleterre/600.

55. Hawkesbury to Whitworth, 4 Apr. 1803, Whitworth Papers FO 323/4.

56. Liverpool to Whitworth, 15 Mar. 1803, Whitworth Papers FO 323/4; Starhemberg to Colloredo, 1 Mar. 1803, HHStA England/144.

57. Hawkesbury to Whitworth, 31 Mar. and 13 Apr. 1803, Whitworth Papers FO 323/4.

58. Coquelle, "Les responsabilités," 294–97.

59. Hawkesbury to Whitworth, 4 Apr. 1803, Whitworth Papers FO 323/4; Andréossy to Talleyrand, 25 ventôse XI (16 Mar. 1803), AE Angleterre/600.

60. Rashleigh to Pole Carew, 9 Apr. 1803, Pole Carew Papers CC/L/36.

61. Hawkesbury to S. Vorontsov, 28 May 1803, FO 65/52.

62. Yorke to Hardwicke, 30 Oct. 1803, Add. MSS 35702, fos. 34–35; Liverpool to Whitworth, 6 Dec. 1802, Whitworth Papers FO 323/4.

63. Vansittart to Addington, 14 Jan. 1803, Sidmouth Papers 152M/1803/OT36.

64. Addington to Redesdale, 7 Jan. 1803, Redesdale Papers X15.

65. Paul W. Schroeder, *The Transformation of European Politics 1763–1848* (New York: Oxford University Press, 1994), 231–45.

66. Andréossy to Talleyrand, 10 ventôse XI (1 Mar. 1803), AE Angleterre/600.

67. Otto to Talleyrand, 7 brumaire XI (29 Oct. 1802), AE Angleterre/600.

68. Paul W. Schroeder, "Napoleon's Foreign Policy: A Criminal Enterprise," *Journal of Military History* 54 (1990): 152–54.

69. Schroeder, "Napoleon's Foreign Policy," 153.

70. Liverpool to Whitworth, 13 Dec. 1802, Whitworth Papers FO 323/4.

71. Hawkesbury to Liverpool, 9 Jan. 1803, MS Loan 72/55, fo. 16.

72. Liverpool to Whitworth, 11 Mar. 1803, Whitworth Papers FO 323/4.

73. *Colchester Diary,* 1:413.

74. Pitt to Rose, 28 Jan. 1803, Stanhope, 3:93.

75. Stanhope, 3:110.

76. Melville to Addington, 25 Mar. 1803, Stanhope, 3:111–12.

77. Pitt to Addington, 15 Apr. 1803, Pellew, 2:122–23.

78. Pitt to Addington, 15 Apr. 1803, Pellew, 2:122.

79. *Colchester Diary,* 1:416; George Rose, *The Diaries and Correspondence of Rt. Hon. George Rose,* 2:34–37.

80. Pitt to Addington, 13 Apr. 1803, Pellew, 2:121.

81. Addington to Pitt, 12 Apr. 1803, Pellew, 2:119–20.

82. Addington to Pitt, 18 Apr. 1803, Pellew, 2:126.

83. Pitt to Addington, 18 Apr. 1803, Pellew, 2:128.

84. Pitt to Addington, 15 Apr. 1803, Pellew, 2:123.

85. Stanhope, 3:121–22.

86. Stanhope, 3:123.

87. Stanhope, 3:114.

88. Pellew, 2:120n.

89. Melville to Pitt, 14 Apr. 1803, Add. MSS 40102, fo. 106.

90. *Colchester Diary,* 1:416.

91. Redesdale to Pitt, 31 Oct. 1803, Chatham Papers PRO 30/8/170/2, fos. 211–14.

92. Pitt to Redesdale, 17 Apr. 1803, Redesdale Papers D2002/C3A.

93. Cornwallis to Ross, 8 Dec. 1803, Marquis Charles Cornwallis, *The Correspondence of Charles, First Marquis Cornwallis,* ed. C. Ross, 3 vols. (London, 1859), 3:506–7.

94. John Ehrman, *The Younger Pitt: The Consuming Struggle* (London: Constable, 1996), 591.

95. Ehrman, *Consuming Struggle,* 591.

96. Duffy, *Younger Pitt,* 1–2.

97. Ehrman, *Consuming Struggle,* 599.

CHAPTER 6

1. Hawkesbury to S. Vorontsov, 26 May 1803, FO 65/52.

2. *SIRIO,* 77:98–100; *VPR,* 1:410; *Parliamentary History,* 36:1489.

3. Hawkesbury to S. Vorontsov, 26 May 1803, FO 65/52.

4. Hawkesbury to S. Vorontsov, 28 May 1803, FO 65/52.

5. Bonaparte to Alexander I, 20 ventôse XI (11 Mar. 1803), *SIRIO,* 77:55; Jacques Petrel, "La Russie et la rupture de la Paix d'Amiens," *Annales de l'Ecole Libre des Sciences Politiques* 12 (1887): 72; Starhemberg to Colloredo, 1 Apr. 1803, HHStA England/144; S. Vorontsov to A. Vorontsov, 18 May 1803, *AKV,* 10:205–6.

6. Petrel, "La Russie," 76, 77, 87; Morkov to S. Vorontsov, 13 June 1803, FO 65/52; Draft of Declaration against France, n.d., FO 27/69.

7. Petrel, "La Russie," 84–92.

8. A. Vorontsov to Morkov, 18 June 1803, *SIRIO,* 77:217.

9. Hawkesbury to S. Vorontsov, 11 July 1803, FO 65/53.

10. Hawkesbury to Warren, 12 July 1803, FO 65/53.

11. Warren to Hawkesbury, 19 July 1803, FO 65/53.

12. Warren to Hawkesbury, 10 Aug. 1803, FO 65/53.

13. Starhemberg to Colloredo, 21 June 1803, HHStA England/144; Paget to Hawkesbury, 21 Jan. 1803, FO 7/67.

14. Starhemberg to Colloredo, 24 July 1801, HHStA England/142; Karl Helleiner, *The Imperial Loans: A Study in Financial and Diplomatic History* (Oxford: Clarendon Press, 1965), 136.

15. Starhemberg to Colloredo, 24 June 1803, HHStA England/144.

16. Starhemberg to Colloredo, 26 July 1803, HHStA England/144. This offer was increased to £500,000 in March 1804, but the Austrians refused. See same to same, 30 Mar. 1804, HHStA England/145.

17. Hawkesbury to Paget, 28 May 1803, FO 7/67.

18. Paget to Hawkesbury, 8 June 1803, FO 7/67.

19. The importance of European opinion in the context of the Anglo-French conflict is examined in Simon Burrows, "The Struggle for European Opinion in the Napoleonic Wars: British Francophone Propaganda, 1803–1814," *French History* 11 (1997): 29–53.

20. Hawkesbury to Liverpool, 16 July 1803, MS Loan 72/55, fo. 30.

21. Hawkesbury to Jackson, 28 June 1803, FO 64/63.

22. Jackson to Hawkesbury, 16 July 1803, FO 64/63; Hawkesbury to Jackson, 6 Dec. 1803, Jackson Papers FO 353/43.

23. Hawkesbury to Warren, 23 Sept. 1803, FO 65/53.

24. Hawkesbury to Warren, 23 Sept. 1803, Warren Papers.

25. Czartoryski to Alexander I, 29 Feb. 1804, *VPR,* 1:619–24, also in *SIRIO,* 77:486–98; Czartoryski to S. Vorontsov, 9 Mar. 1804, *VPR,* 1:638; *Czartoryski Memoirs,* 2:14; Warren to Hawkesbury, 2 Dec. 1803, 17 Feb., 27 Apr., and 12 May 1804, FO 65/53–55.

26. Hawkesbury to Liston, 20 and 29 May 1803, FO 37/61.

27. Admiralty to Admiral Cornwallis, 18 May 1803, FO 72/48.

28. Hawkesbury to Frere, 8 June 1803, FO 72/48.

29. Hawkesbury to Frere, 21 Jan. 1804, FO 72/51.

30. Hawkesbury to Liston, 23 June 1803, FO 22/43.

31. Hill to Hawkesbury, 30 May 1803, FO 22/43.

32. Liston to Hawkesbury, 15 Oct. and 22 Nov. 1803, FO 22/43.

33. Hawkesbury to the king, 21 July 1803, Aspinall, 4:113; Hawkesbury to Silver-hjelm, 25 July 1803, FO 73/30; Hawkesbury to Hobart, 19 Jan. 1804, FO 73/32.

34. Hawkesbury to Elliot, 18 May 1803, FO 70/21.

35. Elliot to Hawkesbury, 19 July 1803, FO 70/21; Hawkesbury to Elliot, 11 Nov. 1803, FO 70/21; Elliot to Hawkesbury, 10 Jan. 1804, FO 70/22; Desmond Gregory, *Sicily: The Insecure Base. A History of the British Occupation of Sicily, 1806–1815* (Rutherford, N.J.: Fairleigh Dickinson University Press, 1988).

36. Hawkesbury to de Souza, June 1803, FO 63/41.

37. Hawkesbury to the king, 30 June 1803, and the king to Hawkesbury, 1 July 1803, Aspinall, 4:111–12; "abstract of Colonel Stewart's final report upon his mission to Portugal," 25 Sept. 1803, and Donald Campbell to the cabinet, 26 Sept. 1803, FO 63/42.

38. Hawkesbury to Fitzgerald, 6 Oct. 1803, FO 63/42.

39. Hawkesbury to Fitzgerald, 21 Jan. 1804, and Fitzgerald to Hawkesbury, 23 Feb. 1804, FO 63/43.

40. Hawkesbury to Drummond, 31 May 1803, FO 78/40.

41. Thornton to Hawkesbury, 3 July 1802, FO 5/35.

42. Hawkesbury to King, 7 May 1802, FO 5/37; Thornton to Hawkesbury, 3 Jan. 1803, FO 5/38; King to secretary of state, 2 Apr. 1803, King, *Life and Correspondence of Rufus King*, 4:241.

43. Thornton to Hammond, 29 Jan. 1804, FO 5/41.

44. Philip Ziegler, *The Sixth Great Power: Barings, 1762–1929* (London: Collins, 1988), 71; Addington to Baring, 16 Dec. 1803, Sidmouth Papers 152M/c1803/OZ214.

45. Fedorak, "In Search of a Necessary Ally," 221–45.

46. Schroeder, "The Collapse of the Second Coalition," 283.

47. Starhemberg to Colloredo, 21 Oct. 1803, HHStA England/144.

48. Starhemberg to Colloredo, 6 Mar. 1804, HHStA England/145.

49. Starhemberg to Colloredo, 1 May 1804, HHStA England/145.

50. Otto to Talleyrand, 19 germinal X (9 Apr. 1802), AE Angleterre/597; King, *Life and Correspondence of Rufus King*, vols. 3 and 4; Add. MSS 38237.

51. George Rose, *The Diaries and Correspondence of Rt. Hon. George Rose*, 2:41–42; Hawkesbury to St. Helens, 30 Mar. 1802, FO 181/3; Norman Gash, *Lord Liverpool: The Life and Political Career of Robert Banks Jenkinson, Second Earl of Liverpool* (London: Weidenfield and Nicolson, 1984), 49–50; S. Vorontsov to Hawkesbury, 16 May 1804, MS Loan 72/43.

52. Schroeder, *Transformation of European Politics*, 244–45.

CHAPTER 7

1. Keith to Pitt, 10 Mar. 1804, Chatham Papers PRO 30/8/149/1, fo. 37.

2. Christopher D. Hall, *British Strategy in the Napoleonic War 1803–15* (Manchester: Manchester University Press, 1992), 79.

3. Richard Glover, *Britain at Bay: Defence against Bonaparte, 1803–14* (London:

George Allen and Unwin, 1973), 14–16; Alan Schom, *Napoleon Bonaparte* (New York: Harper Perennial, 1997), 308–16.

4. Liverpool to Mrs. Johnson, 28 Nov. 1803, Add. MSS 38311, fo. 167.

5. Hobart to Wellesley, 29 Aug. 1803, Add. MSS 37309, fos. 9–10.

6. *Malmesbury Diaries,* 4:272.

7. Keith to York, 21 Oct. 1803, *Keith Papers,* 2:52.

8. Black, *Britain as a Military Power,* 201; J. E. Cookson, *The British Armed Nation* (Oxford: Clarendon Press, 1997), 42

9. *Parliamentary History,* 36:1578.

10. St. Vincent to Keith, 24 June 1803, Add. MSS, 31169, fo. 65.

11. Hobart circular to Lords Lieutenant, 11 Mar. and 28 May 1803, WO 6/190.

12. Glover, *Britain at Bay,* 43.

13. Danby Pickering, ed., *Statutes at Large from Magna Charta to 1806* (Cambridge, 1807), 43 Geo. III, cap. 82, 83, and 85; Hobart to the king, 17 June 1803, Aspinall, 4:107.

14. Pickering, *Statutes at Large,* 43 Geo. III, cap. 96.

15. Twiss, *Lord Chancellor Eldon,* 1:416; Cookson, *British Armed Nation,* 75; 78.

16. Pitt was also lobbying in favor of a large volunteer force, but the view of J. E. Cookson that Pitt forced Addington to expand the volunteers is overstated. Cookson, *British Armed Nation,* 36; 75–79.

17. Philip J. Haythornthwaite, "The Volunteer Force, 1803–04," *Journal of the Society for Army Historical Research* 64 (1986): 193–94.

18. Quoted in Colley, *Britons,* 328.

19. Estcourt to Addington, 27 June 1806, Southerton Estcourt Papers D1571/F664.

20. State of Ordnance: Guns and Equipment, 1801 and 1803, 7 Dec. 1803, Sidmouth Papers 152M/c1803/OM1; Richard Glover, *Peninsular Preparation: The Reform of the British Army, 1795–1809* (Cambridge: Cambridge University Press, 1963), 57; Polden, "Domestic Policies," 346.

21. Yorke to Hardwicke, 10 Sept. 1803, Add. MSS 35703, fo. 106–9.

22. Fortescue, *The County Lieutenancies and the Army,* 69; Pellew, 2:235; Christopher D. Hall, "Factors Influencing British Strategic Planning and Execution during the Napoleonic War" (Ph.D. diss., University of Exeter, 1985), 21–22.

23. Cornwallis to Ross, Dec. 1803, *Cornwallis Correspondence,* 3:509.

24. Glover, *Britain at Bay,* 78; Schom, *Napoleon Bonaparte,* 322–23.

25. York to Hobart, 30 June 1803, WO 1/625.

26. Ibid.

27. Memorandum on Arming, 25 July 1803, WO 1/625.

28. York to General Officers Commanding Districts, 1 July 1803, WO 1/625.

29. York to Hobart, 25 Aug. 1803, WO 30/76.

30. Addington to the king, 1 Jan. 1804, Aspinall, 4:148; Steele to Pitt, 3 Jan. 1804, Chatham Papers PRO 30/8/180/2, fos. 241–2; Starhemberg to Colloredo, 27 Dec. 1803, HHStA England/144.

31. York to Chatham, 4 July 1803, WO 30/76.

32. York to Hobart, 4 July and 25 Aug. 1803, WO 1/625.

33. York to Hobart, 14 Sept. 1803, WO 1/626; Hobart to York, 26 Mar. 1804, WO 1/627.

34. Hobart to York, 6 and 7 Apr. 1804, and York to Hobart, 31 Mar. and 10 Apr. 1804, WO 1/625.

35. York to Hobart, 8 July 1803, WO 30/76.

36. York to Yorke, 24 Oct. 1803, WO 30/76.

37. Pellew, 2:238; Ziegler, 206; Perceval and Manners-Sutton to Yorke, 23 Jan. 1804, Add. MSS 38240, fo. 117; Spencer Walpole, *The Life of the Right Hon. Spencer Perceval, including correspondence with Numerous Distinguished Persons,* 2 vols. (London, 1874), 1:115; York to Addington, 19 Oct. 1803, Sidmouth Papers 152M/c1803/OZ124.

38. York to Hobart, 21 June 1803, WO 30/76; St. Vincent to Hobart, 9 July 1803, WO 1/100.

39. Polden, "Domestic Policies," 362.

40. Sidmouth Papers 152M/c1804/ON7.

41. York to Hobart, 30 June 1803, WO 1/625.

42. Hawkesbury to Liverpool, 1 Nov. 1803, MS Loan 72/55, fo. 34.

43. Pitt to Chatham, 2 Mar. 1803, Stanhope, 3:106.

44. Fedorak, "The Royal Navy and British Amphibious Operations," 141–46.

45. The clear divergence of opinion that had arisen between Grenville and Dundas by 1797 is forcefully demonstrated by Edward Ingram in *Commitment to Empire: Prophesies of the Great Game in Asia, 1797–1800* (Oxford: Clarendon Press, 1981), chapter 2 and Piers Mackesy in *War without Victory: The Downfall of Pitt, 1799–1802* (Oxford: Clarendon Press, 1984), especially 7–18, and "The Strategic Problems of the British War Effort," in *Britain and the French Revolution,* ed. H. T. Dickinson (London: Macmillan, 1989), 161. Moreover, Dundas outlined the schism in a memo of 22 Sept. 1800, and Grenville had his dissent over the sending of the Egyptian expedition noted in the cabinet minutes. "State of the Cabinet," 22 Sept. 1800, Add. MSS 40102, fos. 79–81; Aspinall, 3:424.

46. Yorke to Hardwicke, 28 Mar. 1803, Add. MSS 35702, fos. 155–56.

47. Adm. 2/1360; Adm. 2/145.

48. Hall, *British Strategy,* 103.

49. Reilly, *William Pitt,* 417.

50. Sherrard, *Life of Lord St. Vincent,* 206.

51. Hobart to Admiralty, 5 Mar. 1803, WO 6/183.

52. Hobart to Admiralty, 17 May 1803, WO 6/183.

53. Hobart to Admiralty, 31 Mar. 1803, WO 6/183.

54. Hobart to Admiralty, 1 Apr. and 7 May 1803, Adm. 6/183.

55. Hobart to Wellesley, 16 May 1803, and Hobart to Grinfield, 16 May and 10 June

1803, WO 6/183; Hobart to Grinfield, 16 May and 11 June 1803, Hobart Papers D/MH/H/War/C86 and C87; Hobart to Admiralty, 4 June 1803, WO 6/49.

56. Hall, *British Strategy,* 109.

57. Christopher D. Hall, "Addington at War: Unspectacular but not Unsuccessful," *Historical Research 61* (1988): 311.

58. Hobart to Admiralty, 25 June and 26 July 1803, WO 6/183.

59. Hobart to Admiralty, 6 Sept. 1803, WO 6/183.

60. François Crouzet, "La guerre maritime" and "Le système continental et ses conséquences," in *Napoléon et L'Empire: L'apogée et la chute,* ed. Jean Mistler (Verviers: Marabout, 1979), 50, 152; Kennedy, *Rise and Fall,* 122; Arthur, 182, 188–89, 196–99, 223.

61. Crouzet, "La guerre maritime," 50.

62. Starhemberg to Colloredo, 20 Oct. 1803, HHStA England/144; York to Hobart, 13 Jan. 1804, WO 1/627; Addington to Simcoe, 4 Sept. 1803, Sidmouth Papers 152M/c1803/OZ354; *Parliamentary Debates,* 2:279–82; Vansittart to Addington, 22 Sept. 1803, Sidmouth Papers 152M/c1803/OZ275; Hawkesbury to Hobart, 29 Sept. 1803, Hobart Papers D/MH/H/War/B74; Hobart to Addington, 16 July 1801, Sidmouth Papers 152M/c1801/OM4; King, *Life and Correspondence of Rufus King,* 4:321; Starhemberg to Colloredo, 15 Dec. 1803, HHStA England/144.

63. John Fortescue, *A History of the British Army,* 14 vols. (London: Macmillan, 1899–1930), 5:196–202; Hall, "Addington at War," 310–11.

64. Ziegler, 197–8.

65. Hall, "Addington at War," 306–15.

66. Mackesy, "Strategic Problems of the British War Effort," 157.

67. Brewer, *Sinews of Power,* 191–217; Black, *Britain as a Miliary Power,* 1–4.

68. Private Memoir on Finance, Sidmouth Papers 152M/c1803/OT29.

69. *Parliamentary History,* 36:1594–1602; Private Memoir on Finance, Sidmouth Papers 152M/c1803/OT29.

70. Sidmouth Papers 152M/c1801/OT24; Seligman, *Income Tax,* 78, 115; Sabine, *History,* 33.

71. *Parliamentary History,* 36:1600; Farnsworth, *Addington,* 42–45.

72. Sabine, *History,* 38.

73. Addington's recruiting measures have been discussed in detail by Fortescue, *The County Lieutenancies and the Army;* Glover, *Peninsular Preparation;* J. R. Western, *The English Militia in the Eighteenth Century* (London: Routledge & Kegan Paul, 1965).

74. *Colchester Diary,* 2:29.

75. Glover, *Peninsular Preparation,* 238–44.

76. Ibid., 31.

77. Schroeder, *Transformation of European Politics,* 580–82; "The Collapse of the Second Coalition," 244–90.

CHAPTER 8

1. Queensberry to Macpherson, 15 Mar. 1803, Sidmouth Papers 152M/1803/OZ302 quoted in Pellew, 2:171.

2. Wallis to Pole Carew, 12 Jan. 1804, Pole Carew Papers, CC/L/37.

3. Mulgrave to Lowther, 30 Nov. 1806, Earl of Lonsdale, *Historical Manuscripts Commission: Report on the Manuscripts of the Earl of Lonsdale* (London, 1893), 224–25.

4. Harvey, *Britain in the Early Nineteenth Century,* 142–43; Ingram, *Commitment to Empire,* 24, 94.

5. Liverpool to Hawkesbury, 1 June 1803, Add. MSS 38236, fo. 259.

6. Tierney to Lady Holland, 26 Dec. 1802, Add. MSS 51585, fo. 23.

7. Canning to Frere, 25 Aug. 1803, Add. MSS 38833, fo. 155.

8. Mitchell, *Charles James Fox,* 130–32, 202, 215; Fox to Lauderdale, [1803], Add. MSS 47564, fo. 184; *Parliamentary History,* 36:1408.

9. See the lists in *Parliamentary History,* vol. 36 and *Parliamentary Debates,* vol. 1.

10. Liverpool to Hervey, [1802], Hervey Papers 941/56/8.

11. Mitchell, *Charles James Fox,* 202–9.

12. Tomline to Mrs. Tomline, 10 Jan. 1804, Pretyman Papers HA 119/562/1; Grenville to Thomas Grenville, 14 Jan. 1804, Add. MSS 41852, fos. 188–89.

13. Grenville to Pitt, 31 Jan. 1804, *Dropmore Papers,* 7:211.

14. Fox to Grey, 13 Apr. 1804, Add. MSS 46575, fo. 121.

15. Fox to Grey, 29 Jan. 1804, Add. MSS 47565, fo. 114; Grenville to Pitt, 31 Jan. 1804, *Dropmore Papers,* 7:211–12.

16. Cornwallis to Ross, 13 Feb. 1804, *Cornwallis Correspondence,* 3:510–11.

17. Hobart to Auckland, 30 Jan. 1804, *Auckland Correspondence,* 4:189.

18. Pitt to Grenville, 4 Feb. 1804, *Dropmore Papers,* 7:212–14.

19. Mary Anne Addington's Notes, Sidmouth Papers Box 51 Public Office 2.

20. Stephen Lee, "'A new language in Politicks': George Canning and the Idea of Opposition, 1801–1807," *History* 83 (1998): 472–96.

21. Tomline to Rose, 7 Nov. 1803, Add. MSS 42773, fo. 27.

22. Thomas Richard Bentley, *A Few Cursory Remarks upon the State of Parties during the Administration of Henry Addington. By a Near Observer* (London, 1803); *A Brief Answer to a Few Cursory Remarks on the Present State of Parties by a Near Observer* (London, 1803); *General Review of Men and Measures, Occasioned by Remarks of Near and Accurate Observers, Plain Answers and Replies to Plain Answers etc. etc. by a More Distant Observer, out of the Vortex of Party* (London, 1804); Lord Archibald Hamilton, *Thoughts on the Formation of the Late and Present Administrations* (London, 1804); *Observations on a Ministerial Pamphlet Entitled Cursory Remarks of a Near Observer upon the State of Parties during the Administration of the Right Honourable Henry Addington* (London, 1803); *A Plain Answer to the Misrepresentations and Calumnies contained in the Cursory Remarks of A Near Observer by a More Accurate Observer*

(London, 1803); *Reply of a Near Observer to Some of the Answers of the Cursory Remarks* (London, 1804); *Reply to Lord Archibald Hamilton's Thoughts on the Formation of the Late and Present Administrations* (London, 1804).

23. Pitt to Castlereagh, 21 Sept. 1803, and Castlereagh to Pitt, 6 Oct. 1803, Dacres Adams Papers 30/58/3/107 and 109.

24. Richard Pares, *King George III and the Politicians* (Oxford: Clarendon Press, 1957), 136–37.

25. Hawkesbury to Liverpool, 31 May 1803, MS Loan 72/55, fo. 22.

26. *Malmesbury Diaries*, 4:264.

27. Hawkesbury to Liverpool, 5 June 1803, MS Loan 72/55, fo. 23.

28. Liverpool to Hawkesbury, 7 June 1803, MS Loan 72/49, fo. 64.

29. Lord Sidmouth's Notes, Sidmouth Papers 152M/c1803/Z10.

30. Quoted in Tomline to Mrs. Tomline, 10 Jan. 1804, Pretyman Papers HA 119/562/1.

31. Hawkesbury to Liverpool, 16 July 1803, MS Loan 72/55, fos. 29–30; Eldon to Redesdale, 10 Oct. 1803, Redesdale Papers D2002/C11.

32. *Malmesbury Diaries*, 4:285.

33. Pitt to Tomline, 7 Jan. 1804, Pretyman Papers HA 119/T108/42.

34. Ehrman, *Consuming Struggle*, 599.

35. Lee, "'A new language in Politicks,'" 487.

36. Morpeth to Holland, 22 Jan. 1804, Add. MSS 51577, fo. 35.

37. Hobart to Auckland, 30 Jan. 1804, *Auckland Correspondence,* 4:190–91.

38. Diary of Alexander Hope, Hope of Luffness Muniments GD 364/1/1154; Ehrman, *Consuming Struggle*, 3: 637–54.

39. *Malmesbury Diaries*, 4:288; Cyril Matheson, *The Life of Henry Dundas, First Viscount Melville, 1742–1811,* (London: Constable, 1933), 332–33; Pitt to Melville, 29 Mar. 1804, Earl Stanhope, ed., *Secret Correspondence Connected with Mr. Pitt's Return to Office in 1804,* printed privately (London, 1852), 13–14; Hope Diary, Hope of Luffness Muniments GD 364/1/1154; *Parliamentary Debates,* 1:878; Stanhope, 3:195; Ehrman, *Consuming Struggle,* 630–36; Liverpool to Hervey, 26 Dec. 1804, Hervey Papers 941/56/8; Hardwicke to Yorke, 23 Mar. 1804, Add. MSS 35705, fos. 190–91; *Parliamentary Debates,* 1:891–93; Yorke to Hardwicke, 16 Mar. 1804, Add. MSS 35705, fos. 172–73; *Glenbervie Diaries,* 1:372–73.

40. Foreman, *Georgiana*, 364–74.

41. Melville to Hope, 5 Apr. 1804, Dacres Adams Papers 30/58/5/9; Pitt to Melville, 29 Mar. and 18 Apr. 1804, *Secret Correspondence,* 16, 34; same to same, 4 Apr. 1804, Pitt Papers, John Rylands Library, Eng. MSS 907; Melville to Pitt, 3 and 6 Apr. 1804, Add. MSS 40102, fos. 128–34; Pitt to Tomline, 13 Apr. 1804, Pretyman Papers HA 119/T108/42.

42. Robinson to Jenkinson, 24 Sept. 1804, quoted in Michael Duffy, "The Younger Pitt and the House of Commons," *History* 81 (1998): 218.

43. Holland later claimed that Addington resigned prematurely, as he retained a

majority in Parliament and strong support in the country. Mary Anne Addington's Notes, Sidmouth Papers Box 51, Public Office 2.

44. Hobart to Hawkesbury, 1 Oct. 1803, Hobart Papers D/MH/H/War/B75.

45. Otto to Talleyrand, 2 pluviôse X (22 Jan. 1802), AE Angleterre/597.

46. Ibid.

47. David J. Brown, "The Government of Scotland under Henry Dundas and William Pitt," *History* 83 (1998): 274–75.

48. Maitland to Addington, 16 Sept. 1803, Sidmouth Papers 152M/1803/OZ306.

49. *Glenbervie Diaries,* 1:328; Hardwicke to Yorke, 30 Apr. 1804, Add. MSS 35705, fos. 298–301; same to same, 11 Oct. 1803, Add. MSS 35703, fos. 253–60.

50. St. Vincent to Addington, 10 and 18 Jan. 1804, and Addington to Yorke, 5 Jan. 1804, Sidmouth Papers 152M/c1804/ON26, ON28, and OI2.

51. Bragge's existing correspondence for this period is predominantly concerned with applications for office. Bragge-Bathurst Papers D421/C19.

52. Hardwicke to Addington, 7 Sept. 1801, Sidmouth Papers 152M/c1801/OI10; Rose to Pitt, 7 May 1804, Add. MSS 42772, fo. 196.

53. Addington to Hiley Addington, 24 Dec. 1802, Sidmouth Papers 152M/c1802/F3.

54. Hawkesbury to Liverpool, 31 May 1803, MS Loan 72/55, fo. 21.

55. Yorke to Hardwicke, 12 Aug. 1803, Add. MSS 35702, fos. 326–27; Sheridan to Addington, 29 Aug. 1803, Sidmouth Papers 152M/1803/OZ88; Yorke to Hardwicke, 5 May and 18 Aug. 1803, Add. MSS 35702, fos. 185–88, 339–40; Tierney to Lady Holland, 26 Dec. 1802, Add. MSS 51585, fo. 24; Liverpool to Hawkesbury, 1 June 1803, Add. MSS 38236, fo. 261; Ziegler, 203–4.

56. Hardwicke to Yorke, 15 Nov. 1802, Add. MSS 35702, fos. 48–49; Portland to Crewe, 4 Nov. 1802, Add. MSS 37845, fos. 102; *Malmesbury Diaries,* 4:255; Eldon to Hobart, 12 May 1803, Hobart Papers D/MH/H/War/B65.

57. Cyril Philips, *The East India Company, 1784–1834* (Manchester: Manchester University Press, 1940), 112–41.

58. Yorke to Hardwicke, 16 Mar. 1804, Add. MSS 35705, fos. 172–73.

59. Yorke to Hardwicke, 17 Apr. 1804, Add. MSS 35705, fos. 244–45.

60. Duffy, *The Younger Pitt,* 99–130.

61. Michael Fry, *The Dundas Despotism* (Edinburgh: Edinburgh University Press, 1992), 32–33, 131–33, and 201–3; David J. Brown, "Government of Scotland," 274–76.

62. Maitland to Addington, 16 Sept. 1803, Sidmouth Papers 152M/1803/OZ306.

63. Fry, *Dundas,* 256–57.

64. Bathurst's memorandum, May 1804, *HMC Bathurst,* 34–35; Eldon to Pitt, 22 Apr. 1804, Chatham Papers PRO 30/8/132/1.

65. Yorke to Hardwicke, 24 Apr. 1804, Add. MSS 35705, fos. 268–69.

66. Althorp Papers G57.

67. Michael McCahill, "The House of Lords and the Collapse of Henry Addington's Administration," *Parliamentary History* 6 (1987): 69–94.

68. Pellew, 2:279; Memorandum on the Change of Government, Melville Castle Muniments GD 51/1/76.

69. *Colchester Diary,* 1:500–501.

70. Starhemberg to Colloredo, 1 May 1804, HHStA England/145.

71. Add. MSS 39886, ff. 131–128 reversed.

72. Pellew, 2:291.

73. *Parliamentary Debates,* 2:201–2.

74. Pellew, 2:307.

75. Starhemberg to Colloredo, 6 Mar. 1804, HHStA England/145.

76. Holland, *Memoirs of the Whig Party,* 1:191.

77. Sidmouth to Bond, 1 Jan. 1805, Bond Papers D367/C24.

EPILOGUE

1. Liverpool to Hervey, 26 Dec. 1804, Hervey Papers 941/56/8; Ziegler, 226.

2. A large collection of the letters is in Sidmouth Papers 152M/c1804/OZ.

3. Sidmouth Papers 152M/1804/OZ60.

4. Yorke to Hardwicke, 8 May 1804, Add. MSS 35706, fos. 13–14.

5. Christopher Hibbert, *Nelson: A Personal History* (London: Viking, 1994), 43, 271.

6. Addington to Bragge, 12 Dec. 1804, quoted in Pellew, 2:327.

7. Addington to Pitt, 29 Dec. 1804, Hedlam Papers D/He 271/9.

8. John Kenneth Severn, *A Wellesley Affair: Marquess Wellesley and the Conduct of Anglo-Spanish Diplomacy, 1809–1812* (Tallahassee: University Presses of Florida, 1981), 96.

9. Liverpool to the Bishop of Hereford, 16 July 1804, MS Loan 72/51, fo. 88.

10. Pole to Pole Carew, 1 Dec. 1804, Pole Carew Papers, CC/L/37.

11. Hall, *British Strategy,* 54.

12. Pole to Pole Carew, 26 Dec. 1804 and 5 Jan. 1805, Pole Carew Papers, CC/L/37 and 38.

13. Quoted in Sonia Keppel, *The Sovereign Lady: A Life of Elizabeth Vassall, Third Lady Holland* (London: Hamilton, 1974), 136.

14. Ziegler, 278.

15. Ibid., 288.

16. Addington to Windham, 1 Oct. 1801, Add. MSS 37880, fo. 160; Windham to Addington, 1 Oct. 1801, Add. MSS 37880, fo. 171; Pelham to Windham, 20 Oct. 1801, Add. MSS 37880, fos. 175–6; *Parliamentary History,* 36:14; Pellew, 2:52–53; "Memoirs of Sir Thomas Byam Martin," 10 Sept. 1840, Add. MSS 41378, fo. 61.

17. Schroeder, "The Collapse of the Second Coalition," 289–90.

18. Brewer, *Sinews of Power;* Cookson, *British Armed Nation;* Black, *Britain as a Military Power;* Colley, *Britons;* Philip Harling and Peter Mandler, "From 'Fiscal-Military' State to Laissez-faire State, 1760–1850," *Journal of British Studies* 32 (1993): 44–70; Lawrence Stone, ed., *An Imperial State at War* (London: Routledge, 1994).

19. Harling and Mandler, "From 'Fiscal-Military,'" 48.

20. Colley, *Britons*, 328–37.

21. Ziegler, 374.

22. Ibid., 330–31.

23. Stanhope, 3:1.

Bibliography

MANUSCRIPT SOURCES

Official Correspondence

Archives du Ministère des Affaires Etrangères, Paris
Correspondance Politique, Angleterre

Haus-, Hof-, und Staatsarchiv, Vienna
Staatskanzlei England Korrespondenz
Staatskanzlei England Weisungen

Public Record Office, London

  Admiralty Office Records
Adm. 1/In Letters
Adm. 2/Out Letters
Adm. 3/Board Minutes

  Foreign Office Records
FO 5/United States
FO 7/Austria
FO 22/Denmark
FO 27/France
FO 37/Netherlands
FO 63/Portugal
FO 64/Prussia
FO 65/Russia
FO 70/Sicily
FO 72/Spain
FO 73/Sweden
FO 78/Turkey

  Home Office Records
HO 42/In Letters, Domestic
HO 43/Out Letters, Domestic
HO 100/Ireland

War Office Records
WO 1/In Letters
WO 6/Secretary at War, Out Letters
WO 30/Defence Papers

Private Correspondence

Bodleian Library, Oxford: Yorke Papers

British Library, London: Althorp Papers; Auckland Papers; Bexley Papers; Dropmore Papers; Fox Papers; Frere Papers; Grenville Papers; Hardwicke Papers; Hastings Papers; Holland House Papers; Liverpool Papers; Martin Papers; Melville Papers; Nelson Papers; Paget Papers; Pelham Papers; Perceval Papers; Rose Papers; St. Vincent Papers; Wellesley Papers; Windham Papers

Buckinghamshire Record Office, Aylesbury: Hobart Papers; Grenville Papers

Cambridge University Library: Pitt Papers

Cornwall Record Office, Truro: Pole Carew Papers

Derbyshire Record Office, Matlock: Fitzherbert Papers

Devonshire Record Office, Exeter: Sidmouth Papers

Dorset Record Office, Dorchester: Bond Papers

Durham Record Office, Durham: Headlam Papers

Durham University: Grey Papers

Gloucestershire Record Office, Gloucester: Bragge-Bathurst Papers; Redesdale Papers; Southerton-Estcourt Papers

Hampshire Record Office, Winchester: Tierney Papers; Wickham Papers

John Rylands University, Manchester: Pitt Papers

Kent Record Office, Maidstone: Pratt Papers; Sackville Papers; Stanhope of Chevening Papers

National Maritime Museum, Greenwich: Morice Pole Papers

Public Record Office, London: FO 323/4 Whitworth Papers; FO 353/43 Jackson Papers; PRO 30/8 Chatham Papers; PRO 30/11Cornwallis Papers

Public Record Office of Northern Ireland, Belfast: Castlereagh Papers

Scottish Record Office, Edinburgh: Hope of Luffness Muniments; Melville Castle Muniments

Suffolk Record Office, Bury St. Edmunds: Hervey Papers

Suffolk Record Office, Ipswich: Pretyman Papers

West Yorkshire Archive Service, Leeds: Canning Papers

Private Collections

Adams, G. A. F. E. Wellingborough, Northamptonshire: Dacres Adams Papers

Carew Pole, Sir Richard. Antony House, Cornwall: Pole Carew Papers

Sitwell, Francis. Weston, Northamptonshire: Glenbervie Manuscript Diary

Trustees of the Chatsworth Settlement, Chatsworth, Derbyshire: Chatsworth
    Papers, Fifth Duke's Group
Vernon, Lord. Sudbury, Derbyshire: Warren Papers

PRINTED PRIMARY SOURCES: COLLECTED DOCUMENTS, DIARIES, MEMOIRS

Annual Register

Auckland, William, Lord. *The Journal and Correspondence of William, Lord Auck-
    land*. Ed. G. Hogge. 4 vols. London, 1861.

Bathurst, Henry, Earl. *Historical Manuscripts Commission: Report on the Manu-
    scripts of the Seventh Earl Bathurst*. London: Historical Manuscripts Commis-
    sion, 1923.

Bentley, Thomas Richard. *A Few Cursory Remarks upon the State of Parties during
    the Administration of Henry Addington. By a Near Observer*. London, 1803.

Bonaparte, Joseph. *Mémoires et correspondance politique et militaire du Roi Joseph*,
    pub. par le Baron Du Casse. 9 vols. Paris, 1856.

*A Brief Answer to a Few Cursory Remarks on the Present State of Parties by a Near
    Observer*. London, 1803.

Browning, Oscar, ed. *England and Napoleon in 1803: Being the dispatches of Lord
    Whitworth and others, now first printed from the originals in the Record Office*.
    London, 1887.

Buckingham and Chandos, Richard, duke of. *Memoirs of the Court and Cabinets
    of George III*. 4 vols. London, 1853–55.

Castlereagh, Robert Stewart, Viscount. *Memoirs and Correspondence of Robert
    Stewart, Viscount Castlereagh*. Ed. Marquess of Londonderry. 12 vols. London,
    1848–54.

Colchester, Charles, Lord. *The Diary and Correspondence of Charles Abbot, Lord
    Colchester, Speaker of the House of Commons 1802–1817*. Ed. Charles, Lord
    Colchester. 3 vols. London, 1861.

Cornwallis, Charles, Marquis. *The Correspondence of Charles, First Marquis Corn-
    wallis*. Ed. C. Ross. 3 vols. London, 1859.

*General Review of Men and Measures, Occasioned by Remarks of Near and Accu-
    rate Observers, Plain Answers and Replies to Plain Answers etc. etc. by a More
    Distant Observer, out of the Vortex of Party*. London, 1804.

George III. *The Later Correspondence of George III*. Ed. Arthur Aspinall. 5 vols.
    Cambridge: Cambridge University Press, 1966–70.

George, Prince of Wales. *The Correspondence of George, Prince of Wales, 1770–1812*.
    Ed. Arthur Aspinall. 8 vols. London: Cassell, 1963–71.

Glenbervie, Sylvester Douglas, Lord. *The Diaries of Sylvester Douglas, Lord Glen-
    bervie*. Ed. Francis Bickley. 2 vols. London: Constable, 1928.

Granville, Granville Leveson Gower, Earl. *Lord Granville Leveson Gower: Private Correspondence, 1781–1821.* Ed. Castalia, Countess Granville. 2 vols. London: John Murray, 1916.

Grenville, William, Lord. *Historical Manuscripts Commission: Report on the Manuscripts of J. B. Fortescue, esq. Preserved at Dropmore.* 10 vols. London: Historical Manuscripts Commission, 1892–1927.

Hamilton, Lord Archibald. *Thoughts on the Formation of the Late and Present Administrations.* London, 1804.

Hansard's Parliamentary Debates from the Year 1803 to the Present Time, Published under the Superintendence of T. C. Hansard. 41 vols. London, 1803–20.

Hatherton, Lord. "Extracts from Lord Hatherton's Diary." Ed. A. Aspinall. *Parliamentary Affairs* 17 (1964): 373–88.

Holland, Elizabeth, Lady. *The Journal of Elizabeth, Lady Holland 1791–1811.* Ed. Earl of Ilchester. 2 vols. London: Longman, 1908.

Holland, Henry Richard, Lord. *Memoirs of the Whig Party during My Time.* Ed. Henry Edward, Lord Holland. 2 vols. London, 1852.

Lonsdale, James, earl of. *Historical Manuscripts Commission: Report on the Manuscripts of the Earl of Lonsdale.* London, 1893.

Malmesbury, James, earl of. *The Diaries and Correspondence of James Harris, First Earl of Malmesbury.* Ed. third earl of Malmesbury. 4 vols. London, 1844.

Marsden, William. *A Brief Memoir of the Life and Writings of the Late William Marsden Written by Himself with Notes from His Correspondence.* Ed. Mrs. E. W. Marsden. London, 1838.

Minto, Gilbert, earl of. *Life and Letters of Gilbert Elliot, First Earl of Minto, from 1751–1806.* Ed. countess of Minto. 3 vols. London, 1874.

Napoleon I, emperor of France. *Correspondance de Napoléon Ier: Publiée par ordre de l'Empereur Napoléon III.* 32 vols. Paris, 1858–70.

———. *Letters and Documents of Napoleon, 1769–1822.* Ed. John Howard. London: Cresset, 1961.

———. *Lettres inédites de Napoléon.* Ed. Leon Lecestre. 2 vols. Paris, 1897.

———. *Napoleon's Letters.* Ed. J. M. Thompson. London: J. M. Dent and Sons, 1954.

Narochnitskii, A. L. et al., ed. *Vneshniaia politika Rossii XIX i nachala XX veka: Dokumenty rossiiskogo ministerstva inostrannykh del.* First series. 15 vols. Moscow: Komissiia po izdaniiu diplomaticheskikh dokumentov, 1960.

Observations on a Ministerial Pamphlet Entitled Cursory Remarks of a Near Observer upon the State of Parties during the Administration of the Right Honourable Henry Addington. London, 1803.

Parliamentary History of England: From the Earliest Period to the Year 1803. 36 vols. London, 1806–20.

A Plain Answer to the Misrepresentations and Calumnies contained in the Cursory Remarks of A Near Observer by a More Accurate Observer. London, 1803.

Pickering, Danby, ed. *Statutes at Large from Magna Charta to 1806.* Cambridge, 1807.

Times. (London, 1800–1804).

Reply of a Near Observer to Some of the Answers of the Cursory Remarks. London, 1804.

Reply to Lord Archibald Hamilton's Thoughts on the Formation of the Late and Present Administrations. London, 1804.

Rose, George. *The Diaries and Correspondence of Rt. Hon. George Rose.* Ed. L. V. Harcourt. 2 vols. London, 1860.

St. Vincent, John, earl of. *Letters of Admiral of the Fleet, the Earl of St. Vincent, 1801–1804.* Ed. David. B. Smith. 2 vols. London: Navy Records Society, 1922–27.

Sbornik Imperatorskogo Russkogo istoricheskogo obshchestva. 140 vols. St. Petersburg, 1867–1916.

Southey, Robert. *Letters from England.* Ed. Jack Simmons. London: Cresset, 1951.

Stanhope, Philip Henry, Earl, ed. *Secret Correspondence Connected with Mr. Pitt's Return to Office in 1804.* London: printed privately, 1852.

Vorontsov, Count Semen de. *Arkhiv kniazia Vorontsova.* Ed. P. I. Bartenev. 40 vols. Moscow, 1870–97.

Wellesley, Richard, Marquess. *Despatches, Minutes and Correspondence of the Marquess Wellesley.* Ed. Montgomery Martin. 5 vols. London, 1837.

———. *The Wellesley Papers.* Ed. L. S. Benjamin. 2 vols. London: Herbert Jenkins, 1914.

Windham, William. *The Diary of the Rt. Hon. William Windham, 1784 to 1810.* Ed. Mrs. Henry Baring. London, 1866.

SECONDARY SOURCES

Alter, J.-M. "The Early Life and Political Career of Robert Banks Jenkinson, Second Earl of Liverpool, 1790–1812." Ph.D. diss., University College Wales, Aberystwyth, 1988.

Anderson, M. S. *Britain's Discovery of Russia, 1553–1815.* London: Macmillan, 1958.

———. *Europe in the Eighteenth Century, 1713–1783.* London: Longman, 1961.

Anderson, Roger C. *Naval Wars in the Baltic during the Sailing Ship Epoch, 1522–1850.* London: C. Gilbert-Wood, 1910.

Anson, W. V. *Life of John Jervis, Admiral Lord St. Vincent.* London: Murray, 1913.

Arthur, Charles B. *The Remaking of the English Navy by Admiral St. Vincent—Key to Victory over Napoleon: The Great Unclaimed Naval Revolution, 1795–1805.* London: University Press of America, 1986.

Ashbourne, Edward, Lord. *Pitt: Some Chapters of His Life and Times.* London, 1898.

Baxter, J. L., and F. K. Donnelly. "The Revolutionary Underground in the West Riding: Myth or Reality." *Past and Present* 64 (1974): 113–35.

Beeley, H. "A Project of Alliance with Russia in 1802." *English Historical Review* 49 (1934): 497–502.

Black, Jeremy. *Britain as a Military Power, 1688–1815*. London: UCL Press, 1999.

————. *Natural and Necessary Enemies: Anglo-French Relations in the Eighteenth Century*. London: Duckworth, 1986.

Bohstedt, John. *Riots and Community Politics in England and Wales, 1790–1810*. Cambridge, Mass.: Harvard University Press, 1983.

Booth, Alan. "Food Riots in the North West of England, 1790–1801." *Past and Present* 78 (1977): 84–107.

Bowman, H. M. *Preliminary Stages of the Peace of Amiens*. Toronto: University Library, 1901.

Breihan, John R. "The Addington Party and the Navy in British Politics, 1801–1806." In *New Aspects of Naval History*, ed. Craig L. Symonds. Annapolis: Naval Institute Press, 1981.

Brenton, E. P. *Life and Correspondence of John, Earl of St. Vincent*. 2 vols. London, 1838.

Brewer, John. *The Pleasures of the Imagination: English Culture in the Eighteenth Century*. Chicago: University of Chicago Press, 1997.

————. *The Sinews of Power: War, Money and the English State 1688–1783*. London: Unwin Hyman, 1989.

Brown, David J. "The Government of Scotland under Henry Dundas and William Pitt." *History* 83 (1998): 265–79.

Brown, Judith. "The Early Career of Robert Banks Jenkinson, Second Earl of Liverpool, 1790–1812: The Making of the Arch Mediocrity." Ph.D. diss., University of Delaware, 1980.

Bryant, Arthur. *The Years of Endurance, 1793–1802*. London: Collins, 1942.

————. *The Years of Victory, 1802–1812*. London: Collins, 1945.

Burrows, Simon. "Culture and Misperception: The Law and the Press in the Outbreak of War in 1803." *International History Review* 18 (1996): 793–818.

————. "The Struggle for European Opinion in the Napoleonic Wars: British Francophone Propaganda, 1803–1814." *French History* 11 (1997): 29–53.

Campbell, John, Lord. *Lives of the Lord Chancellors and Keepers of the Great Seal of England*. 4th ed. 10 vols. London, 1857.

Cannan, Edwin. *The Paper Pound of 1797–1821*. London: P. S. King and Son, 1919.

Charlesworth, Andrew. ed. *An Atlas of Rural Protest in Britain, 1548–1900*. London: Croon Helm, 1982.

Christie, Ian R. *Stress and Stability in Late Eighteenth-Century Britain: Reflections on the British Avoidance of Revolution*. Oxford: Clarendon Press, 1984.

————. *Wars and Revolutions: Britain, 1760–1815*. London: Edward Arnold, 1982.

Colley, Linda. *Britons: Forging the Nation, 1707–1837*. New Haven, Conn.: Vintage, 1992.

Cookson, J. E. *The British Armed Nation*. Oxford: Clarendon Press, 1997.

Coquelle, P. "Les responsabilités de la rupture de la Paix d'Amiens en 1803." *Revue d'histoire diplomatique* 16 (1902): 267–302.

Cox, N. G. "Aspects of British Radicalism: The Suppression and Re-emergence of the Constitutional Democratic Tradition, 1795–1809." Ph.D. diss., University of Cambridge, 1971.

Crouzet, François. "La guerre maritime" and "Le système continental et ses conséquences." In *Napoléon et l'Empire*, ed. Jean Mistler, 2: 27–51. Verviers: Marabout, 1979.

Deutch, Harold C. *The Genesis of Napoleonic Imperialism*. Cambridge, Mass.: Harvard University Press, 1938.

Dickinson, H. T., ed. *Britain and the French Revolution, 1789–1815*. London: Macmillan, 1989.

Dinwiddy, J. R. "The 'Black Lamp' in Yorkshire, 1801–1802." *Past and Present* 64 (1974): 113–135.

Duffy, Michael. "British Diplomacy and the French Wars, 1789–1815." In *Britain and the French Revolution, 1789–1815*, ed. H. T. Dickinson. London: Macmillan, 1989.

———. "British War Policy: The Austrian Alliance, 1793–1801." D.Phil. diss., Oxford: 1971.

———. *Soldiers, Sugar, and Seapower: The British Expedition to the West Indies and the War against Revolutionary France*. Oxford: Clarendon Press, 1987.

———. *The Younger Pitt*. London: Longman, 2000.

———. "The Younger Pitt and the House of Commons." *History* 81 (1998): 217–24.

Ehrman, John. *The Younger Pitt: The Consuming Struggle*. London: Constable, 1996.

Elliott, Marianne. *Partners in Revolution: The United Irishmen and France*. London: Yale University Press, 1982.

Emsley, Clive. *British Society and the French Wars, 1793–1815*. London: Macmillan, 1979.

Farnsworth, Arthur. *Addington, Author of the Modern Income Tax*. London: Stevens & Sons, 1951.

Fedorak, Charles John. "Catholic Emancipation and the Resignation of William Pitt in 1801." *Albion* 24 (1992): 49–64.

———. "The French Capitulation in Egypt and the Preliminary Anglo-French Treaty of Peace in October 1801: A Note." *International History Review* 15 (1993): 525–34.

———. "In Search of a Necessary Ally: Addington, Hawkesbury, and Russia, 1801–1804." *International History Review* 13 (1991): 221–45.

———. "Maritime versus Continental Strategy: Britain and the Defeat of

Napoleon." *Proceedings of the Consortium on Revolutionary Europe* 20 (1990): 176–82.

———. "The Royal Navy and British Amphibious Operations during the Revolutionary and Napoleonic Wars." *Military Affairs* 52 (1988): 141–46.

Feiling, Keith. *The Second Tory Party, 1714–1832.* London: Macmillan, 1938.

Feldbaek, Ole. "The Anglo-Russian Rapprochement of 1801: A Prelude to the Peace of Amiens." *Scandinavian Journal of History* 3 (1978): 205–27.

———. *Denmark and the Armed Neutrality, 1800–1801.* Copenhagen: Akademisk Forlag, 1980.

Foreman, Amanda. *Georgiana: The Duchess of Devonshire.* London: Harper Collins, 1998.

Fortescue, John. *The County Lieutenancies and the Army, 1803–1814.* London: Macmillan, 1909.

———. *A History of the British Army.* 14 vols. London: Macmillan, 1899–1930.

Fry, Michael. *The Dundas Despotism.* Edinburgh: Edinburgh University Press, 1992.

Gash, Norman. *Lord Liverpool: The Life and Political Career of Robert Banks Jenkinson, Second Earl of Liverpool.* London: Weidenfield and Nicolson, 1984.

Gayer, Arthur, W. W. Rostow, and A. J. Schwartz. *The Growth of the British Economy, 1790–1850.* 2 vols. Oxford: Clarendon Press, 1953.

Gielgud, Adam. *Memoirs of Prince Adam Czartoryski and His Correspondence with Alexander I.* 2 vols. London, 1888.

Gill, Conrad. "The Relations between England and France in 1802." *English Historical Review* 24 (1909): 61–78.

Glover, Richard. *Britain at Bay: Defence against Bonaparte, 1803–14.* London: George Allen & Unwin, 1973.

———. *Peninsular Preparation: The Reform of the British Army, 1795–1809.* Cambridge: Cambridge University Press, 1963.

Gregory, Desmond. *Malta, Britain, and the European Powers, 1793–1815.* Madison, N.J.: Fairleigh Dickinson University Press, 1996.

———. *Sicily: The Insecure Base. A History of the British Occupation of Sicily, 1806–1815.* Rutherford, N.J.: Fairleigh Dickinson University Press, 1988.

Grimsted, Patricia Kennedy. *The Foreign Ministers of Alexander I: Political Attitudes and the Conduct of Russian Diplomacy, 1801–1825.* Los Angeles: University of California Press, 1969.

Grunwald, Constantin de. *Trois siècles de diplomatie russe.* Paris: Calmann-Levy, 1945.

Hall, Christopher, D. "Addington at War: Unspectacular but not Unsuccessful." *Historical Research* 61 (1988): 306–15.

———. *British Strategy in the Napoleonic War 1803–15.* Manchester: Manchester University Press, 1992.

———. "Factors Influencing British Strategic Planning and Execution during the Napoleonic Wars." Ph.D. diss., University of Exeter, 1985.

Harling, Philip. *The Waning of "Old Corruption": The Politics of Economical Reform in Britain, 1779–1846*. Oxford: Clarendon Press, 1996.

Harling, Philip and Peter Mandler. "From 'Fiscal-Military' State to Laissez-faire State, 1760–1850." *Journal of British Studies* 32 (1993): 44–70.

Harvey, A. D. *Britain in the Early Nineteenth Century*. New York: St. Martin's Press, 1978.

———. "European Attitudes to Britain during the French Revolution and Napoleonic Era." *History* 63 (1978): 356–65.

Haythornthwaite, Philip J. "The Volunteer Force, 1803–04." *Journal of the Society for Army Historical Research* 64 (1986): 193–204.

Helleiner, Karl. *The Imperial Loans: A Study in Financial and Diplomatic History*. Oxford: Clarendon Press, 1965.

Hibbert, Christopher. *George III: A Personal History*. London: Viking, 1998.

———. *Nelson: A Personal History*. London: Viking, 1994.

Hone, J. Ann. *For the Cause of Truth: Radicalism in London, 1796–1821*. Oxford: Clarendon Press, 1983.

Ingram, Edward. "British Policy towards Persia and the Defence of British India, 1798–1807." Ph.D. diss., London School of Economics: 1968.

———. *Commitment to Empire: Prophesies of the Great Game in Asia, 1797–1800*. Oxford: Clarendon Press, 1981.

———. "The Geopolitics of the First British Expedition to Egypt—IV: Occupation and Withdrawal, 1801–3." *Middle Eastern Studies* 31 (1995): 317–46.

———. *In Defence of British India: Great Britain in the Middle East, 1775–1842*. London: Frank Cass, 1984.

Keir, D. K. *The Constitutional History of Modern Britain since 1485*. 7th ed. London: Adam & Charles Black, 1964.

Kennedy, Paul. *The Rise and Fall of British Naval Mastery*. London: Allen Lane, 1976.

Kenny, J. J. "Lord Whitworth and the Conspiracy against Tsar Paul I: The New Evidence of the Kent Archives." *Slavic Review* 36 (1977): 205–19.

Keppel, Sonia. *The Sovereign Lady: A Life of Elizabeth Vassall, Third Lady Holland*. London: Hamilton, 1974.

King, Charles R. *The Life and Correspondence of Rufus King*. 6 vols. New York, 1896.

Kissinger, Henry. *A World Restored: The Politics of Conservatism in a Revolutionary Period*. New York: Grosset & Dunlap, 1964.

Kraehe, Enno E. *Metternich's German Policy*. 2 vols. Princeton: Princeton University Press, 1983.

Langford, Paul. *The Eighteenth Century, 1688–1815*. London: A. & C. Black, 1976.

Lee, Stephen. "'A new language in Politicks': George Canning and the Idea of Opposition, 1801–1807." *History* 83 (1998): 472–96.

McCahill, Michael. "The House of Lords and the Collapse of Henry Addington's Administration." *Parliamentary History* 6 (1987): 69–94.

McGrew, Roderick E. *Paul I of Russia, 1754–1801.* Oxford: Clarendon Press, 1992.

Mackesy, Piers. "The Strategic Problems of the British War Effort." In *Britain and the French Revolution, 1789–1815,* ed. H. T. Dickinson. London: Macmillan, 1989.

————. *War without Victory: The Downfall of Pitt, 1799–1802.* Oxford: 1984.

MacLeod, Emma Vincent. *A War of Ideas: British Attitudes to the Wars against Revolutionary France, 1792–1802.* Aldershot: Ashgate, 1998.

MacLeod, Henry. *The Theory and Practice of Banking.* 2 vols. London, 1876.

Manning, J. A. *Lives of the Speakers of the House of Commons.* London, 1851.

Matheson, Cyril. *The Life of Henry Dundas, First Viscount Melville, 1742–1811.* London: Constable, 1933.

Mitchell, L. G. *Charles James Fox.* Oxford: Oxford University Press, 1992.

Morriss, R. A. "Labour Relations in the Royal Naval Dockyards, 1801–5." *Mariner's Mirror* 63 (1976): 337–45.

————. *The Royal Dockyards during the Revolutionary and Napoleonic Wars.* Leicester: Leicester University Press, 1983.

Newman, Gerald. *The Rise of English Nationalism: A Cultural History, 1740–1830.* London: Weidenfield & Nicolson, 1987.

O'Brien, P. K. "English Government Revenue, 1793–1815: A Study in Fiscal and Financial Policy in the Wars against France." D.Phil. diss., University of Oxford, 1967.

Olphin, H. K. *George Tierney.* London: G. Allen & Unwin, 1934.

Oman, Charles. *The Unfortunate Colonel Despard and Other Stories.* London: E. Arnold & Co., 1922.

Pares, Richard. *King George III and the Politicians.* Oxford: Clarendon Press, 1953.

Parkinson, C. Northcote. *War in the Eastern Seas, 1793–1815.* London: George Allen & Unwin, 1954.

Pellew, George. *The Life and Correspondence of the Right Honourable Henry Addington, First Viscount Sidmouth.* 3 vols. London, 1847.

Petrel, Jacques. "La Russie et la rupture de la Paix d'Amiens." *Annales de l'Ecole Libre des Sciences Politiques* 12 (1887): 70–101.

Philips, Cyril. *The East India Company, 1784–1834.* Manchester: Manchester University Press, 1940.

Philippson, Martin. "La Paix d'Amiens et la politique générale de Napoléon Ier." *Revue historique* 75 (1901): 286–318.

Polden, Patrick. "Domestic Policies of the Addington Administration, 1801–1804." Ph.D. diss., University of Reading, 1975.

Pool, Bernard. *Navy Board Contracts, 1660–1832: Contract Administration under the Navy Board.* London: Longman, 1966.

Pretyman Tomline, George. *Memoirs of the Life of William Pitt.* 3 vols. London, 1821; a fourth volume was printed privately in 1904.

Ragsdale, Hugh. *Detente in the Napoleonic Era.* Lawrence, Kansas: Regents Press, 1980.

Reilly, Robin. *William Pitt the Younger.* New York: Putnam, 1979.

Roberts, Michael. "Great Britain, Denmark and Russia, 1763–1770." In *Studies in Diplomatic History,* ed. Ragnhild Hatton and M. S. Anderson. London: Longman, 1970.

———. *Splendid Isolation, 1763–1780.* The Stenton Lecture of 1969. University of Reading, 1970.

Rodger, A. B. *The War of the Second Coalition, 1798–1801: A Strategic Commentary.* Oxford: Clarendon Press, 1964.

Roider, Karl A. *Baron Thugut and Austria's Response to the French Revolution.* Princeton, N. J.: Princeton University Press, 1987.

Rose, John Holland. "The Struggle with Revolutionary France, 1793–1801." and "The Contest with Napoleon, 1802–1812." In *The Cambridge History of British Foreign Policy,* ed. A. Ward and G. P. Gooch, 1: 216–392. Cambridge: Cambridge University Press, 1922.

———. *William Pitt and the Great War.* London: G. Bell & Sons, 1911.

Rudé, George. *Hanoverian London, 1714–1808.* London: Secker and Warburg, 1971.

Russell, Lord John. *Memorials and Correspondence of Charles James Fox.* 4 vols. London, 1853–57.

Sabine, B. E. V. *A History of Income Tax.* London: George Allen & Unwin, 1966.

Schom, Alan. *Napoleon Bonaparte.* New York: Harper Perennial, 1997.

Schroeder, Paul W. "The Collapse of the Second Coalition." *Journal of Modern History* 59 (1987): 244–90.

———. "Napoleon's Foreign Policy: A Criminal Enterprise." *Journal of Military History* 54 (1990): 147–62.

———. *The Transformation of European Politics 1763–1848.* New York: Oxford University Press, 1994.

Scott, H. M. "Great Britain, Poland and the Russian Alliance, 1763–1767." *Historical Journal* 19 (1976): 53–74.

Seligman, Edwin R. A. *The Income Tax: A Study of the History Theory and Practice of Income Tax at Home and Abroad.* New York: Macmillan, 1911.

Severn, John Kenneth. *A Wellesley Affair: Marquess Wellesley and the Conduct of Anglo-Spanish Diplomacy, 1809–1812.* Tallahassee: University Presses of Florida, 1981.

Sherrard, O. A. *A Life of Lord St. Vincent.* London: G. Allen & Unwin, 1933.

Smith, E. A. *Lord Grey, 1764–1845.* Oxford: Clarendon Press, 1990.

Sorel, Albert. *L'Europe et la Révolution française.* 8 vols. Paris: E. Plon, Nourrit et cie, 1949.

Stanhope, Philip Henry, Earl. *The Life of Pitt.* 3rd ed. 3 vols. London, 1879.

Stevenson, John. "Food Riots in England, 1792–1818." In *Popular Protest and Public Order,* ed. R. Quinault and J. Stevenson. London: George Allen & Unwin, 1974.

Stone, Lawrence, ed. *An Imperial State at War.* London: Routledge, 1994.

Thompson, E. P. *The Making of the English Working Class.* Harmondsworth: Penguin, 1982.

Twiss, Horace. *The Public and Private Life of Lord Chancellor Eldon, with Selections from his Correspondence.* 3 vols. London, 1844.

Walpole, Spencer. *The Life of the Right Hon. Spencer Perceval, including correspondence with Numerous Distinguished Persons.* 2 vols. London, 1874.

Watson, J. Steven. *The Reign of George III, 1760–1815.* Oxford: Clarendon Press, 1960.

Wells, Roger. *Dearth and Distress in Yorkshire, 1793–1802.* York: Borthwick Institute of Historical Research, 1977.

———. *Insurrection: The British Experience, 1795–1803.* Gloucester: Alan Sutton, 1983.

———. *Wretched Faces: Famine in Wartime England, 1793–1801.* London: Alan Sutton, 1988.

Western, J. R. *The English Militia in the Eighteenth Century.* London: Routledge & Kegan Paul, 1965.

———. "The Volunteer Movement as an Anti-Revolutionary Force, 1793–1801." *English Historical Review* 71 (1956): 603–14.

Wickwire, Franklin, and Mary Wickwire. *Cornwallis: The Imperial Years.* Chapel Hill: University of North Carolina Press, 1980.

Ziegler, Philip. *Addington: The Life of Henry Addington, First Viscount Sidmouth, 1757–1844.* London: Collins, 1965.

———. *The Sixth Great Power: Barings, 1762–1929.* London: Collins, 1988.

Index

ABOUT THE AUTHOR

Charles John Fedorak has been the Director of Information and Privacy Branch, Ministry of Education, Government of British Columbia since 1998. He received his Ph.D. in International History from the London School of Economics.

ABOUT THE BOOK

Henry Addington: Prime Minister, 1801–1804 was designed and typeset by Kachergis Book Design in Pittsboro, North Carolina. The typeface for the text, Minion, was designed by Robert Slimbach and reflects the classical typography of the Renaissance. The display type, Cateneo, was designed by Richard Lipton and Jacqueline Sakwa for Bitstream. It is based on calligraphy drawn by Bennardino Cateneo, writing master at the University of Siena, c. 1544–1560.

   Henry Addington: Prime Minister, 1801–1804 was printed on sixty-pound Glatfelter Writers Offset and bound by Thomson-Shore, Dexter, Michigan.